NANUET PUBLIC LIBRARY

3 2824 01018 5523

S0-BTC-261

the AMAZING SPIDER-GIRL

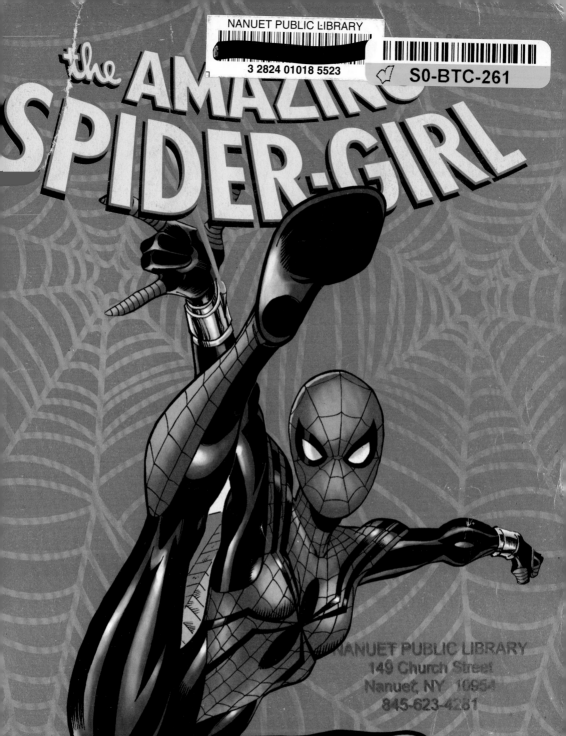

NANUET PUBLIC LIBRARY
149 Church Street
Nanuet, NY 10954
845-623-4281

WHATEVER HAPPENED TO THE DAUGHTER OF SPIDER-MAN?

the AMAZING SPIDER-GIRL

WHATEVER HAPPEN TO THE DAUGHTER SPIDER-MAN?

Script, Plot & Pencils
Tom DeFalco & Ron Frenz

Inks
Sal Buscema

Colors
Gotham

Letters
Dave Sharpe

Cover Art
Ron Frenz, Sal Buscema &
Paul Mounts

Editor
Molly Lazer

Spider-Girl #0

Writer
Tom DeFalco

Featuring Artwork by
Pat Olliffe, Ron Frenz, John Romita Sr.,
J. Scott Campbell, Al Williamson, Sal Buscema,
Bill Sienkiewicz, Scott Koblish & Tim Townsend

Cover Art
Ron Frenz, Sal Buscema & Gotham

Editor
Molly Lazer

Collection Editor
Jennifer Grünwald

Assistant Editors
Michael Short &
Cory Levine

Associate Editor
Mark D. Beazley

**Senior Editor,
Special Projects**
Jeff Youngquist

**Senior Vice
President Of Sales**
David Gabriel

Book Designer
Dayle Chesler

**Vice President
of Creative**
Tom Marvelli

Editor In Chief
Joe Quesada

Publisher
Dan Buckley

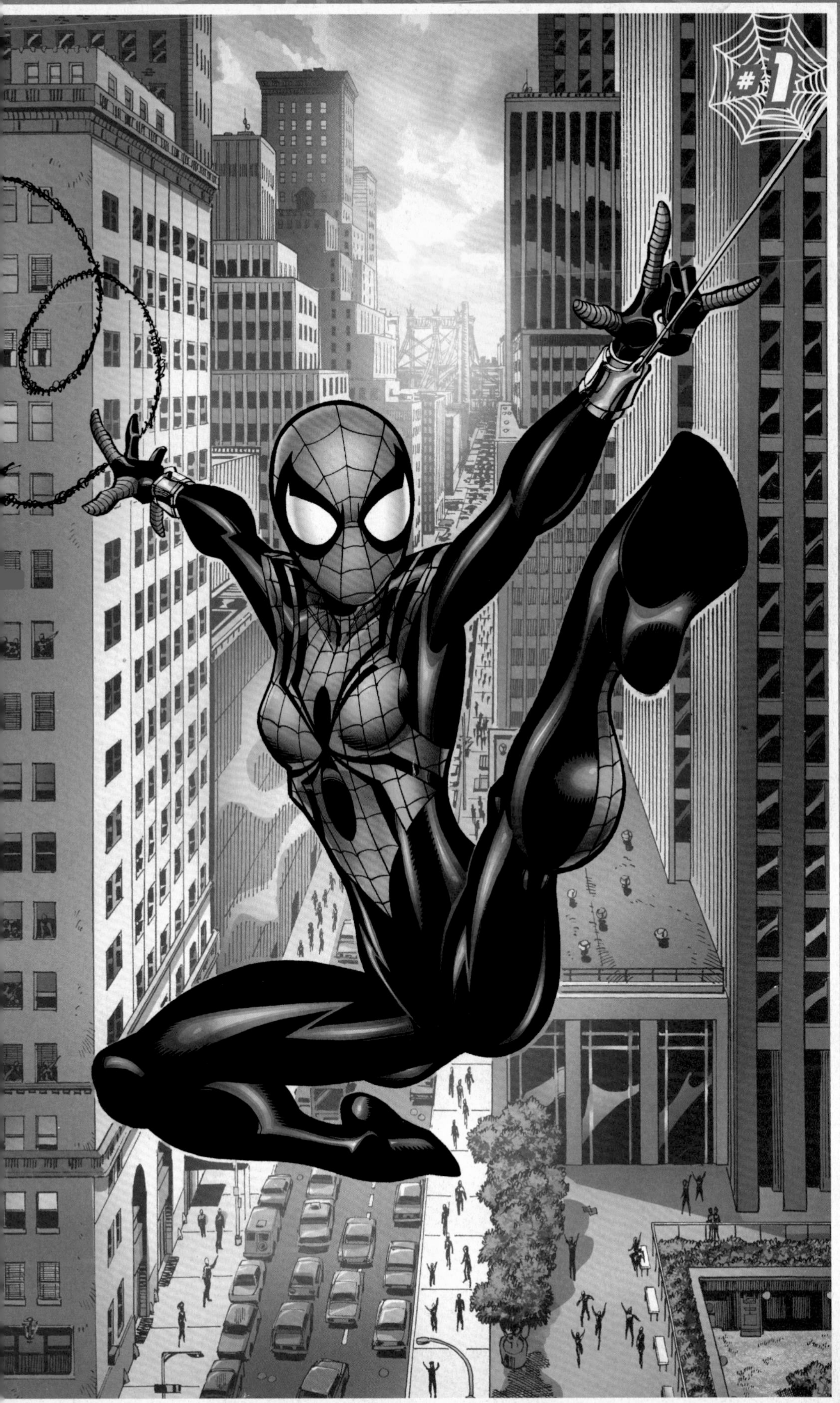
#1

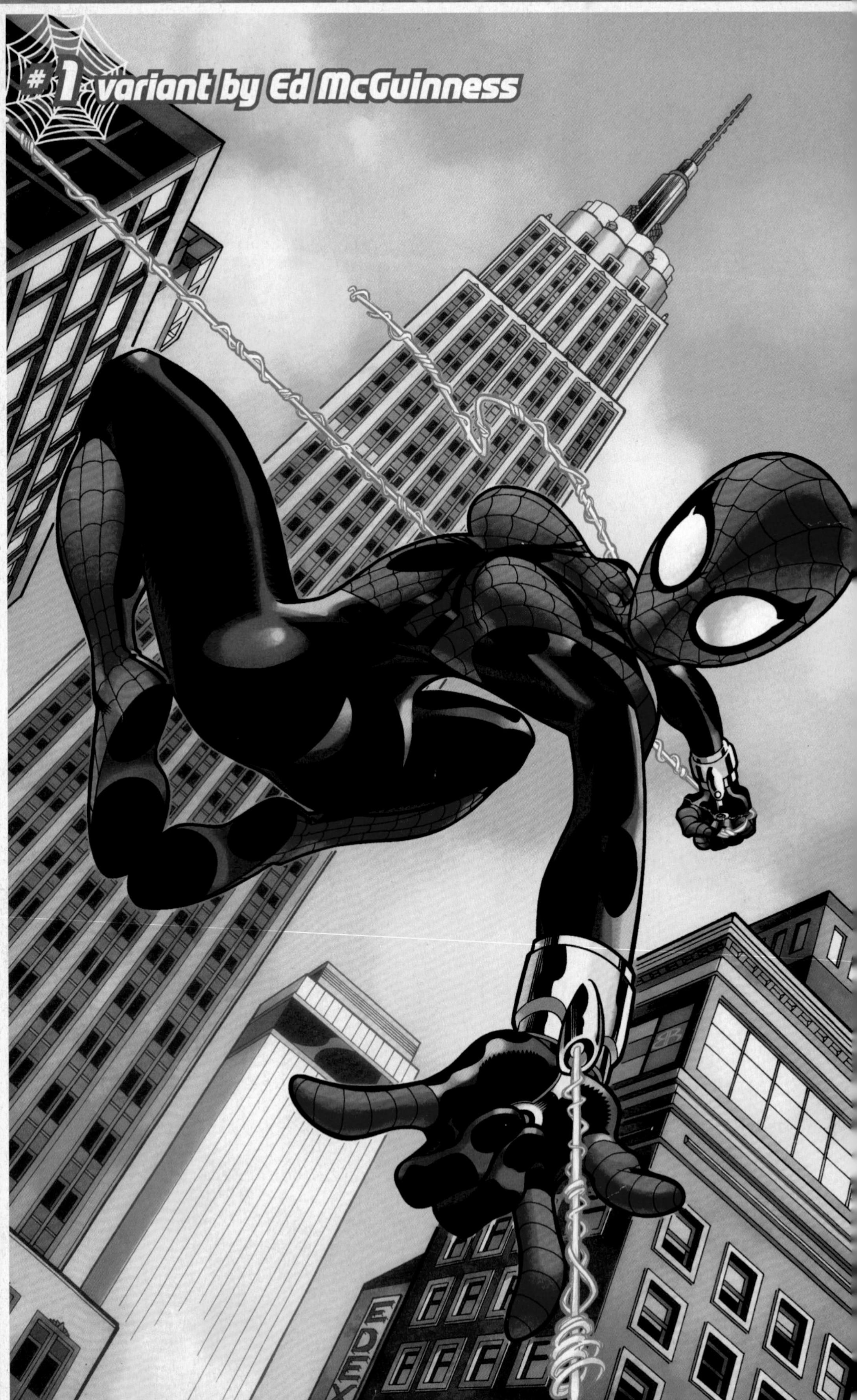

#1 variant by Ed McGuinness

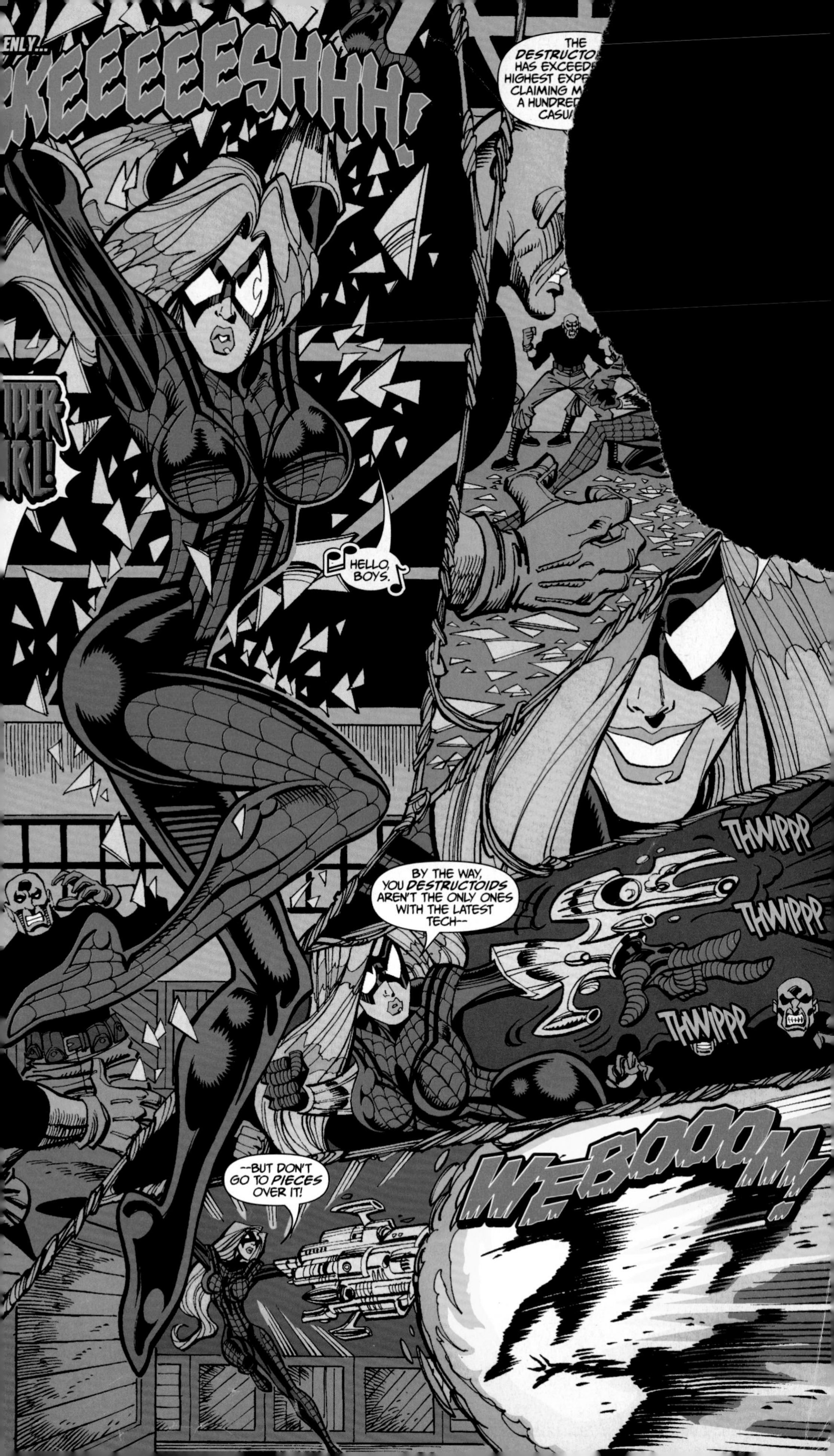

ENLY...
KEEEEEEESHHH!
THE DESTRUCTO HAS EXCEED HIGHEST EXPE CLAIMING M A HUNDRED CASU
IDER- IRL!
HELLO, BOYS.
BY THE WAY, YOU DESTRUCTOIDS AREN'T THE ONLY ONES WITH THE LATEST TECH--
THWIPPP
THWIPPP
THWIPPP
--BUT DON'T GO TO PIECES OVER IT!
WEBOOOM!

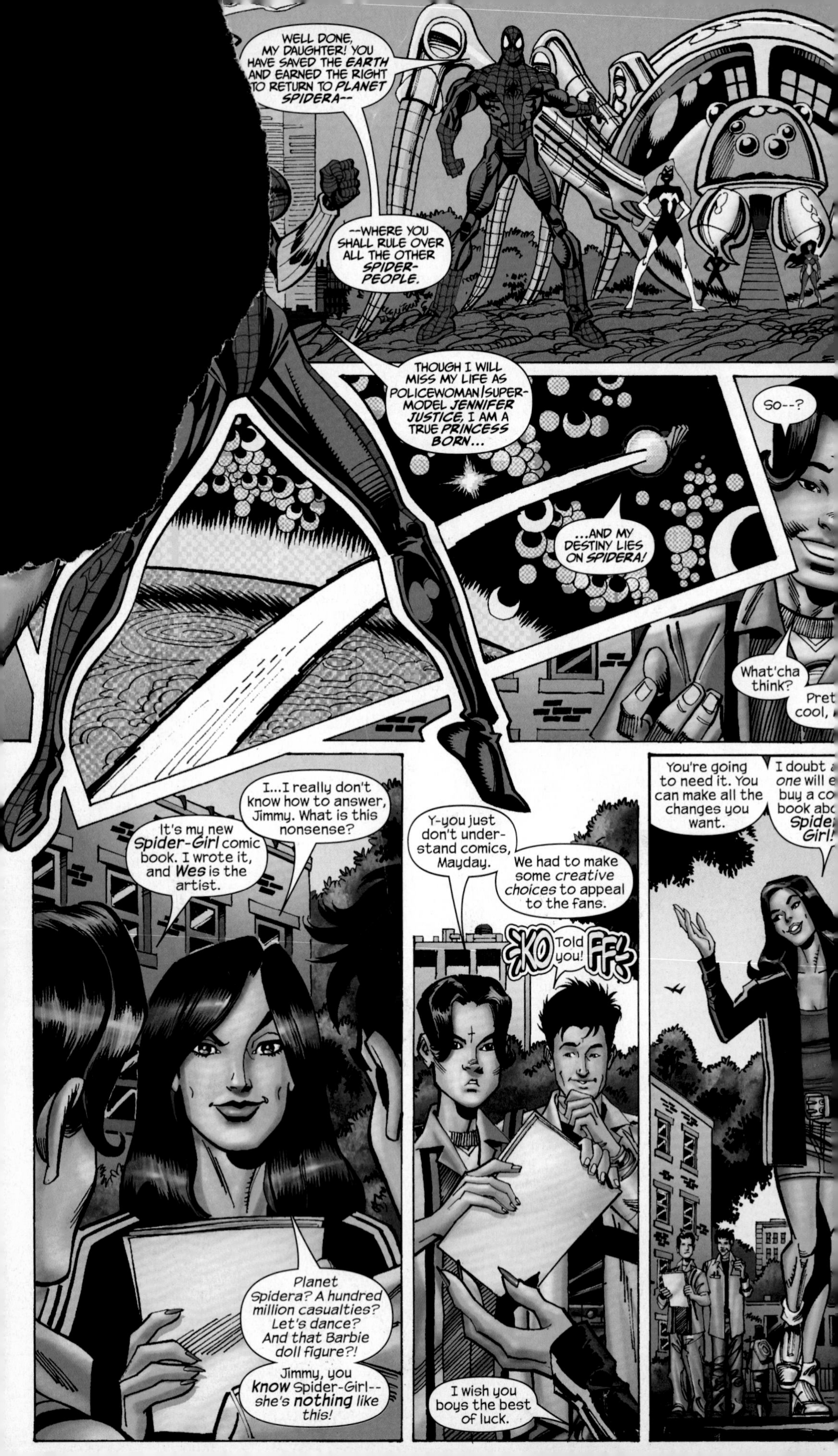
WELL DONE, MY DAUGHTER! YOU HAVE SAVED THE EARTH AND EARNED THE RIGHT TO RETURN TO PLANET SPIDERA--
--WHERE YOU SHALL RULE OVER ALL THE OTHER SPIDER-PEOPLE.
THOUGH I WILL MISS MY LIFE AS POLICEWOMAN/SUPER-MODEL JENNIFER JUSTICE, I AM A TRUE PRINCESS BORN...
...AND MY DESTINY LIES ON SPIDERA!
SO--?
What'cha think?
Pret
cool,
It's my new Spider-Girl comic book. I wrote it, and Wes is the artist.
I...I really don't know how to answer, Jimmy. What is this nonsense?
Planet Spidera? A hundred million casualties? Let's dance? And that Barbie doll figure?!
Jimmy, you know Spider-Girl--she's nothing like this!
Y-you just don't under-stand comics, Mayday.
We had to make some creative choices to appeal to the fans.
KO
Told you!
FF
I wish you boys the best of luck.
You're going to need it. You can make all the changes you want.
I doubt
one will
buy a co
book abo
Spide
Girl!

Whatever happened to the daughter of Spider-Man?

PART 1

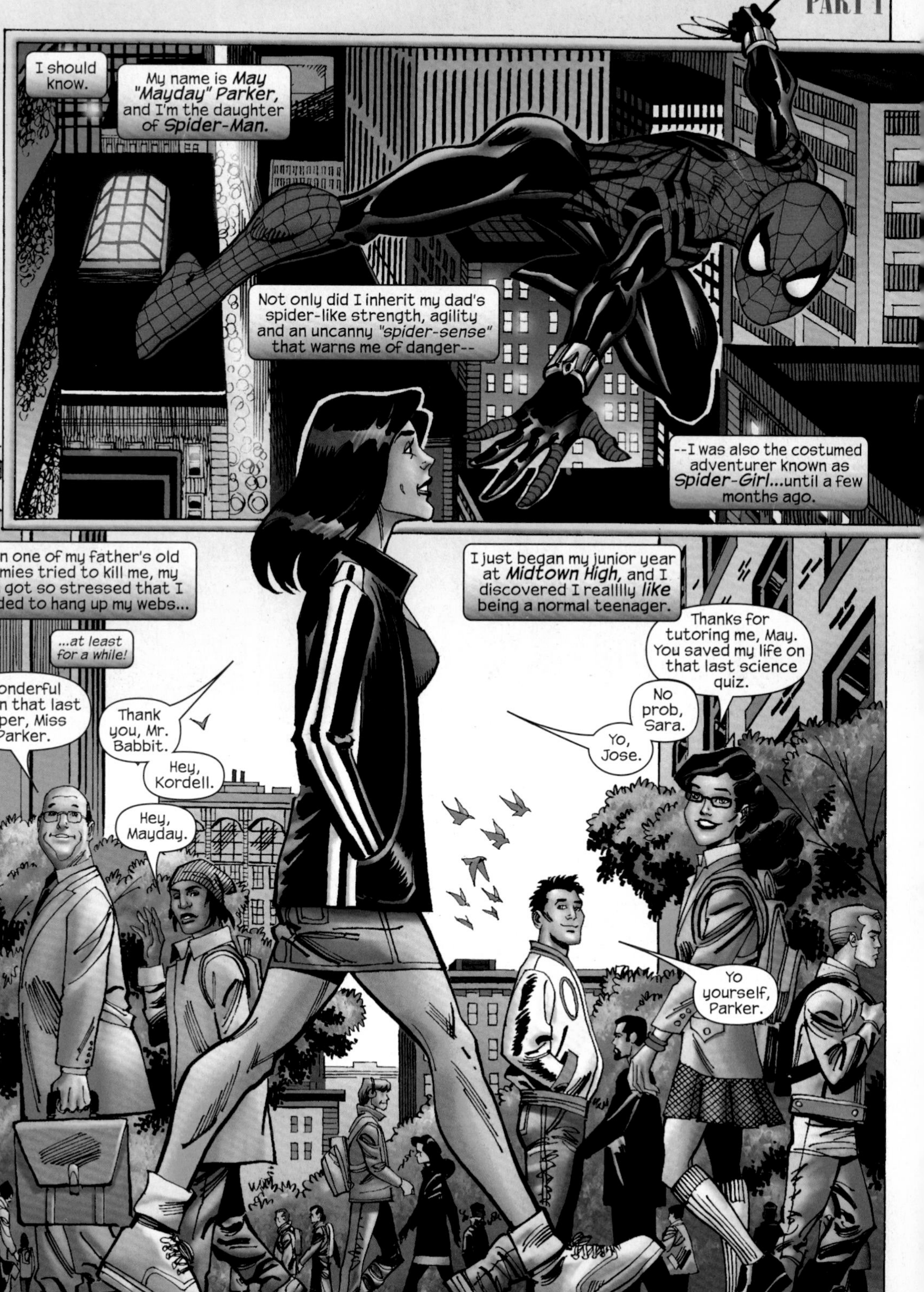

I should know.
My name is May "Mayday" Parker, and I'm the daughter of Spider-Man.
Not only did I inherit my dad's spider-like strength, agility and an uncanny "spider-sense" that warns me of danger--
--I was also the costumed adventurer known as Spider-Girl...until a few months ago.
hen one of my father's old nemies tried to kill me, my om got so stressed that I ecided to hang up my webs...
...at least for a while!
I just began my junior year at Midtown High, and I discovered I realllly like being a normal teenager.
Wonderful on that last paper, Miss Parker.
Thank you, Mr. Babbit.
Hey, Kordell.
Hey, Mayday.
Thanks for tutoring me, May. You saved my life on that last science quiz.
No prob, Sara.
Yo, Jose.
Yo yourself, Parker.

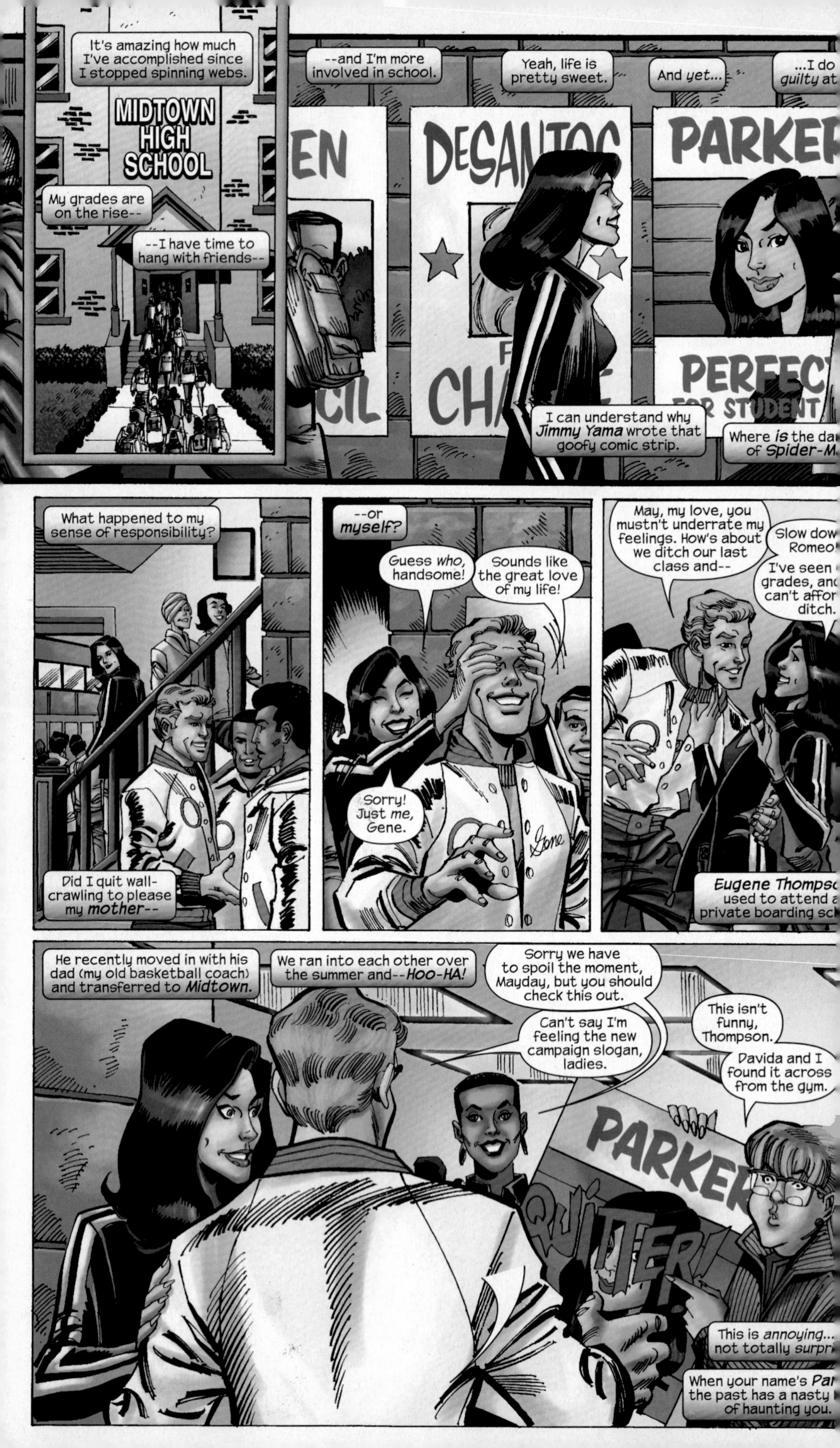

It's amazing how much I've accomplished since I stopped spinning webs.
MIDTOWN HIGH SCHOOL
My grades are on the rise--
--I have time to hang with friends--
--and I'm more involved in school.
Yeah, life is pretty sweet.
And yet...
...I do
guilty at
EN
DESANTOS
PARKER
CIL
CHA
PERFEC
FOR STUDENT
I can understand why Jimmy Yama wrote that goofy comic strip.
Where is the da
of Spider-M
What happened to my sense of responsibility?
Did I quit wall-crawling to please my mother--
--or myself?
Guess who, handsome!
Sounds like the great love of my life!
Sorry! Just me, Gene.
May, my love, you mustn't underrate my feelings. How's about we ditch our last class and--
Slow dow
Romeo!
I've seen
grades, and
can't affor
ditch.
Eugene Thomps
used to attend a
private boarding sc
He recently moved in with his dad (my old basketball coach) and transferred to Midtown.
We ran into each other over the summer and--HOO-HA!
Sorry we have to spoil the moment, Mayday, but you should check this out.
Can't say I'm feeling the new campaign slogan, ladies.
This isn't funny, Thompson.
Davida and I found it across from the gym.
PARKER QUITTER!
This is annoying...
not totally surpr
When your name's Par
the past has a nasty
of haunting you.

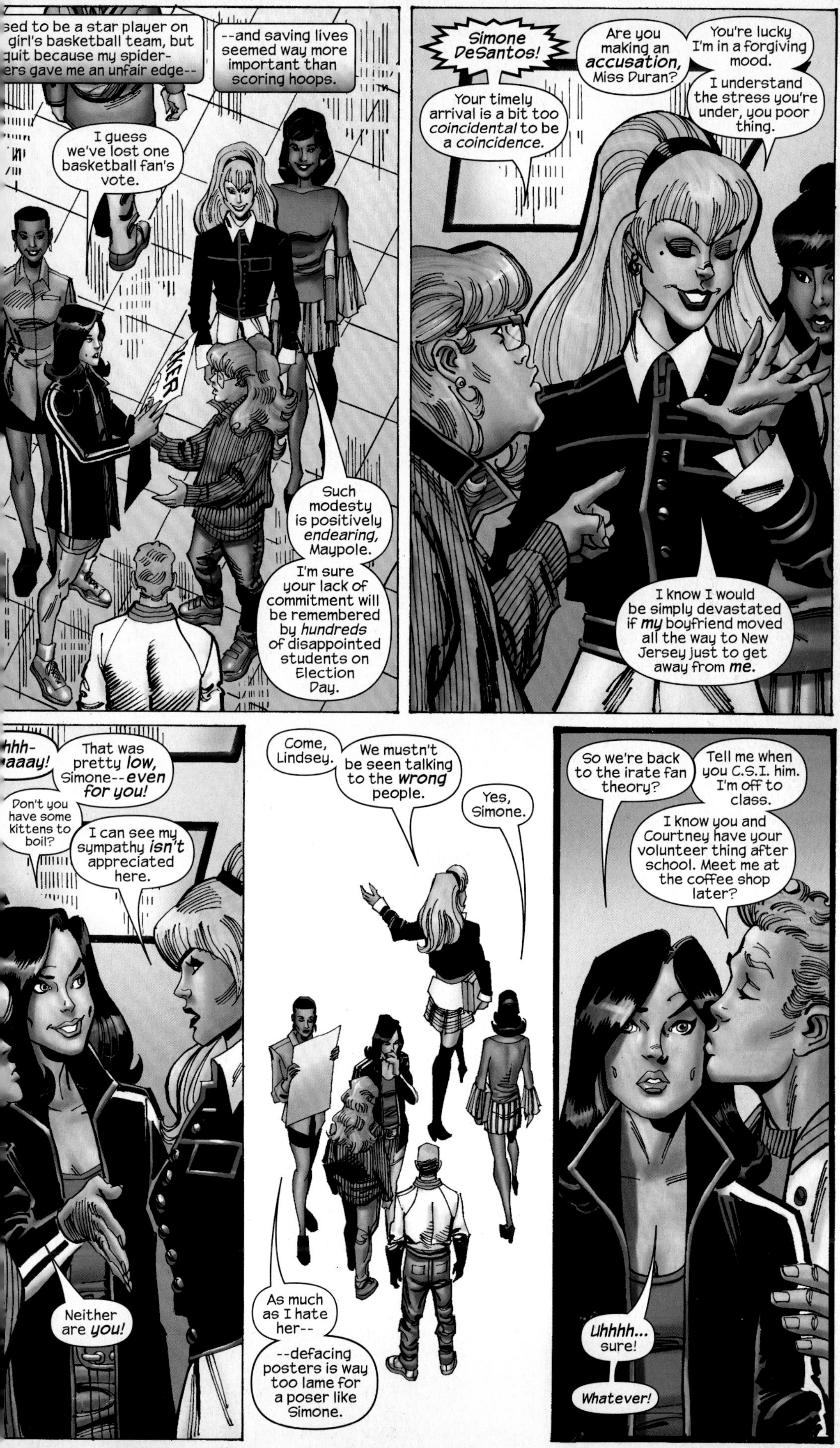
sed to be a star player on girl's basketball team, but quit because my spider- ers gave me an unfair edge--
--and saving lives seemed way more important than scoring hoops.
I guess we've lost one basketball fan's vote.
Such modesty is positively *endearing,* Maypole.
I'm sure your lack of commitment will be remembered by *hundreds* of disappointed students on Election Day.
Simone DeSantos!
Your timely arrival is a bit too *coincidental* to be a *coincidence.*
Are you making an *accusation,* Miss Duran?
You're lucky I'm in a forgiving mood.
I understand the stress you're under, you poor thing.
I know I would be simply devastated if *my* boyfriend moved all the way to New Jersey just to get away from *me.*
hhh- aaay!
That was pretty *low,* Simone--*even for you!*
Don't you have some kittens to boil?
I can see my sympathy *isn't* appreciated here.
Neither are *you!*
Come, Lindsey.
We mustn't be seen talking to the *wrong* people.
Yes, Simone.
As much as I hate her--
--defacing posters is way too lame for a poser like Simone.
So we're back to the irate fan theory?
Tell me when you C.S.I. him. I'm off to class.
I know you and Courtney have your volunteer thing after school. Meet me at the coffee shop later?
Uhhhh... sure!
Whatever!

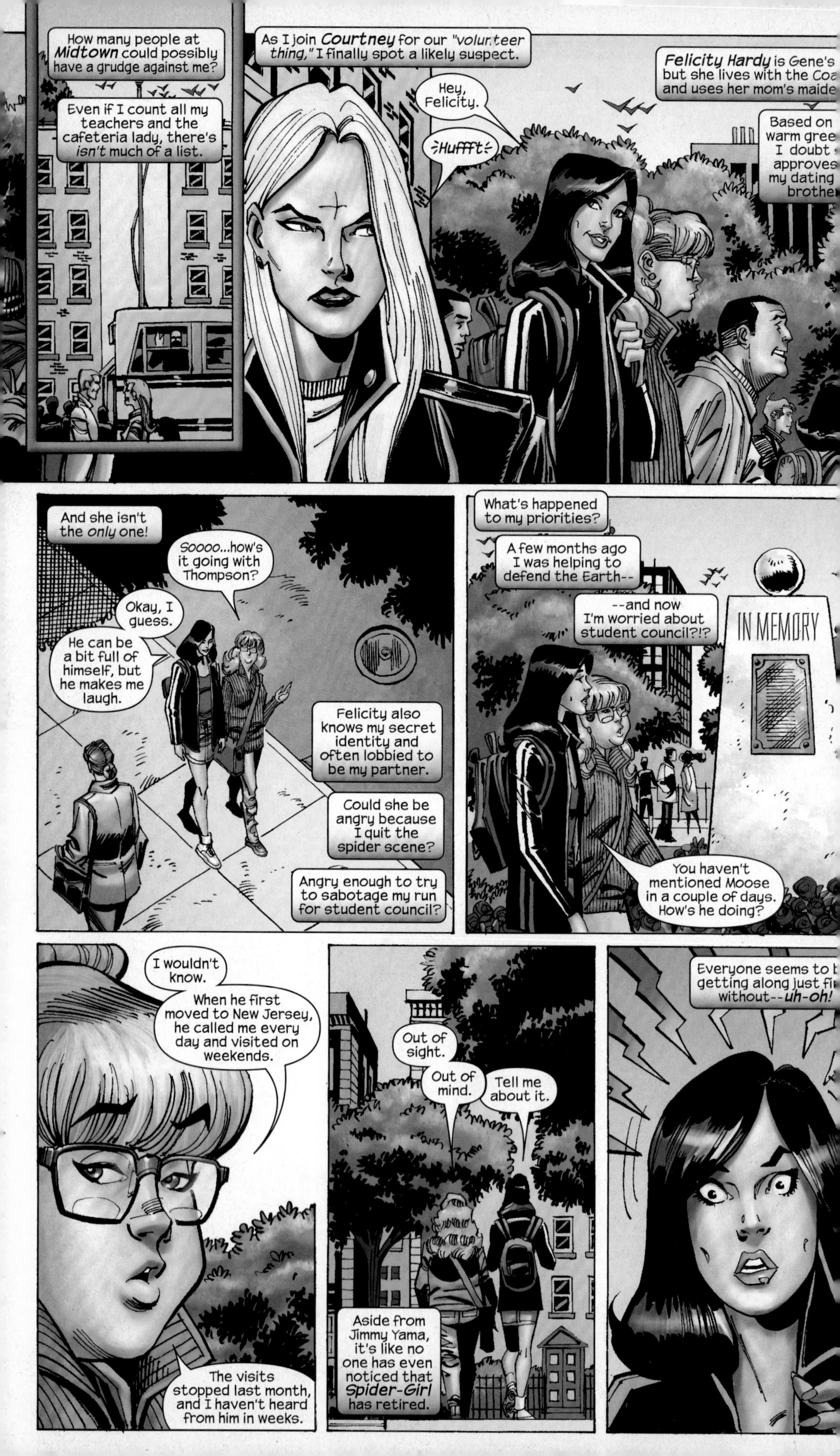
How many people at Midtown could possibly have a grudge against me?
Even if I count all my teachers and the cafeteria lady, there's isn't much of a list.
As I join Courtney for our "volunteer thing," I finally spot a likely suspect.
Hey, Felicity.
Hufffft
Felicity Hardy is Gene's
but she lives with the Coa
and uses her mom's maide
Based on
warm gree
I doubt
approves
my dating
brothe
And she isn't the only one!
Soooo...how's it going with Thompson?
Okay, I guess.
He can be a bit full of himself, but he makes me laugh.
Felicity also knows my secret identity and often lobbied to be my partner.
Could she be angry because I quit the spider scene?
Angry enough to try to sabotage my run for student council?
What's happened to my priorities?
A few months ago I was helping to defend the Earth--
--and now I'm worried about student council?!?
IN MEMORY
You haven't mentioned Moose in a couple of days. How's he doing?
I wouldn't know.
When he first moved to New Jersey, he called me every day and visited on weekends.
The visits stopped last month, and I haven't heard from him in weeks.
Out of sight.
Out of mind.
Tell me about it.
Aside from Jimmy Yama, it's like no one has even noticed that Spider-Girl has retired.
Everyone seems to b
getting along just fi
without--uh-oh!

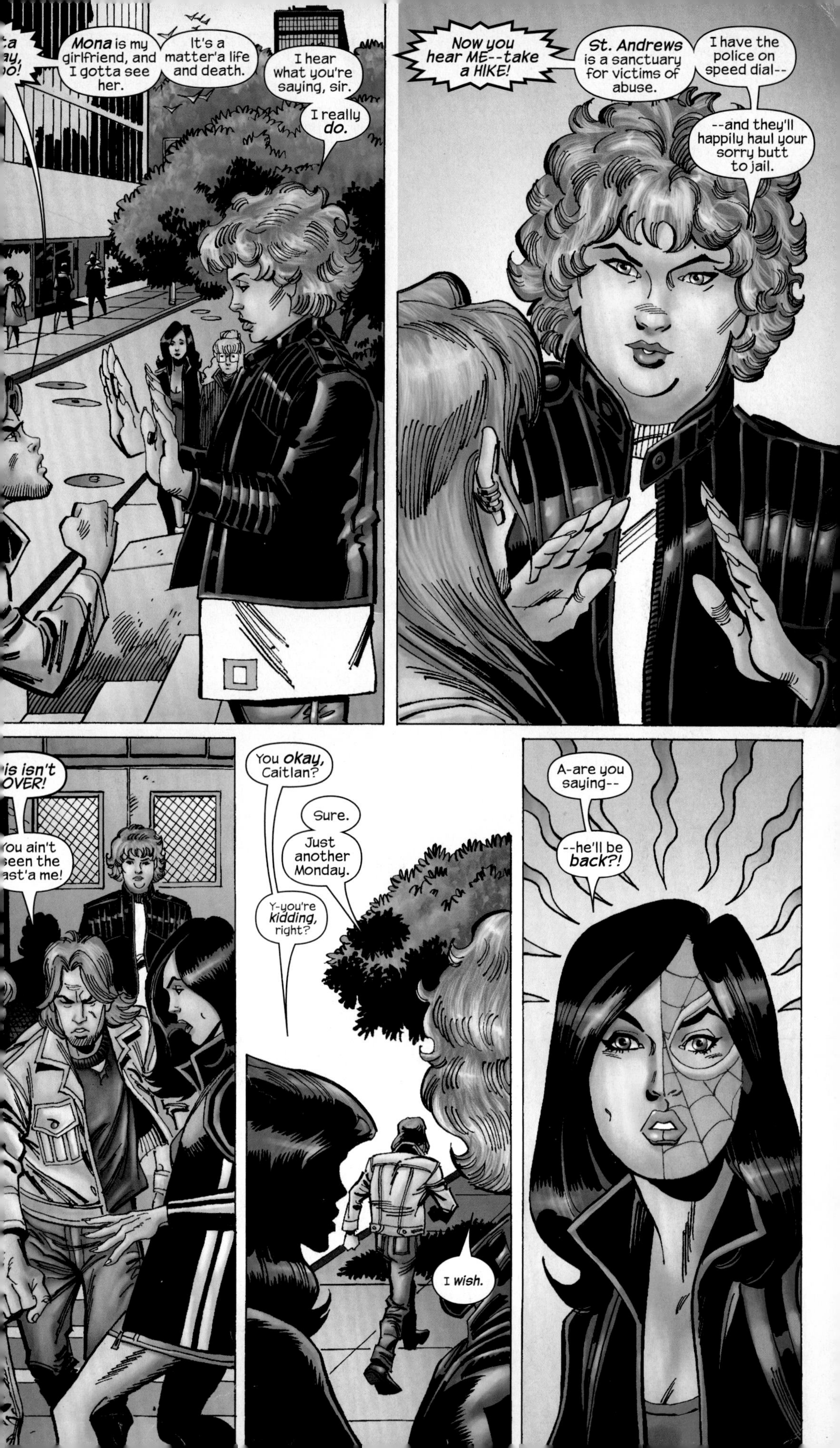
Mona is my girlfriend, and I gotta see her.
It's a matter'a life and death.
I hear what you're saying, sir.
I really do.
Now you hear ME--take a HIKE!
St. Andrews is a sanctuary for victims of abuse.
I have the police on speed dial--
--and they'll happily haul your sorry butt to jail.
You okay, Caitlan?
Sure.
Just another Monday.
Y-you're kidding, right?
I wish.
A-are you saying--
--he'll be back?!

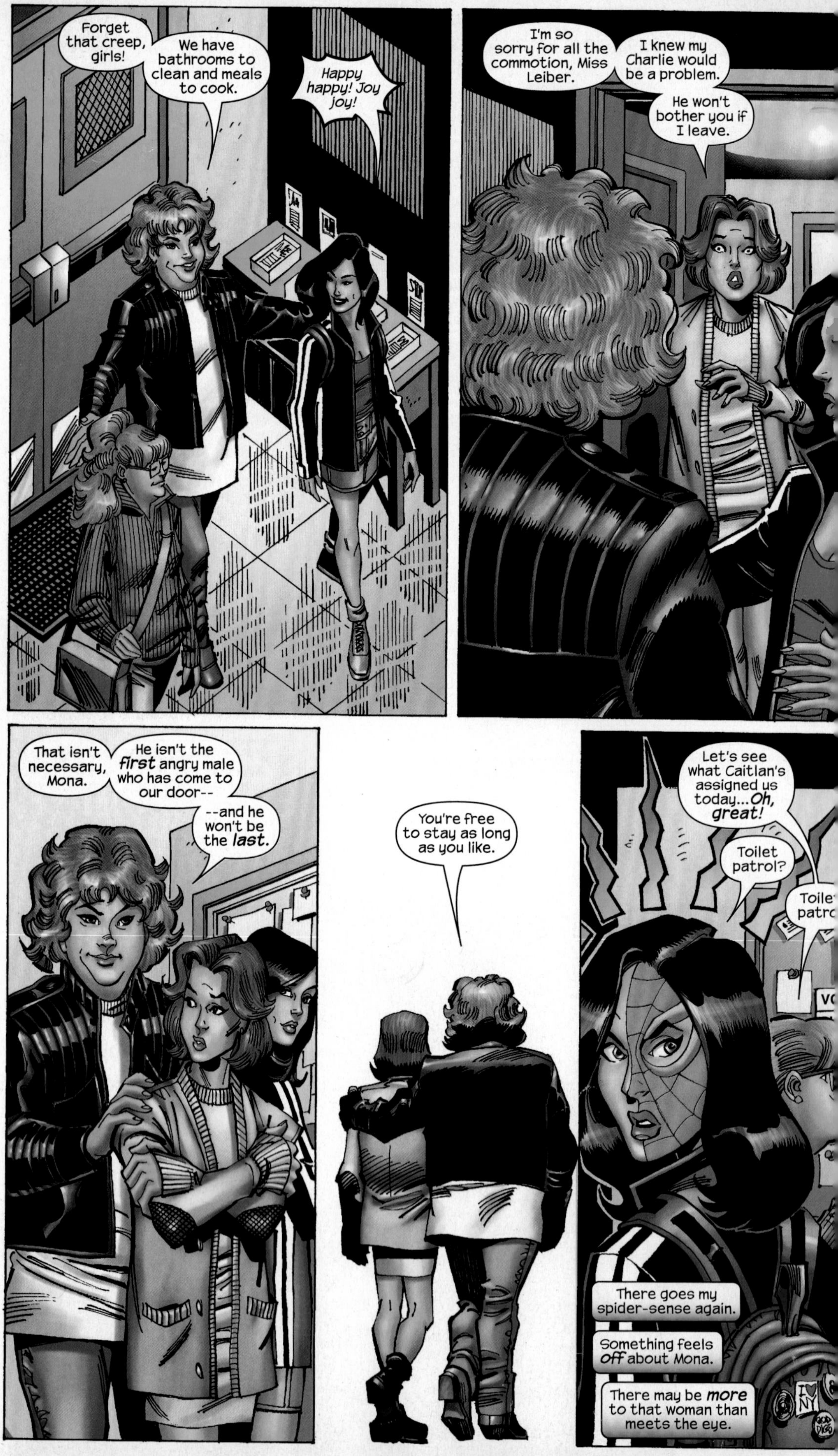
Forget that creep, girls!
We have bathrooms to clean and meals to cook.
Happy happy! Joy joy!
I'm so sorry for all the commotion, Miss Leiber.
I knew my Charlie would be a problem.
He won't bother you if I leave.
That isn't necessary, Mona.
He isn't the *first* angry male who has come to our door--
--and he won't be the *last*.
You're free to stay as long as you like.
Let's see what Caitlan's assigned us today...*Oh, great!*
Toilet patrol?
There goes my spider-sense again.
Something feels *off* about Mona.
There may be *more* to that woman than meets the eye.

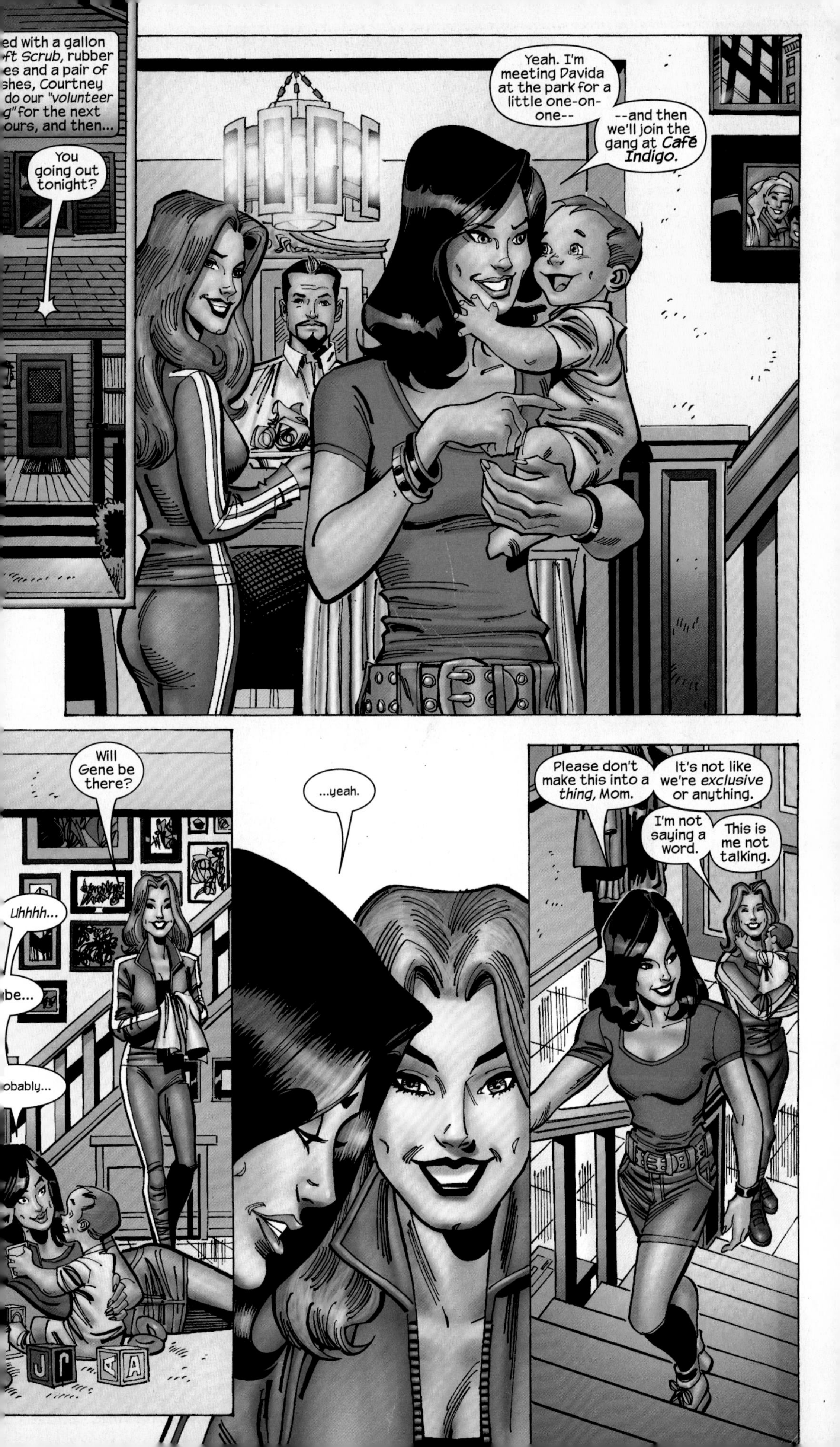

ed with a gallon ft Scrub, rubber es and a pair of shes, Courtney do our "volunteer g" for the next ours, and then...
You going out tonight?
Yeah. I'm meeting Davida at the park for a little one-on-one--
--and then we'll join the gang at *Café Indigo.*
Will Gene be there?
Uhhhh...
be...
obably...
...yeah.
Please don't make this into a *thing,* Mom.
It's not like we're *exclusive* or anything.
I'm not saying a word.
This is me not talking.

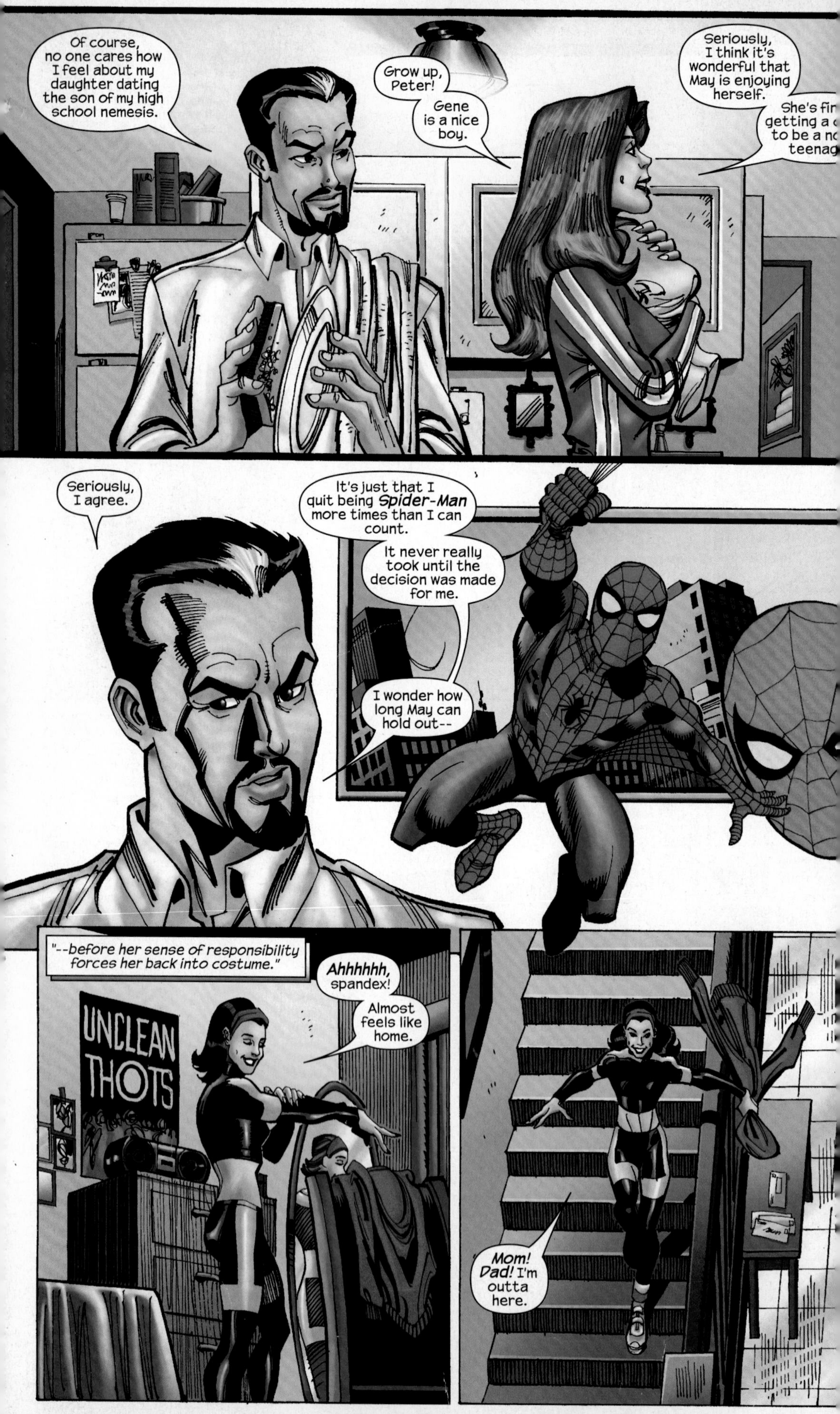

Of course, no one cares how I feel about my daughter dating the son of my high school nemesis.
Grow up, Peter!
Gene is a nice boy.
Seriously, I think it's wonderful that May is enjoying herself.
She's fir getting a c to be a nc teenag
Seriously, I agree.
It's just that I quit being Spider-Man more times than I can count.
It never really took until the decision was made for me.
I wonder how long May can hold out--
"--before her sense of responsibility forces her back into costume."
UNCLEAN THOTS
Ahhhhhh, spandex!
Almost feels like home.
Mom! Dad! I'm outta here.

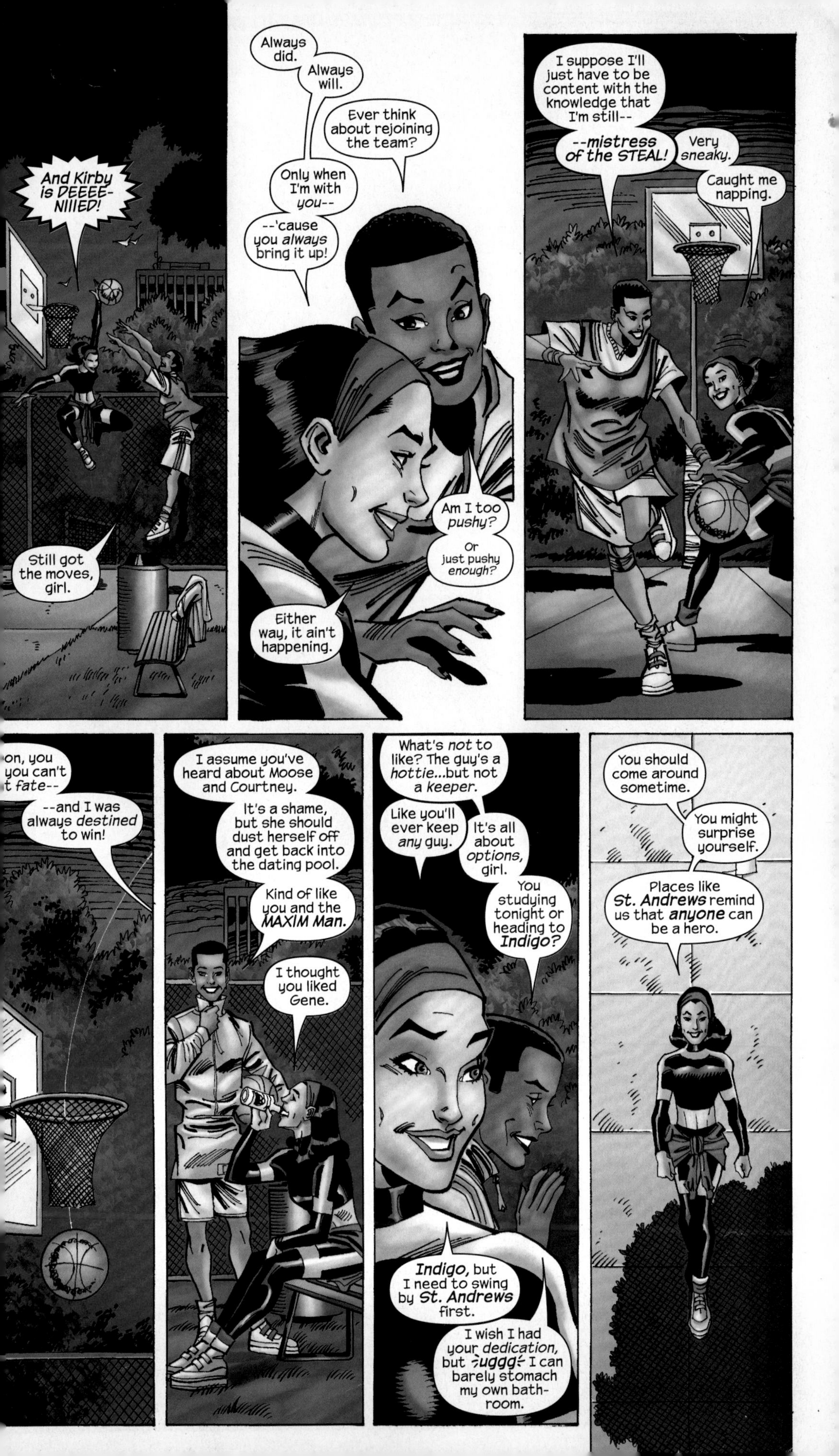
And Kirby is DEEEE-NIIIED!
Still got the moves, girl.
Always did.
Always will.
Ever think about rejoining the team?
Only when I'm with *you*--
--'cause you *always* bring it up!
Am I too *pushy*?
Or just pushy *enough*?
Either way, it ain't happening.
I suppose I'll just have to be content with the knowledge that I'm still--
--**mistress of the STEAL!**
Very *sneaky*.
Caught me napping.
on, you you can't t *fate*--
--and I was always *destined* to win!
I assume you've heard about Moose and Courtney.
It's a shame, but she should dust herself off and get back into the dating pool.
Kind of like you and the ***MAXIM Man.***
I thought you liked Gene.
What's *not* to like? The guy's a *hottie*...but not a *keeper*.
Like you'll ever keep *any* guy.
It's all about *options*, girl.
You studying tonight or heading to ***Indigo?***
Indigo, but I need to swing by ***St. Andrews*** first.
I wish I had your *dedication*, but *ugggh* I can barely stomach my own bath-room.
You should come around sometime.
You might surprise yourself.
Places like ***St. Andrews*** remind us that ***anyone*** can be a hero.

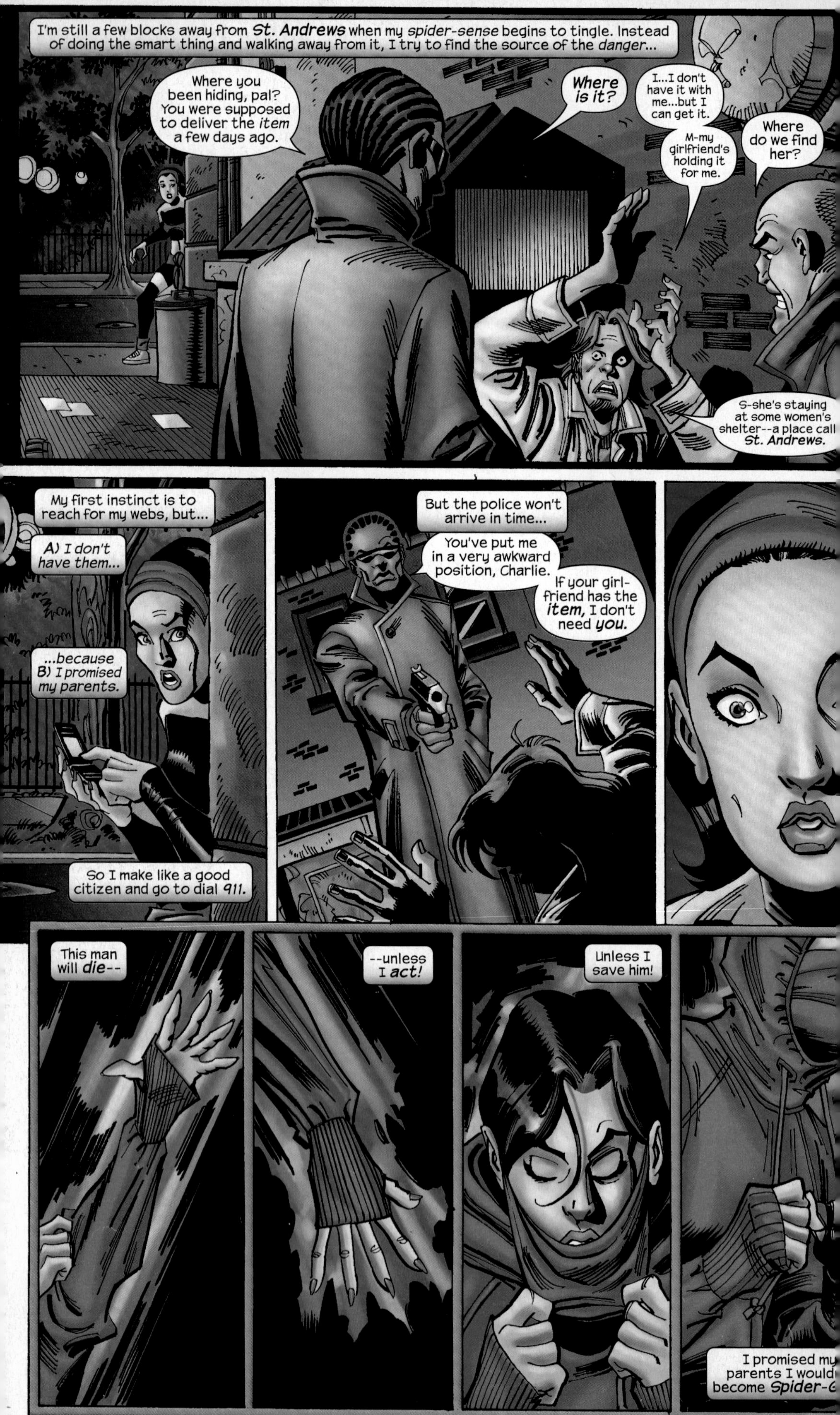
I'm still a few blocks away from St. Andrews when my spider-sense begins to tingle. Instead of doing the smart thing and walking away from it, I try to find the source of the danger...
Where you been hiding, pal? You were supposed to deliver the item a few days ago.
Where is it?
I...I don't have it with me...but I can get it.
M-my girlfriend's holding it for me.
Where do we find her?
S-she's staying at some women's shelter--a place call St. Andrews.
My first instinct is to reach for my webs, but...
A) I don't have them...
...because B) I promised my parents.
So I make like a good citizen and go to dial 911.
But the police won't arrive in time...
You've put me in a very awkward position, Charlie.
If your girl-friend has the item, I don't need you.
This man will die--
--unless I act!
Unless I save him!
I promised my parents I would become Spider-G

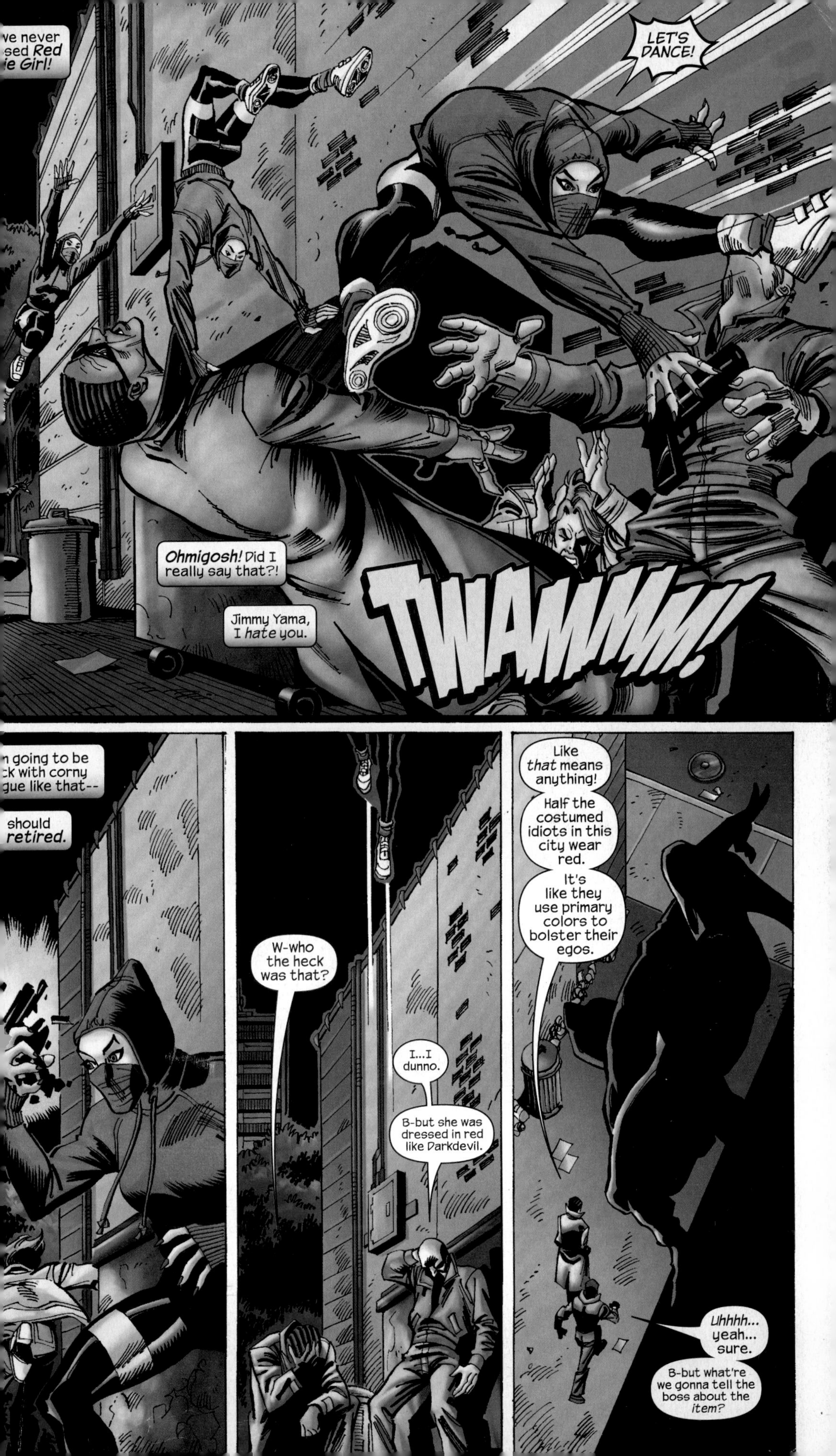
ve never
sed *Red*
ie Girl!
LET'S DANCE!
Ohmigosh! Did I really say that?!
Jimmy Yama, I *hate* you.
TWAMMM!
n going to be
ck with corny
gue like that--
should
retired.
W-who the heck was that?
I...I dunno.
B-but she was dressed in red like Darkdevil.
Like *that* means anything!
Half the costumed idiots in this city wear red.
It's like they use primary colors to bolster their egos.
Uhhhh... yeah... sure.
B-but what're we gonna tell the boss about the *item?*

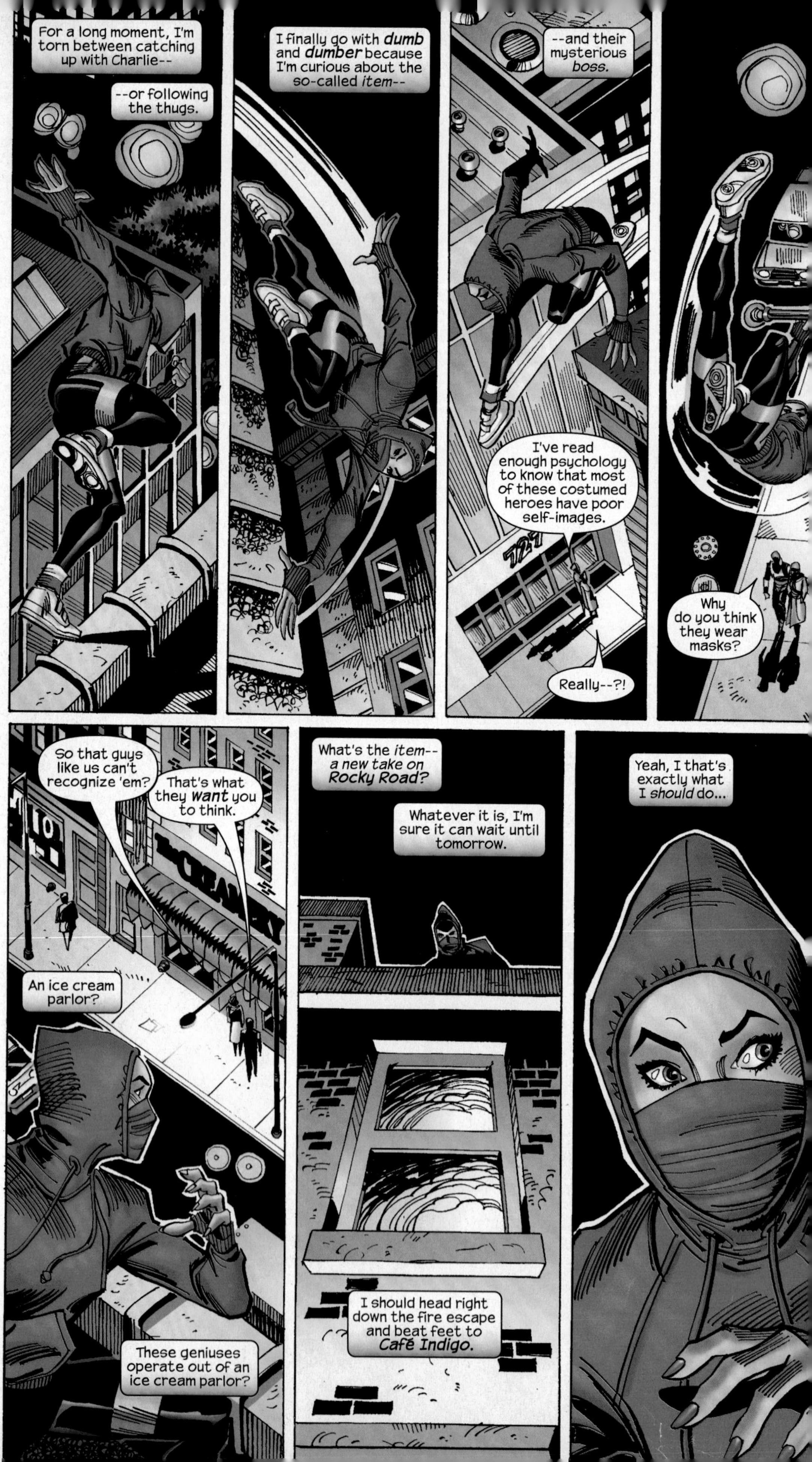

For a long moment, I'm torn between catching up with Charlie--
--or following the thugs.
I finally go with dumb and dumber because I'm curious about the so-called item--
--and their mysterious boss.
I've read enough psychology to know that most of these costumed heroes have poor self-images.
Really--?!
Why do you think they wear masks?
So that guys like us can't recognize 'em?
That's what they want you to think.
An ice cream parlor?
These geniuses operate out of an ice cream parlor?
What's the item--a new take on Rocky Road?
Whatever it is, I'm sure it can wait until tomorrow.
I should head right down the fire escape and beat feet to Café Indigo.
Yeah, I that's exactly what I should do...

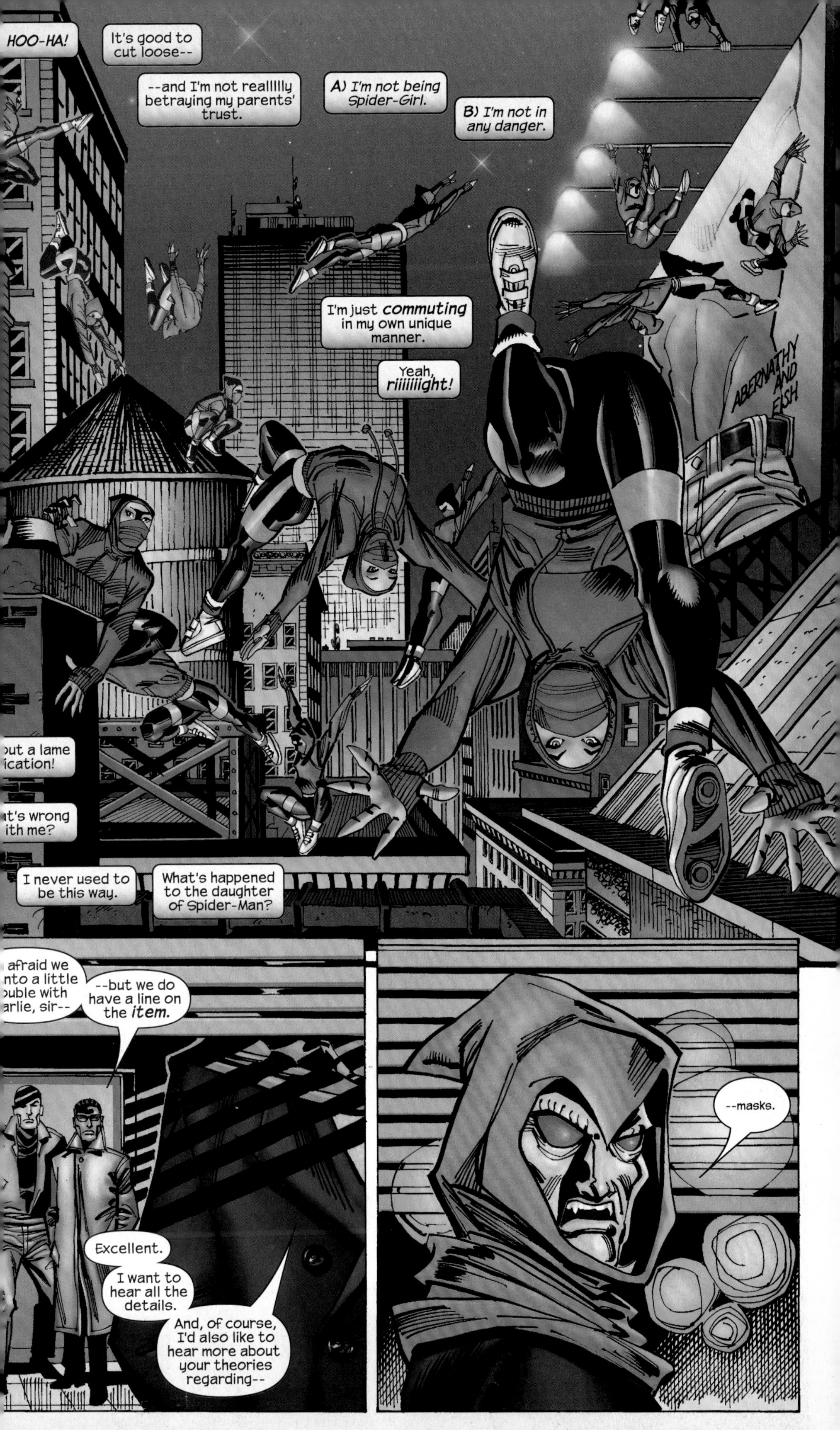

HOO-HA!
It's good to cut loose--
--and I'm not realllly betraying my parents' trust.
A) I'm not being Spider-Girl.
B) I'm not in any danger.
I'm just commuting in my own unique manner.
Yeah, riiiiiight!
ABERNATHY AND FISH
ut a lame ication!
t's wrong ith me?
I never used to be this way.
What's happened to the daughter of Spider-Man?
afraid we nto a little uble with arlie, sir--
--but we do have a line on the item.
Excellent.
I want to hear all the details.
And, of course, I'd also like to hear more about your theories regarding--
--masks.

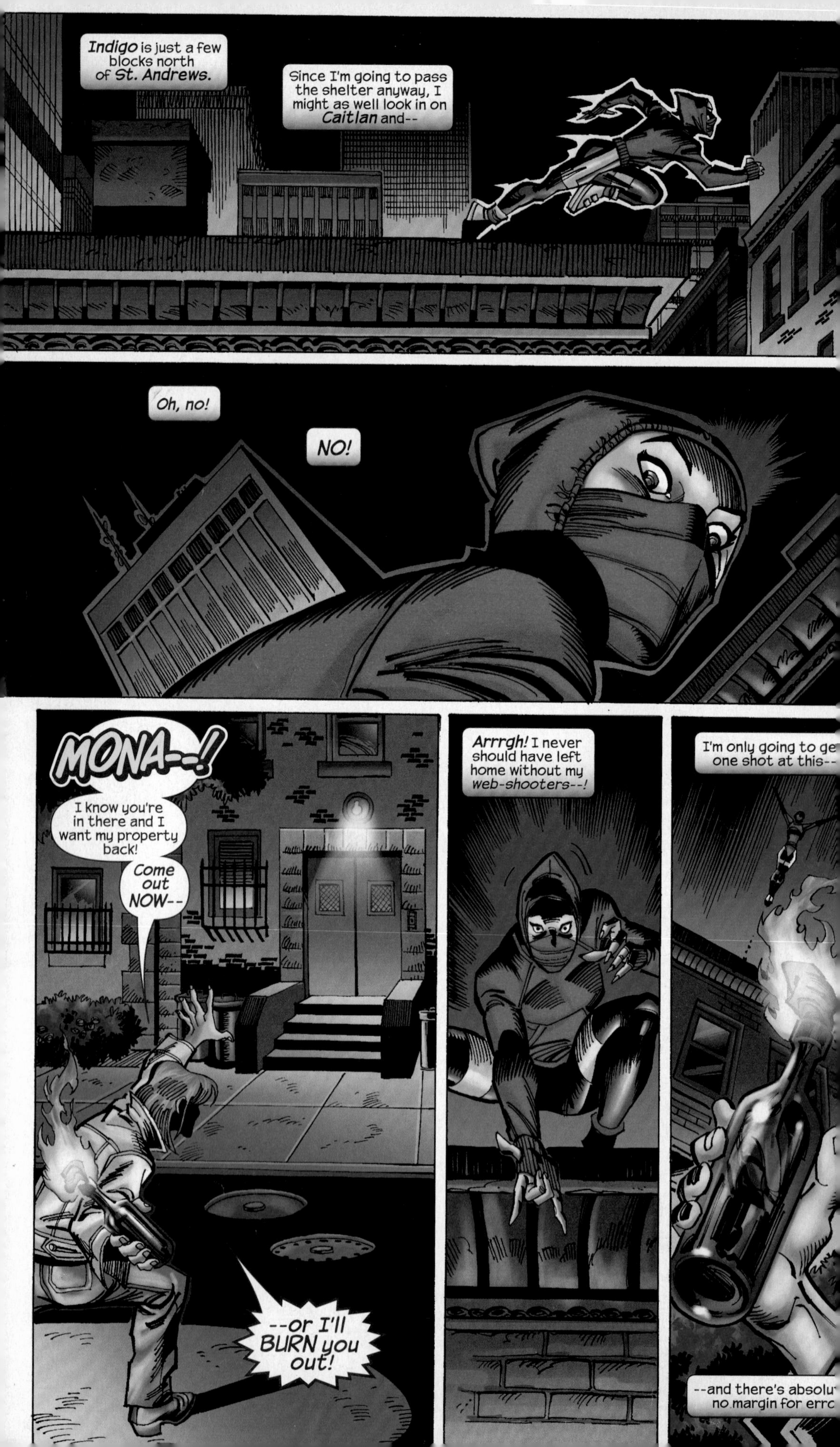

Indigo is just a few blocks north of St. Andrews.
Since I'm going to pass the shelter anyway, I might as well look in on Caitlan and--
Oh, no!
NO!
MONA--!
I know you're in there and I want my property back!
Come out NOW--
--or I'll BURN you out!
Arrrgh! I never should have left home without my web-shooters--!
I'm only going to ge one shot at this--
--and there's absolu no margin for errc

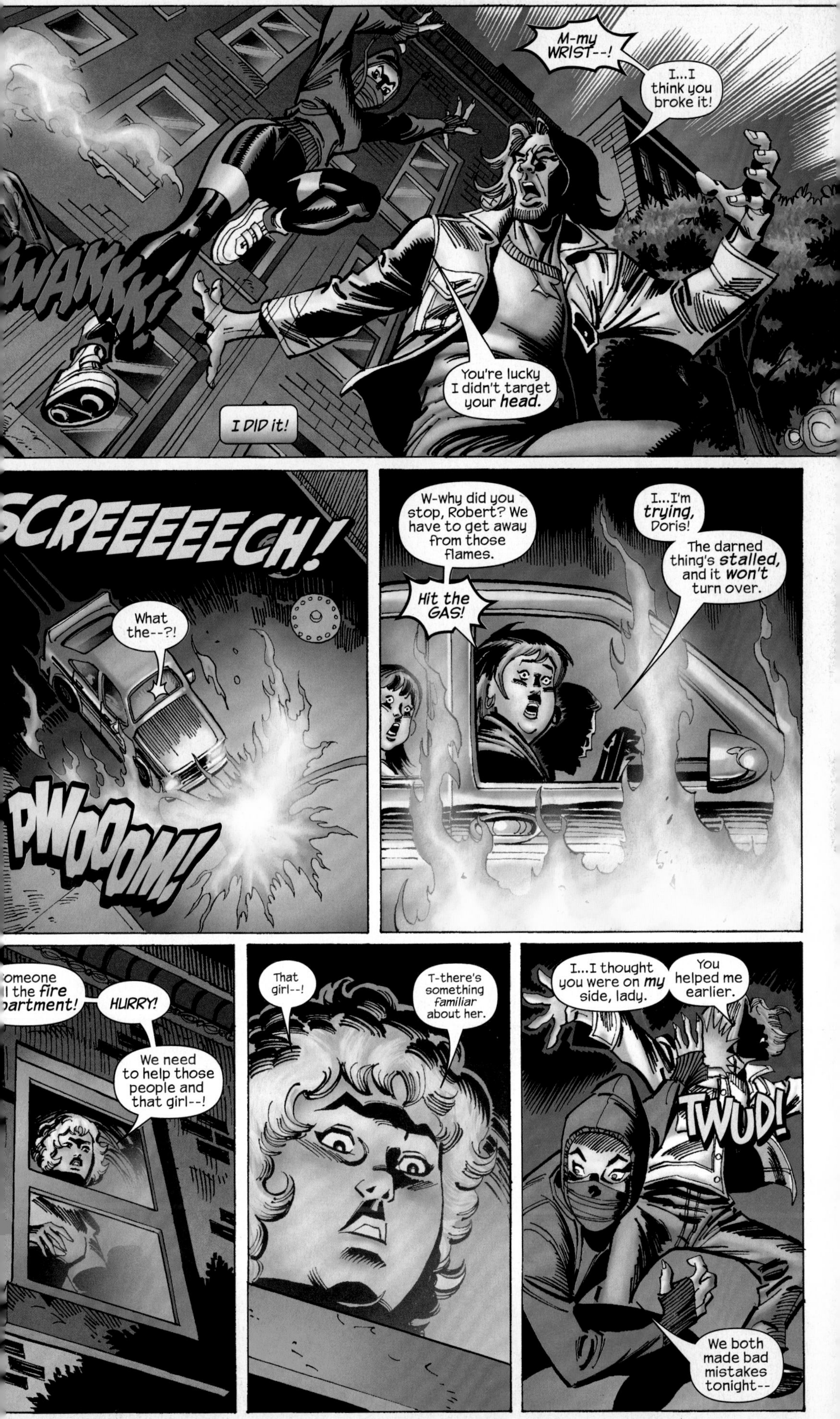

M-my WRIST--!
I...I think you broke it!
WAKKK!
You're lucky I didn't target your head.
I DID it!
SCREEEEECH!
What the--?!
PWOOOM!
W-why did you stop, Robert? We have to get away from those flames.
Hit the GAS!
I...I'm trying, Doris!
The darned thing's stalled, and it won't turn over.
omeone l the fire artment!
HURRY!
We need to help those people and that girl--!
That girl--!
T-there's something familiar about her.
I...I thought you were on my side, lady.
You helped me earlier.
TWUD!
We both made bad mistakes tonight--

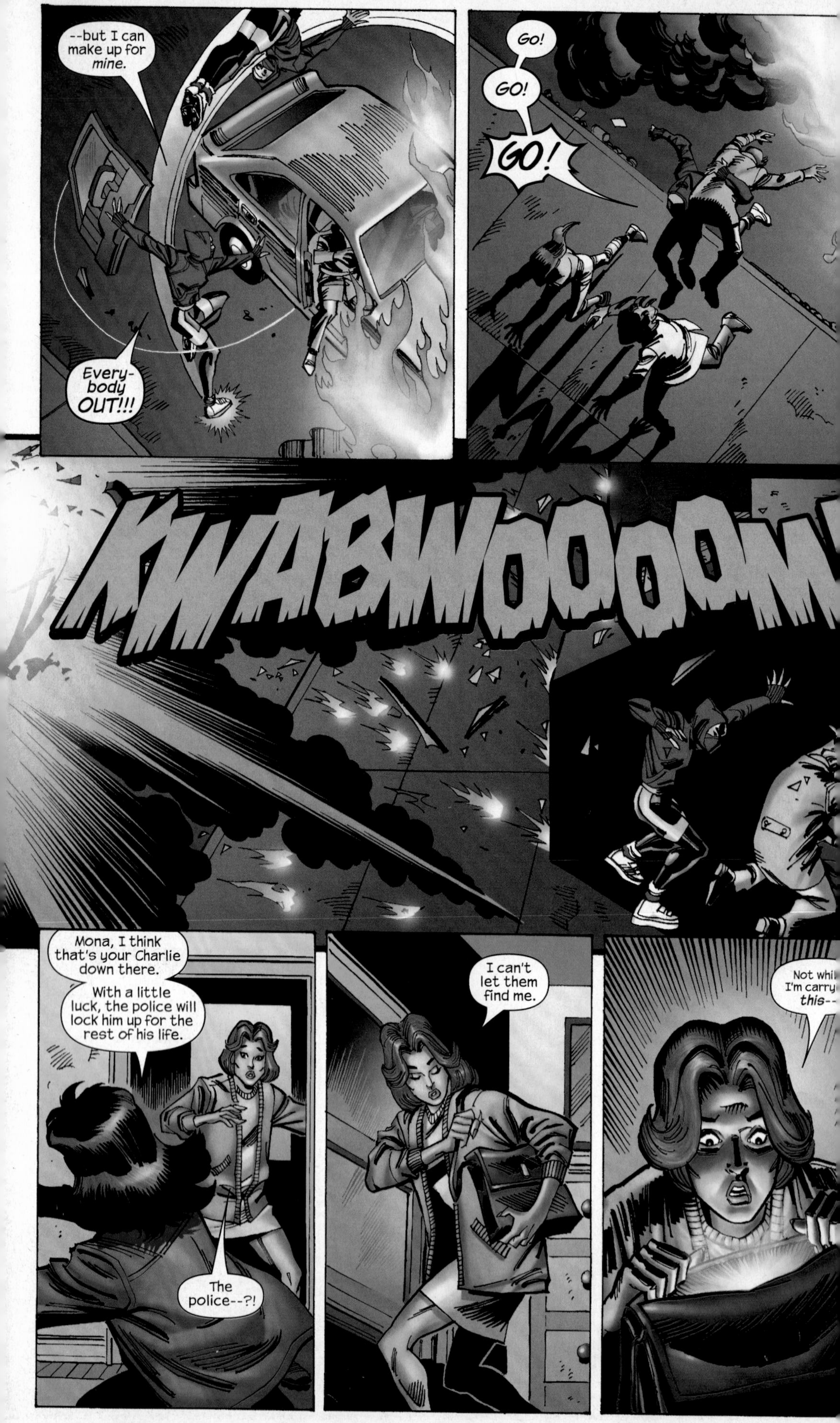
--but I can make up for *mine*.
Every-body OUT!!!
GO!
GO!
GO!
KWABWOOOOM
Mona, I think that's your Charlie down there.
With a little luck, the police will lock him up for the rest of his life.
The police--?!
I can't let them find me.
Not whi I'm carry *this*--

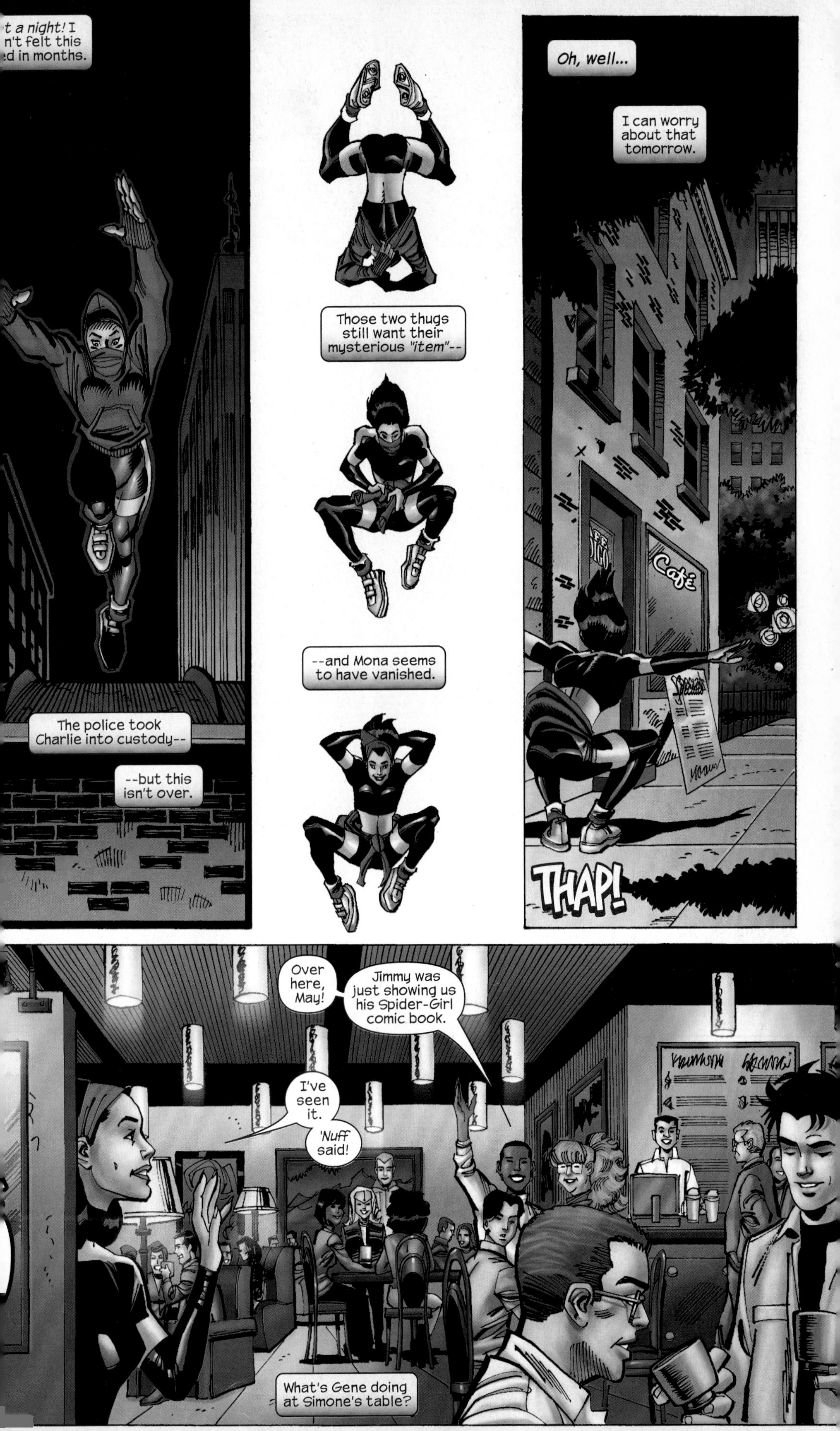

t a night! I n't felt this d in months.
The police took Charlie into custody--
--but this isn't over.
Those two thugs still want their mysterious "item"--
--and Mona seems to have vanished.
Oh, well...
I can worry about that tomorrow.
Café
THAP!
Over here, May!
Jimmy was just showing us his Spider-Girl comic book.
I've seen it.
'Nuff said!
What's Gene doing at Simone's table?

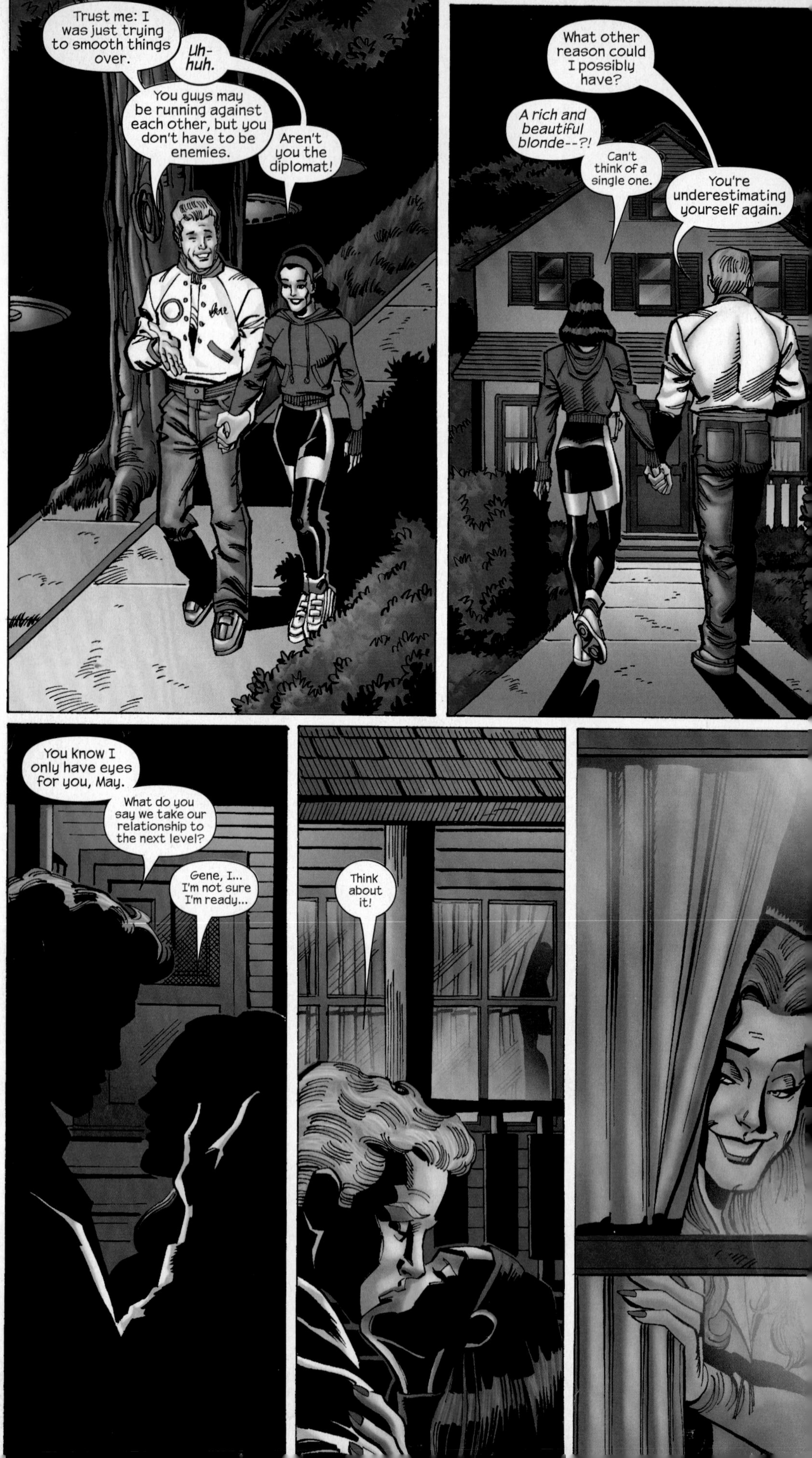
Trust me: I was just trying to smooth things over.
Uh-huh.
You guys may be running against each other, but you don't have to be enemies.
Aren't you the diplomat!
What other reason could I possibly have?
A rich and beautiful blonde--?!
Can't think of a single one.
You're underestimating yourself again.
You know I only have eyes for you, May.
What do you say we take our relationship to the next level?
Gene, I... I'm not sure I'm ready...
Think about it!

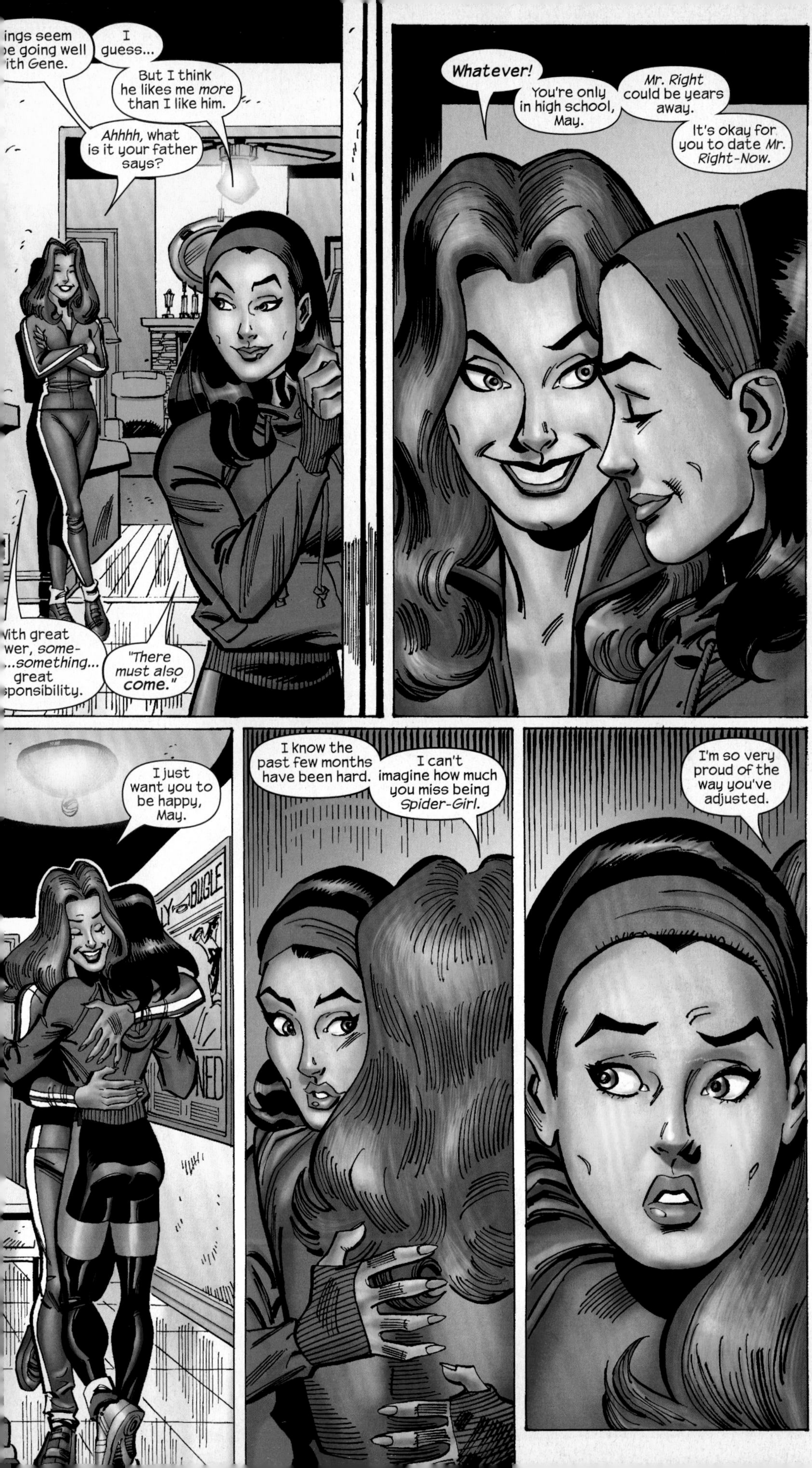
ings seem
e going well
ith Gene.
I guess...
But I think he likes me *more* than I like him.
Ahhhh, what is it your father says?
ith great
wer, *some-*
...something...
great
ponsibility.
"There must also **come.**"
Whatever!
You're only in high school, May.
Mr. Right could be years away.
It's okay for you to date *Mr. Right-Now.*
I just want you to be happy, May.
I know the past few months have been hard.
I can't imagine how much you miss being *Spider-Girl.*
I'm so very proud of the way you've adjusted.

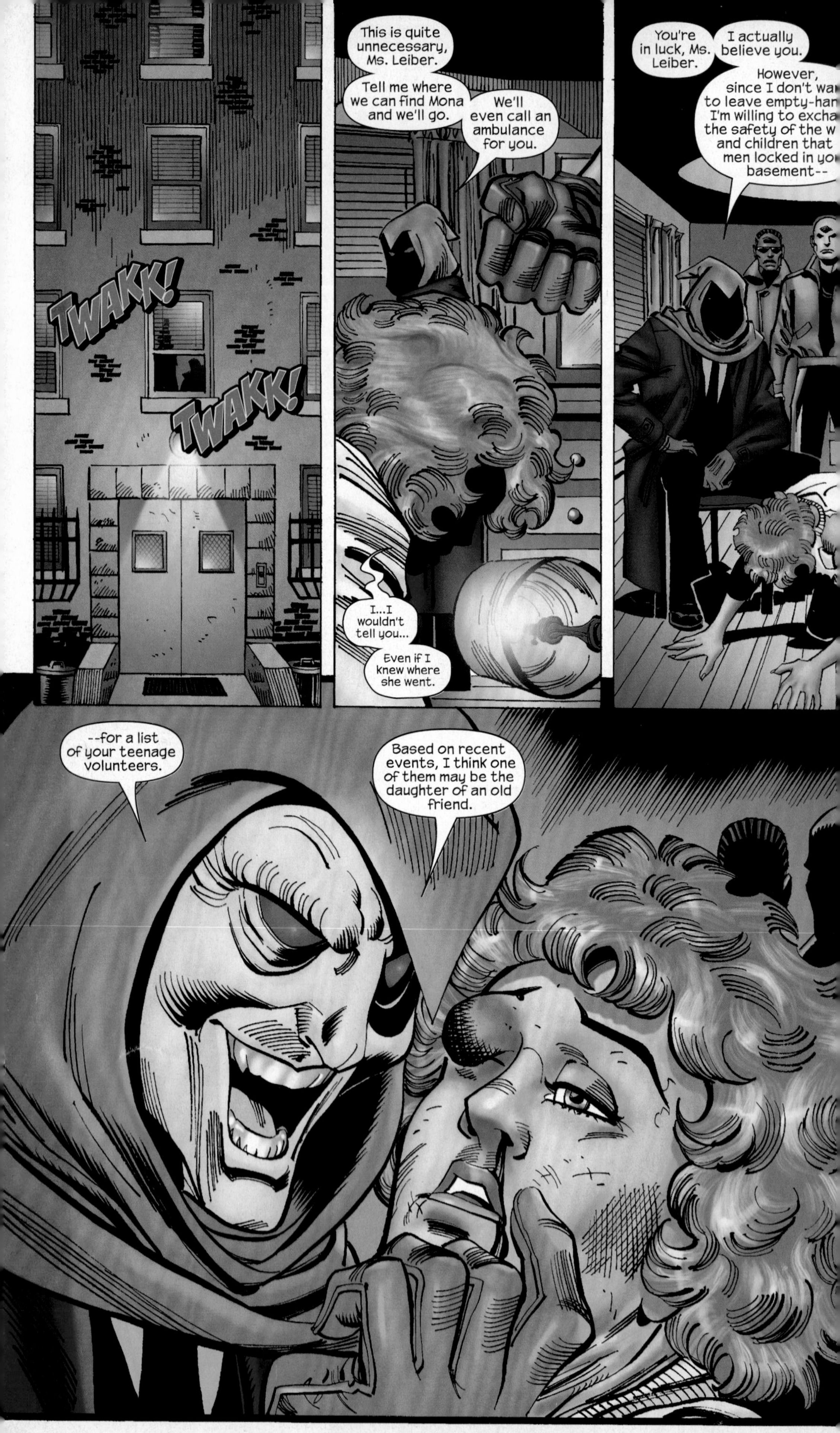
TWAKK!
TWAKK!
This is quite unnecessary, Ms. Leiber.
Tell me where we can find Mona and we'll go.
We'll even call an ambulance for you.
I...I wouldn't tell you...
Even if I knew where she went.
You're in luck, Ms. Leiber.
I actually believe you.
However, since I don't wa to leave empty-han I'm willing to excha the safety of the w and children that men locked in yo basement--
--for a list of your teenage volunteers.
Based on recent events, I think one of them may be the daughter of an old friend.

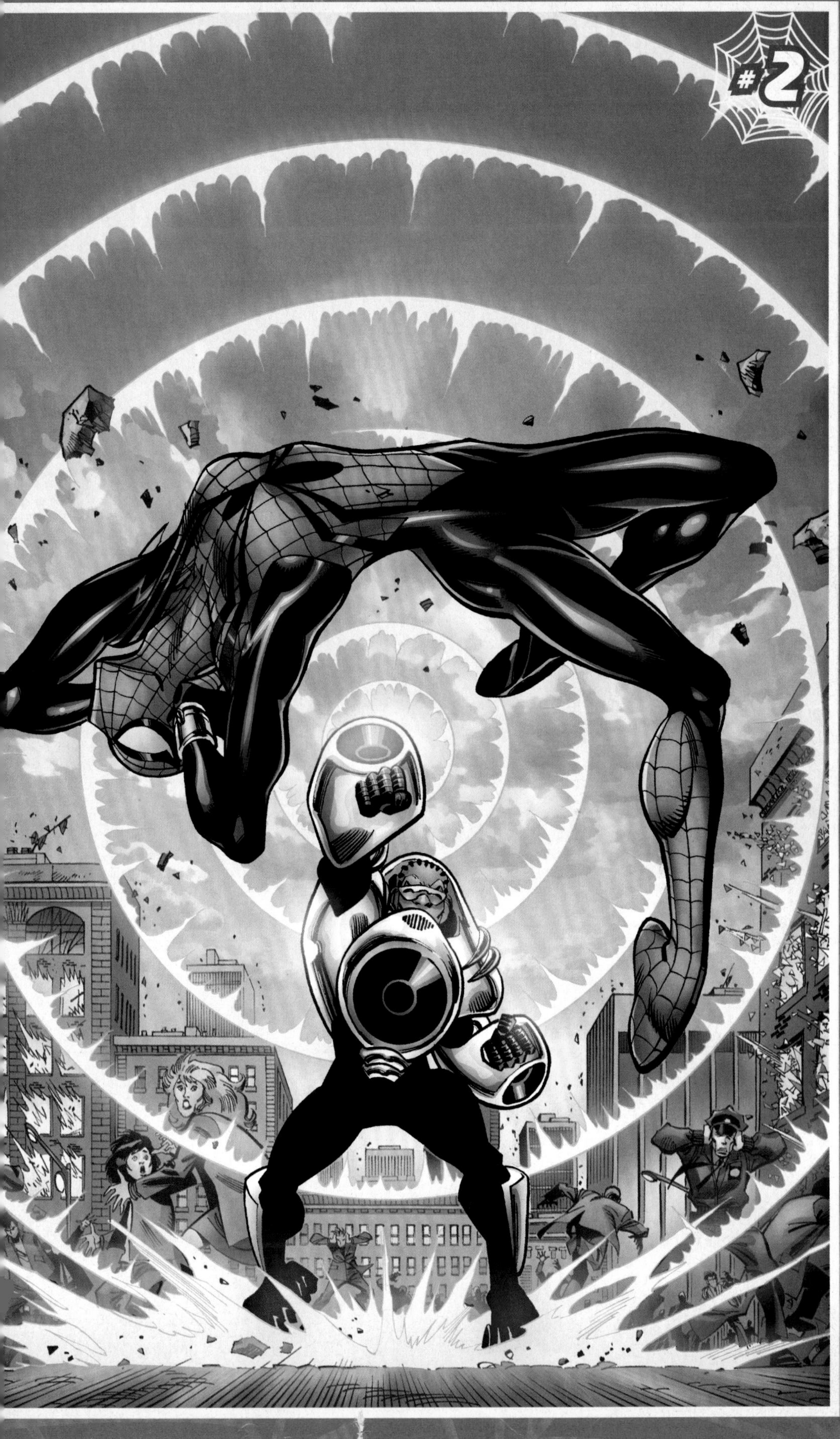
#2

D-did someone hurt one of them poor ladies?

Please step back, sir.

There's nothing to see here.

Officer, can you confirm that *Caitlan Leiber,* the managing director of *St. Andrews Shelter,* was brutally beaten last night?

Please step back, ma'am.

But *officer,* the public has a *right* to know--!

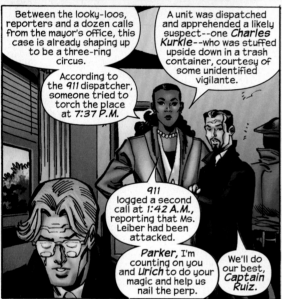

Between the looky-loos, reporters and a dozen calls from the mayor's office, this case is already shaping up to be a three-ring circus.

According to the *911* dispatcher, someone tried to *torch* the place at 7:37 P.M.

A unit was dispatched and apprehended a likely suspect--one *Charles Kurkle*--who was stuffed upside down in a trash container, courtesy of some unidentified vigilante.

911 logged a second call at 1:42 A.M., reporting that Ms. Leiber had been attacked.

Parker, I'm counting on you and *Urich* to do your magic and help us nail the perp.

We'll do our best, *Captain Ruiz.*

Find anything, *Phil?*

Nothing ou of the ordina *Pete.*

Dozens of hair and fiber samples, but they probably belong to the residents.

What have you got for me, *Drasco?*

An unknown number of masked men entered the premises at approximately 1:05 A.M. and herded everyone except the *vic* upstairs.

There may be *more* to this case than meets the eye, Pete...

...especially since we both know someone who *volunteers* here.

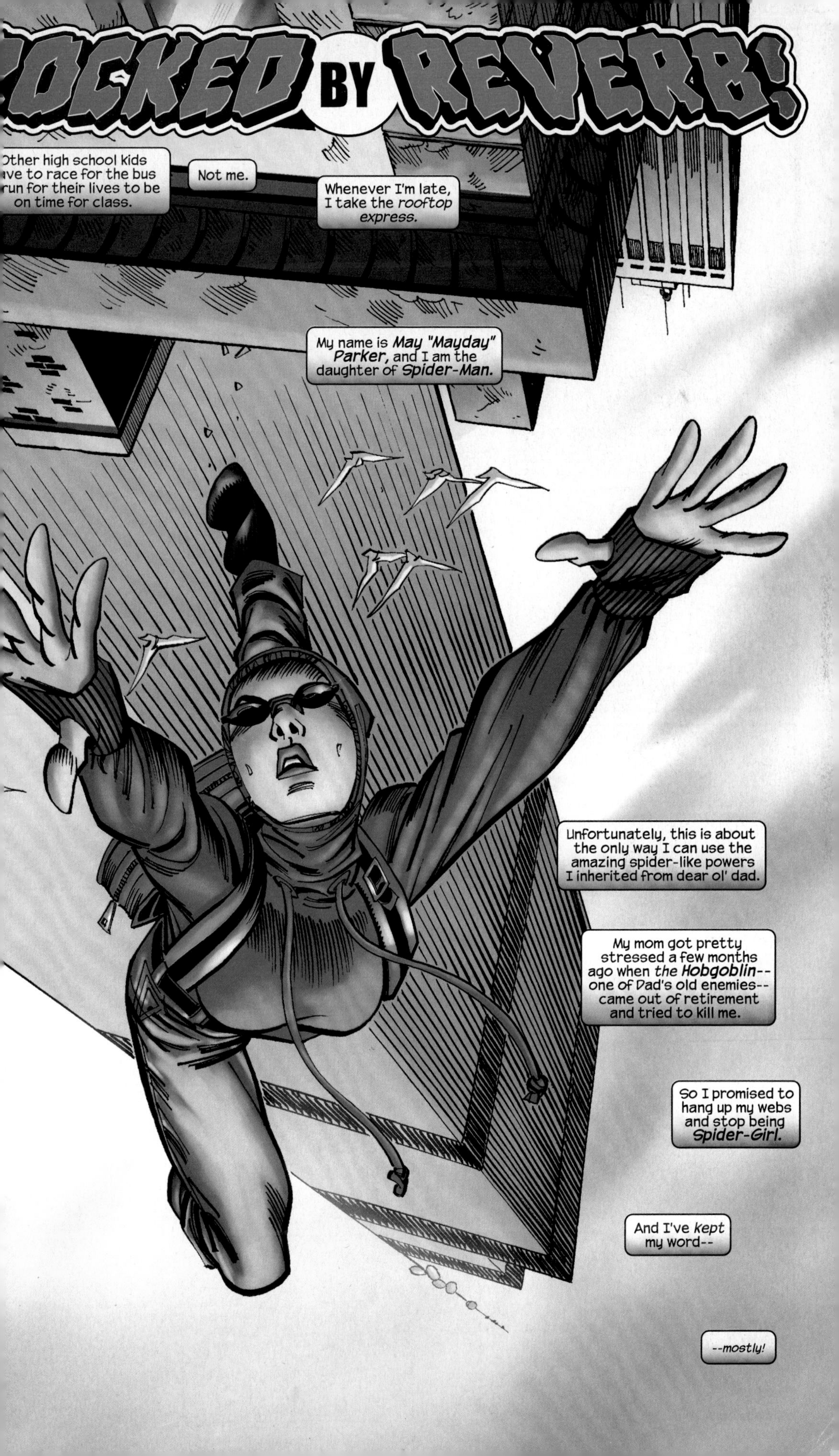

OCKED BY REVERB!
Other high school kids ave to race for the bus run for their lives to be on time for class.
Not me.
Whenever I'm late, I take the rooftop express.
My name is May "Mayday" Parker, and I am the daughter of Spider-Man.
Unfortunately, this is about the only way I can use the amazing spider-like powers I inherited from dear ol' dad.
My mom got pretty stressed a few months ago when the Hobgoblin--one of Dad's old enemies--came out of retirement and tried to kill me.
So I promised to hang up my webs and stop being Spider-Girl.
And I've kept my word--
--mostly!

Okay.

Okay!

If you want to get technical, I may be violating the *spirit* of the agreement--

--which probably explains why I'm riding the *gallopin'* guilts!

Sure, I can rationalize my actions.

I'm a candidate for student council, so I can't afford to be late.

Guess that means I'm a two-faced politician--

--as well as a dishonest daughter.

Hey, May--!

We've been looking all over for you.

What's the problem, guys? Did we have another campaign meeting scheduled for this morning?

Have you seen today's *Daily Bugle?* Someone tried to burn down *St. Andrew's* last night.

And if that wasn't bad enough, Caitlan got mugged sometime after midnight.

What--?!

The details are still kind of sketchy. I figure I'll head over after school and get the real scoop.

You want to come?

Can't do it, Courtney. May and I have a campaign meeting.

How about I go to *Davida's* meeting and meet you later?

Sounds like a plan.

I knew about the atter arson. That's when I f violated my mother's tr deciding to play *he*

I was trying to solv problem, but I might h just made things *wor*

Did my actions spar some sort of retribu against Caitlan?

Am I som responsib her att

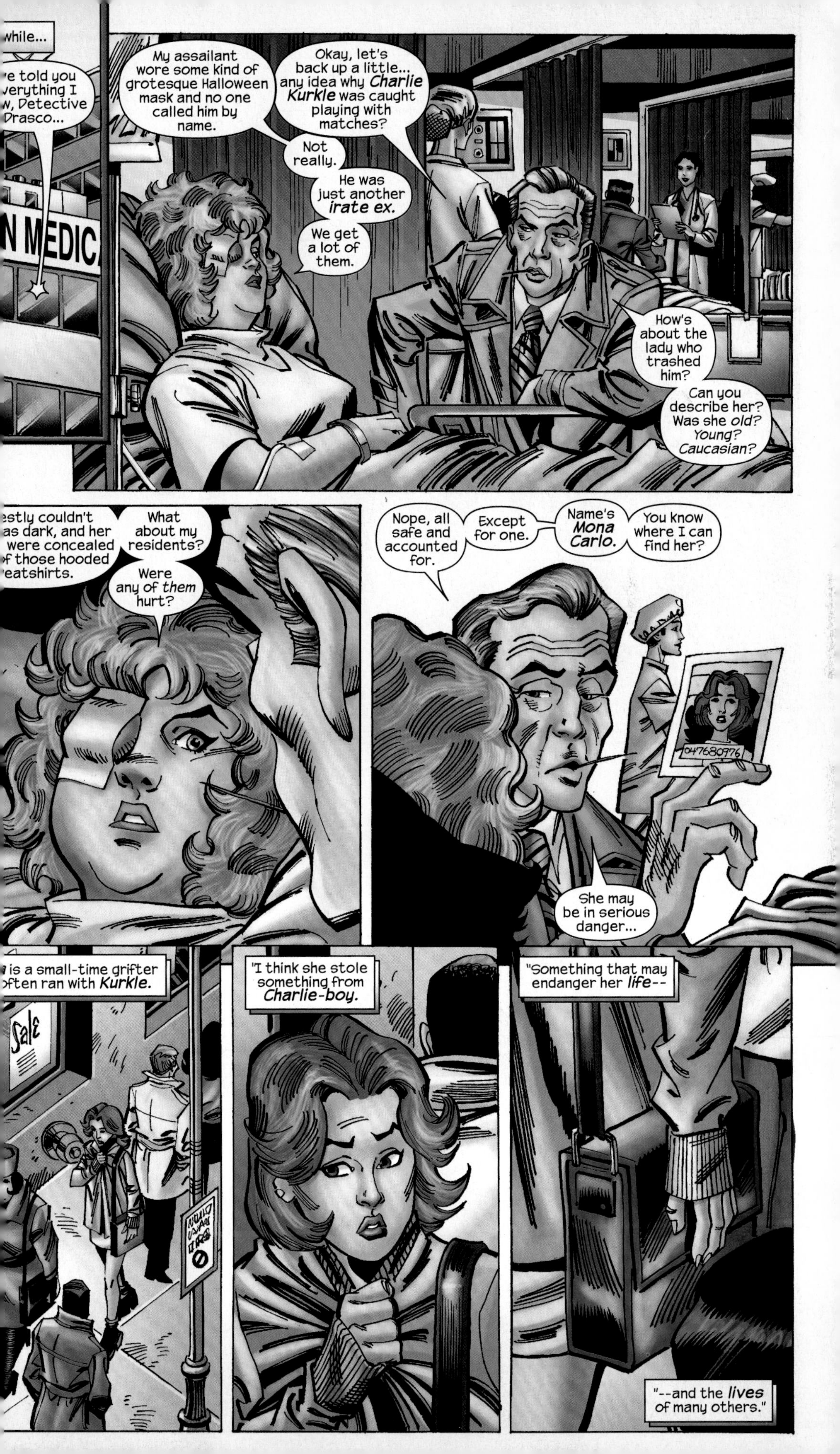
while...
'e told you
verything I
w, Detective
Drasco...
My assailant wore some kind of grotesque Halloween mask and no one called him by name.
Okay, let's back up a little... any idea why Charlie Kurkle was caught playing with matches?
Not really.
He was just another irate ex.
We get a lot of them.
N MEDIC
How's about the lady who trashed him?
Can you describe her? Was she old? Young? Caucasian?
estly couldn't
as dark, and her
were concealed
f those hooded
eatshirts.
What about my residents?
Were any of them hurt?
Nope, all safe and accounted for.
Except for one.
Name's Mona Carlo.
You know where I can find her?
047680976
She may be in serious danger...
is a small-time grifter
ften ran with Kurkle.
Sale
"I think she stole something from Charlie-boy.
"Something that may endanger her life--
"--and the lives of many others."

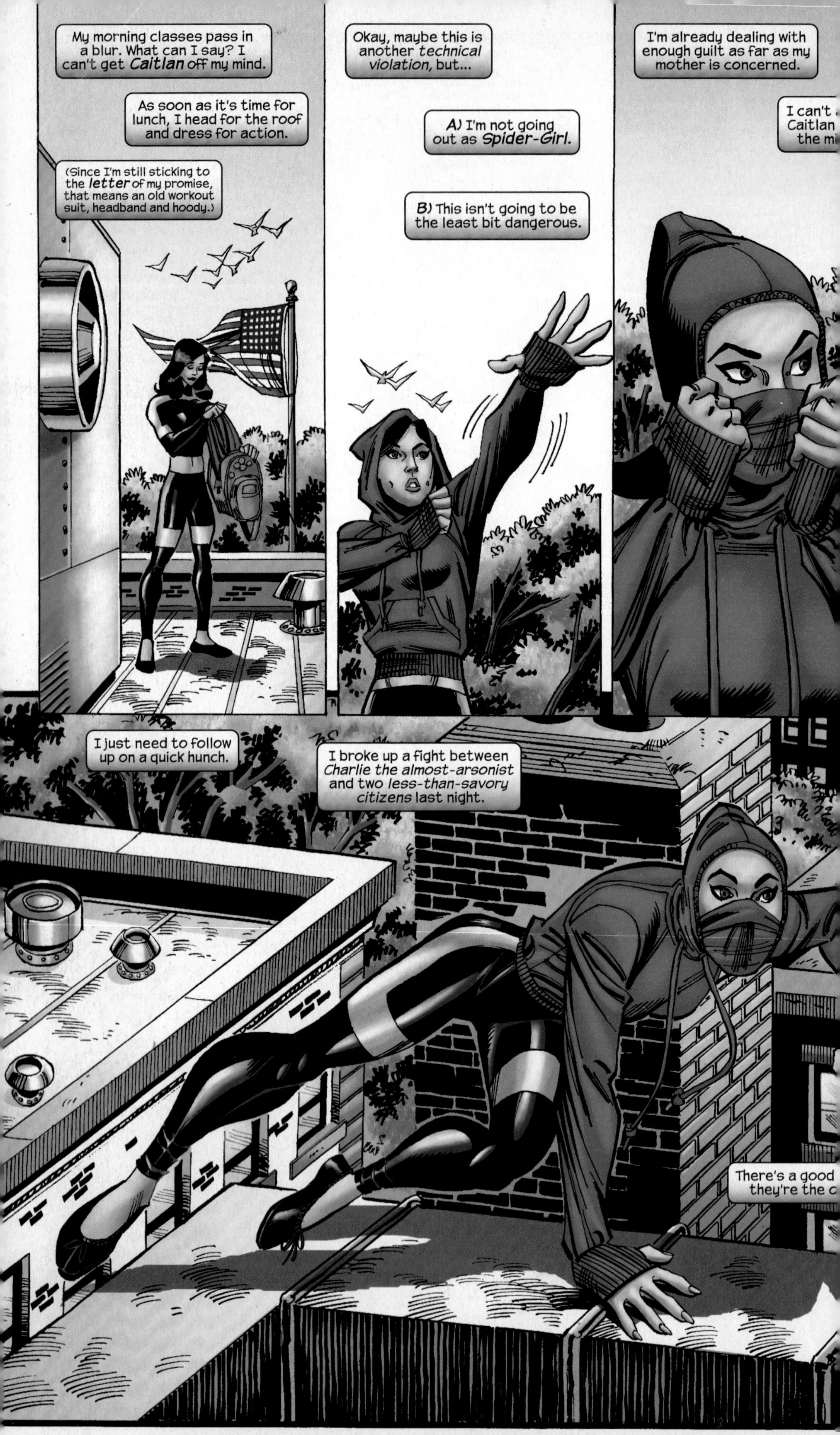
My morning classes pass in a blur. What can I say? I can't get *Caitlan* off my mind.
As soon as it's time for lunch, I head for the roof and dress for action.
(Since I'm still sticking to the *letter* of my promise, that means an old workout suit, headband and hoody.)
Okay, maybe this is another *technical violation*, but...
A) I'm not going out as *Spider-Girl*.
B) This isn't going to be the least bit dangerous.
I'm already dealing with enough guilt as far as my mother is concerned.
I can't
Caitlan
I just need to follow up on a quick hunch.
I broke up a fight between *Charlie the almost-arsonist* and two *less-than-savory citizens* last night.
There's a good
they're the

...ho hurt
...aitlan!

...nce our
...ssion with
...oman from
...Andrew's
...ed so dis-
...pointing--

--I have placed a rather sizable reward on the street for any information that can lead us to *Mona Carlo.*

There is a *war* coming, gentlemen. A war that will determine the next *kingpin of crime!* The item in her possession could help me *win* that war.

You want us to join the search, boss?

No, Barney. I have other, more elaborate plans for you and Rudolf.

I assume you've both heard of *Spider-Girl.* She vanished a few months ago and no one seems to know what's become of her.

I have recently come to suspect that she has a personal connection to *St. Andrew's.*

Since I wish to renew our acquaintance, I want you to target the shelter's teenage volunteers.

Attack them one at a time until you flush her out.

Uhhh...

Sure.

You're the *boss.*

Only...what are we supposed to do if *Spider-Girl* actually shows?

...n
...lent
...tion,
...olf.

You will employ this equipment to subdue her.

I based the design on some advanced *sonic technology* that recently came into my possession.

The outfit's weaponry should be self-explanatory, but I included an instruction manual.

If you can capture her *alive,* please do so.

If not, *c'est la vie!*

Now, if you will excuse me, I am needed else-where...

This could be your big break, Barney.

You always wanted to be one of those costumed guys.

Forget it, Rudy!

No way *I'm* climbing into no experimental super-suit.

This is the ice cream parlor that I tracked those two thugs to.

Might as well see if they're home.

If I'm real lucky, they're already overwhelmed with guilt--

--and have left a couple of neatly typed confessions for me to find.

Otherwise, I'm not sure how to proceed.

I have no real detective skills--

--and doubt I'd recognize an *honest-to-gosh* clu unless it jump up and bit me

The boss was talking to *you* when he--*Hey!*

Something moving around upstairs?

This discussion isn't over. You're not getting out of this that easy.

Okay, but while I'm gone--

--you might as well flip through the manual.

Y'know... just in case!

I'm not laughing, Barney.

≈UFFFT≈

≈MAKT

Barney--?

Barney--?

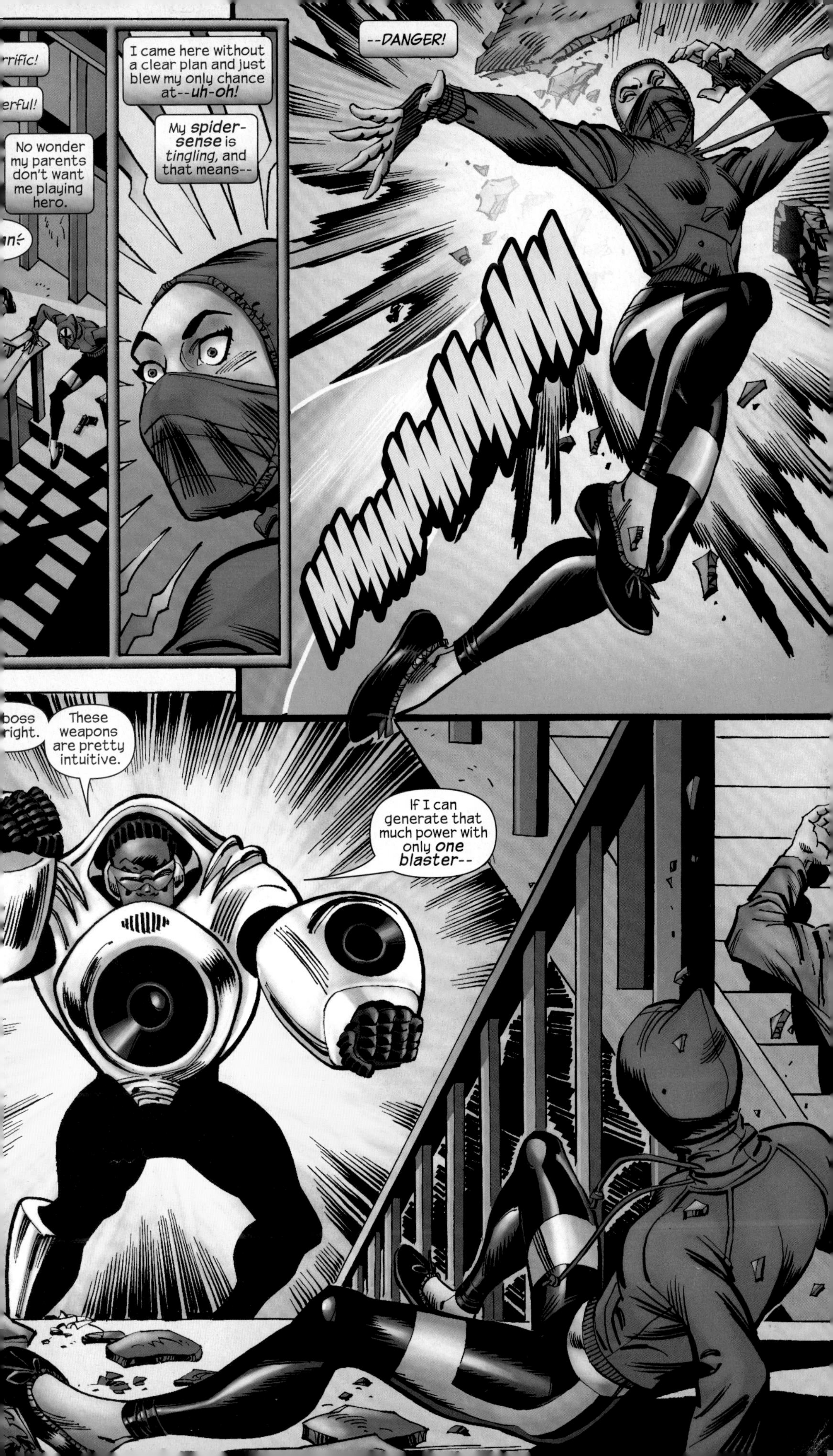
rrific!
erful!
No wonder my parents don't want me playing hero.
I came here without a clear plan and just blew my only chance at--*uh-oh!*
My *spider-sense* is *tingling,* and that means--
--*DANGER!*
MMMMMMMMMM
boss right.
These weapons are pretty intuitive.
If I can generate that much power with only *one blaster*--

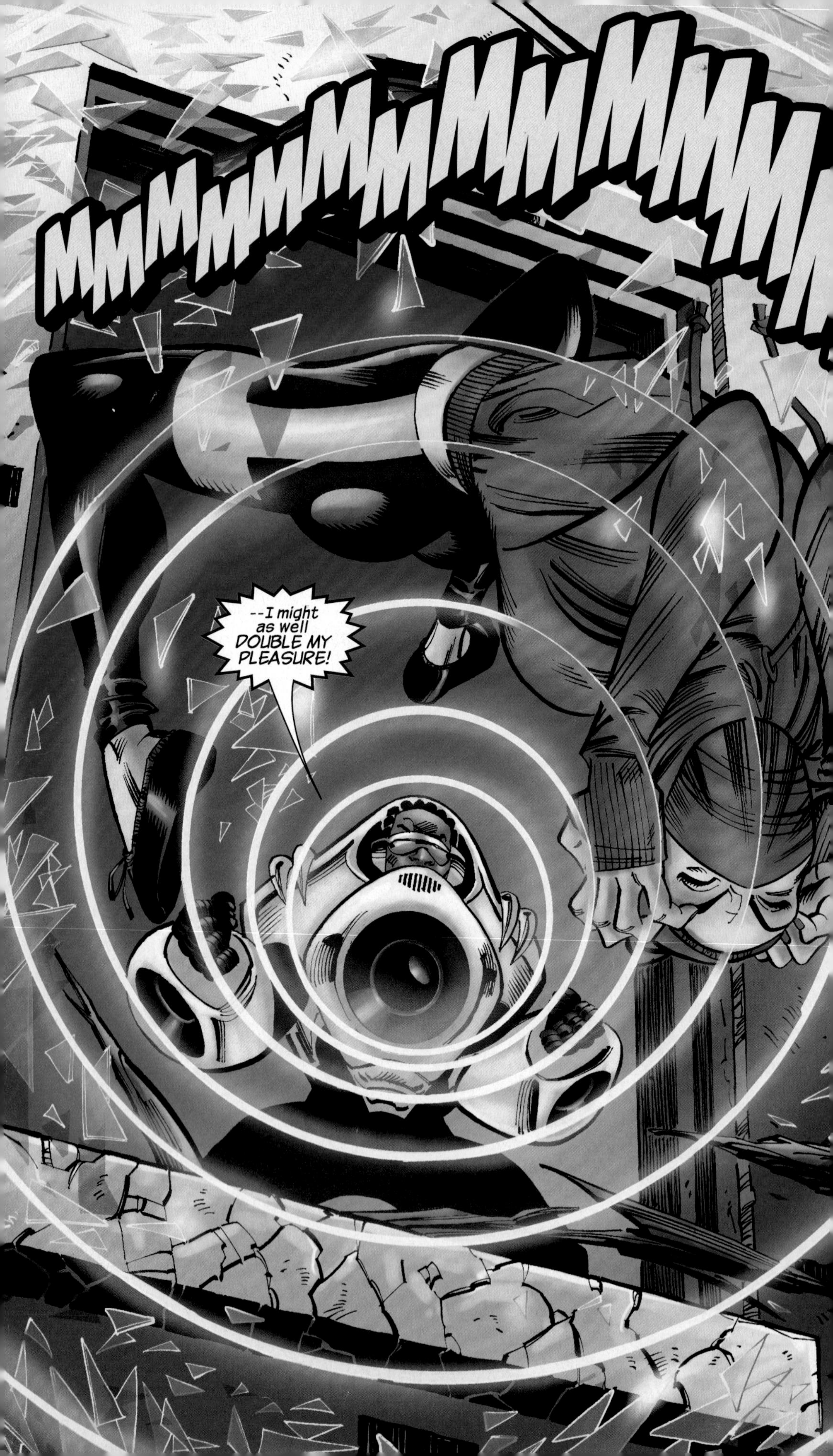
MMMMMMMMMMMMMMMM
--I might as well DOUBLE MY PLEASURE!

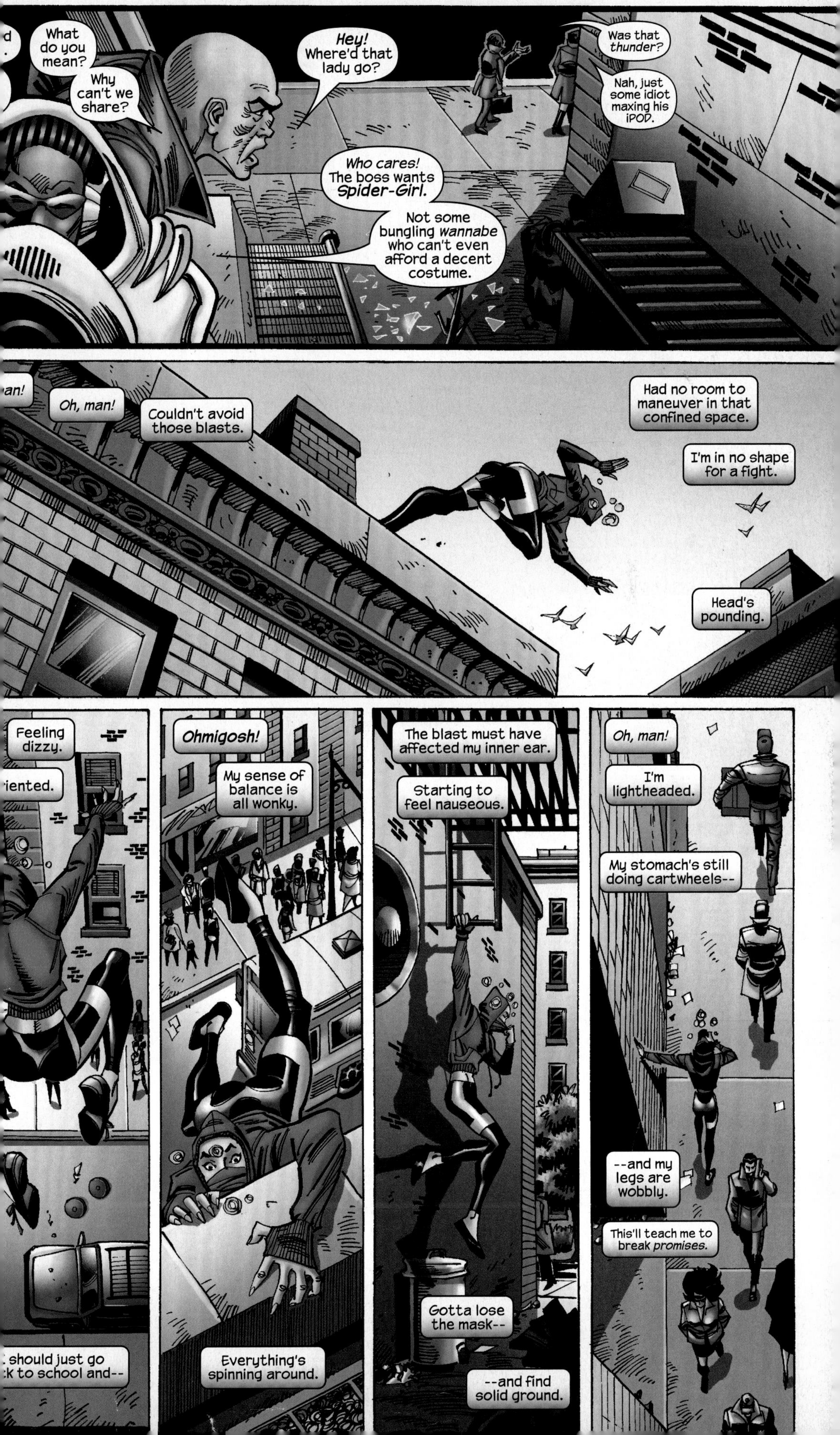
What do you mean?
Why can't we share?
Hey! Where'd that lady go?
Was that thunder?
Nah, just some idiot maxing his iPOD.
Who cares! The boss wants Spider-Girl.
Not some bungling wannabe who can't even afford a decent costume.
Oh, man!
Couldn't avoid those blasts.
Had no room to maneuver in that confined space.
I'm in no shape for a fight.
Head's pounding.
Feeling dizzy.
iented.
should just go
k to school and--
Ohmigosh!
My sense of balance is all wonky.
Everything's spinning around.
The blast must have affected my inner ear.
Starting to feel nauseous.
Gotta lose the mask--
--and find solid ground.
Oh, man!
I'm lightheaded.
My stomach's still doing cartwheels--
--and my legs are wobbly.
This'll teach me to break promises.

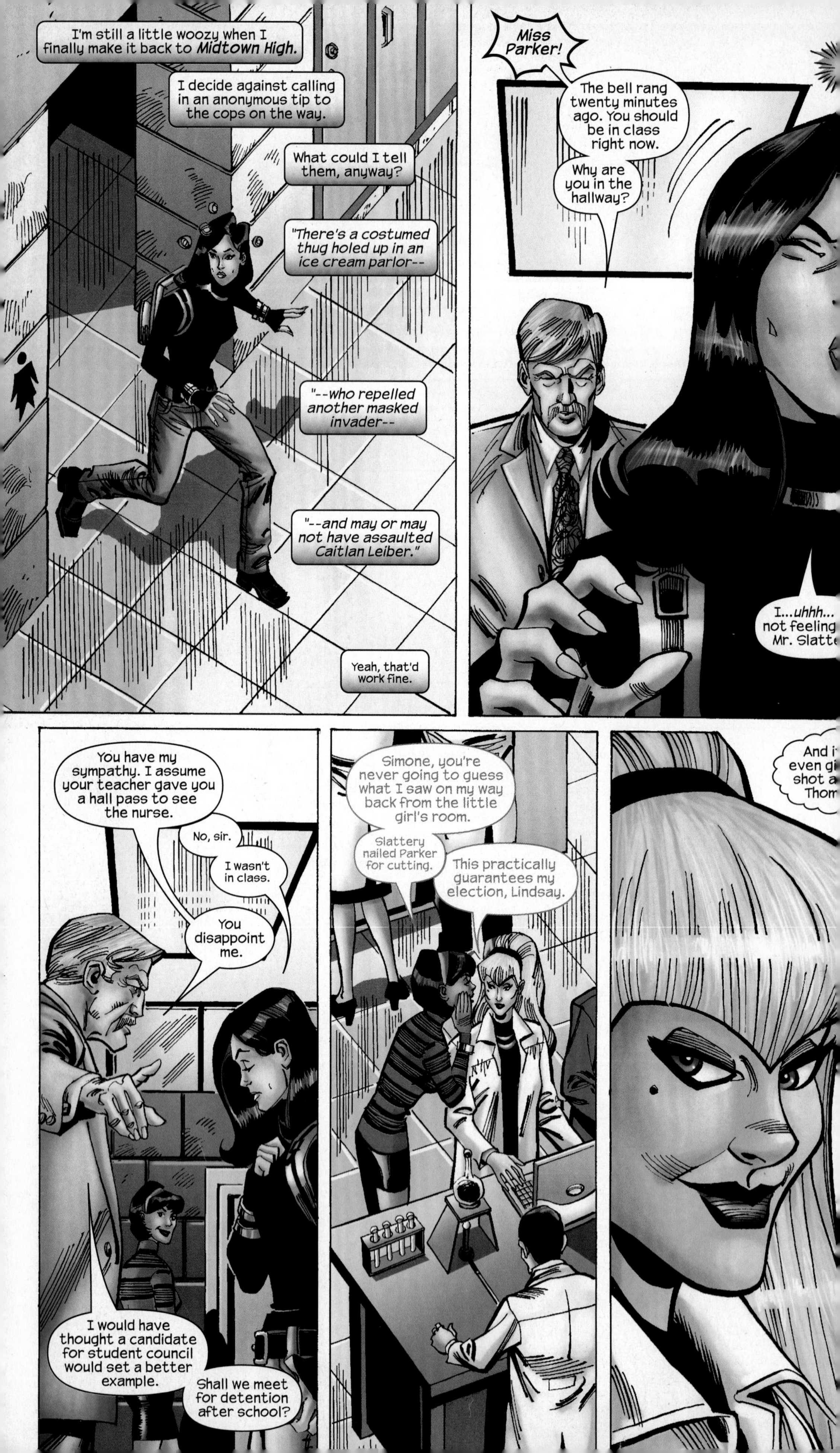
I'm still a little woozy when I finally make it back to *Midtown High.*
I decide against calling in an anonymous tip to the cops on the way.
What could I tell them, anyway?
"There's a costumed thug holed up in an ice cream parlor--
"--who repelled another masked invader--
"--and may or may not have assaulted Caitlan Leiber."
Yeah, that'd work fine.
Miss Parker!
The bell rang twenty minutes ago. You should be in class right now.
Why are you in the hallway?
I...*uhhh...* not feeling Mr. Slatte
You have my sympathy. I assume your teacher gave you a hall pass to see the nurse.
No, sir.
I wasn't in class.
You disappoint me.
I would have thought a candidate for student council would set a better example.
Shall we meet for detention after school?
Simone, you're never going to guess what I saw on my way back from the little girl's room.
Slattery nailed Parker for cutting.
This practically guarantees my election, Lindsay.
And i even gi shot a Thom

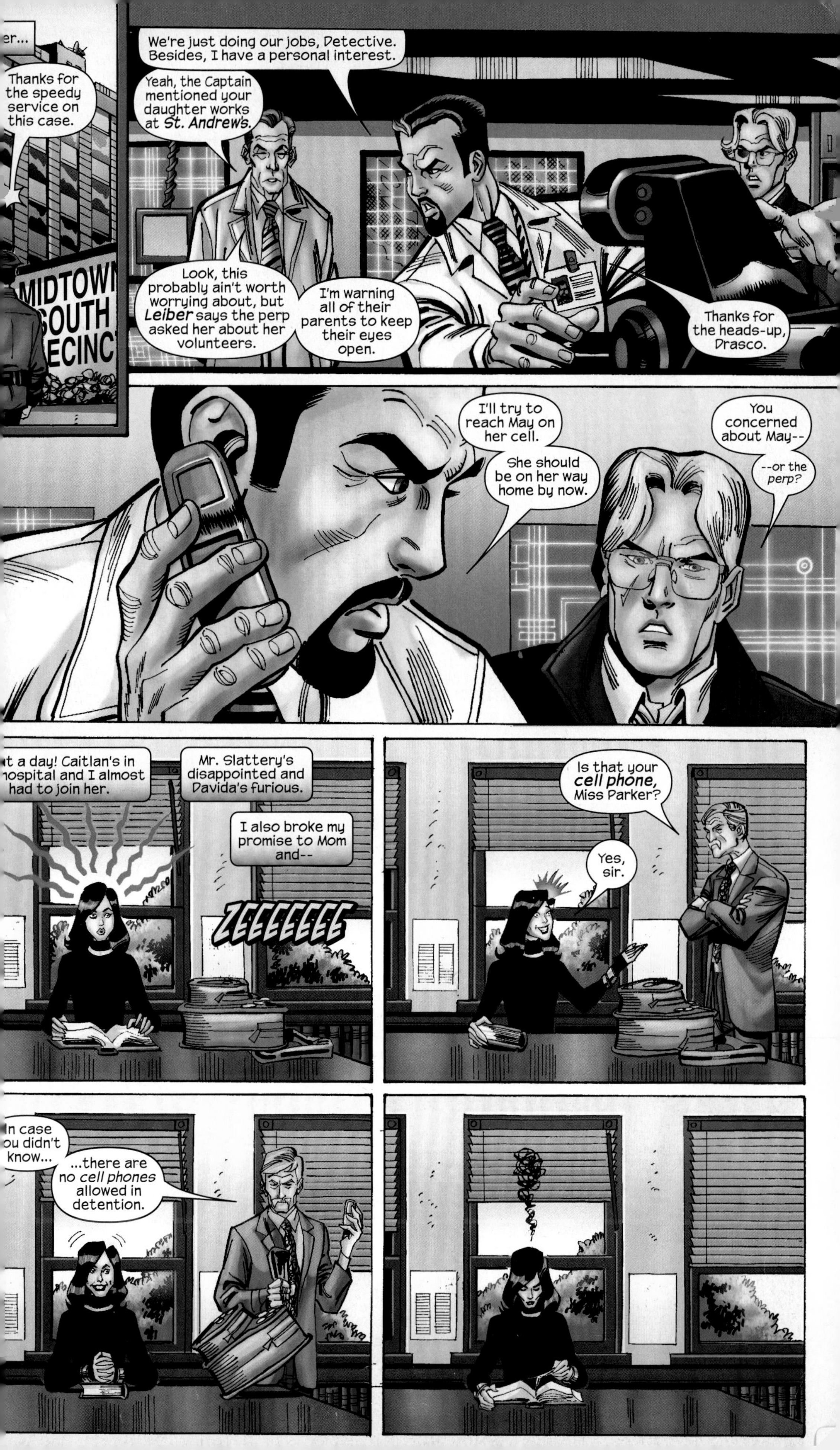

er...
Thanks for the speedy service on this case.
We're just doing our jobs, Detective. Besides, I have a personal interest.
Yeah, the Captain mentioned your daughter works at St. Andrew's.
MIDTOWN SOUTH ECINCT
Look, this probably ain't worth worrying about, but Leiber says the perp asked her about her volunteers.
I'm warning all of their parents to keep their eyes open.
Thanks for the heads-up, Drasco.
I'll try to reach May on her cell.
She should be on her way home by now.
You concerned about May--
--or the perp?
t a day! Caitlan's in hospital and I almost had to join her.
Mr. Slattery's disappointed and Davida's furious.
I also broke my promise to Mom and--
ZEEEEEEE
Is that your cell phone, Miss Parker?
Yes, sir.
In case ou didn't know...
...there are no cell phones allowed in detention.

No answer, Parker?

You know how teenagers are. They always screen their parents.

I'll give my wife a call.

Sorry, Peter. I haven't heard from her, but that's the way it's been ever since she decided to run for student council.

What--

Yes, she usually goes to St. Andrew's with Courtney.

I'll call th immediate

ZEEEEEEEL

My, my, you're even more *popular* than I suspected.

It could be *important*, sir.

I doubt it.

I am afraid Miss Parker is currently in detention--

--and will not be taking calls for the next forty-seven minutes.

D-detention--?

She's in detention?!

I suppose she's *safe* for the moment--

--but *Courtney* may not be!

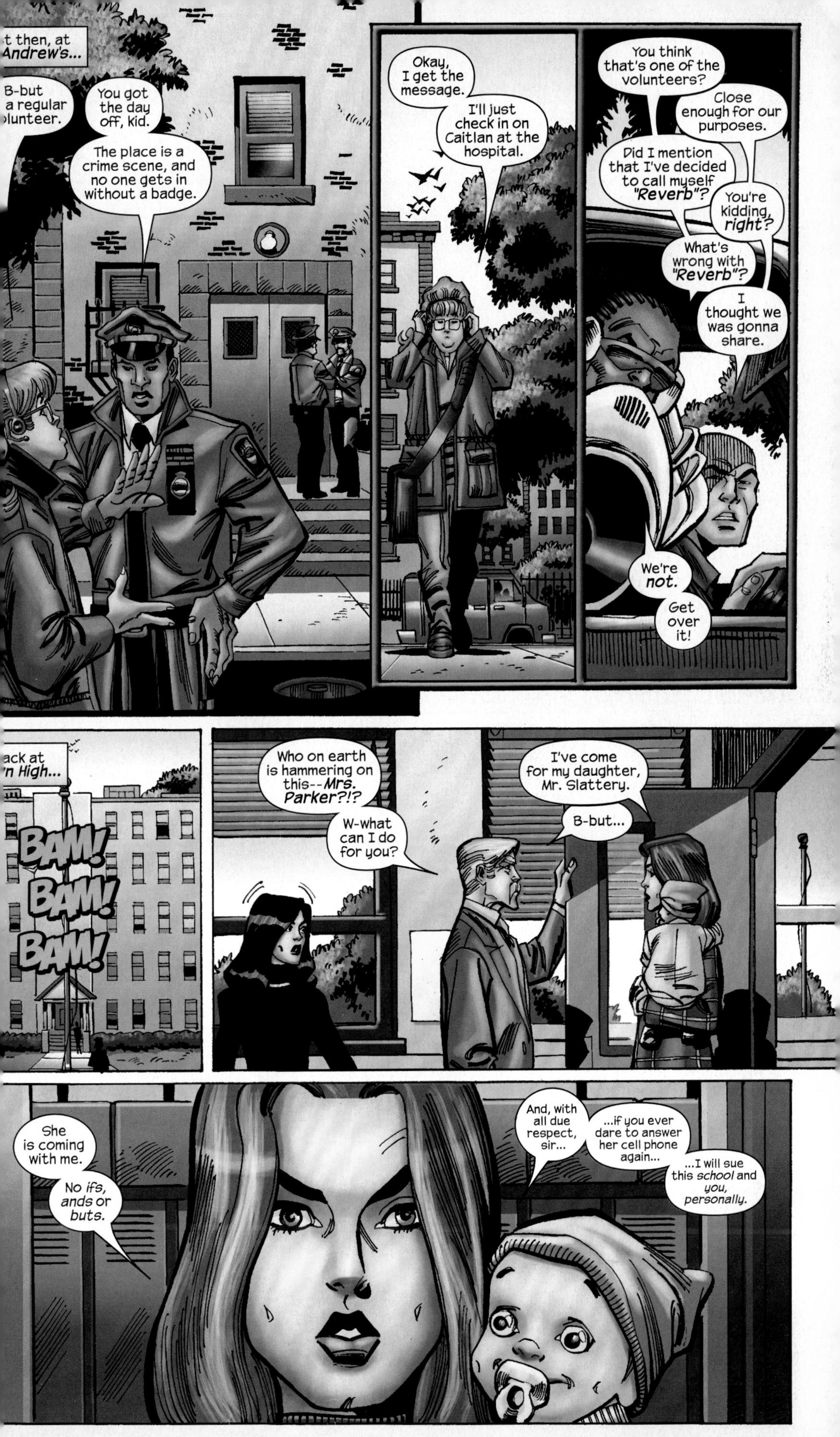
...t then, at
...Andrew's...
B-but
...a regular
...olunteer.
You got the day off, kid.
The place is a crime scene, and no one gets in without a badge.
Okay, I get the message.
I'll just check in on Caitlan at the hospital.
You think that's one of the volunteers?
Close enough for our purposes.
Did I mention that I've decided to call myself "Reverb"?
You're kidding, right?
What's wrong with "Reverb"?
I thought we was gonna share.
We're not.
Get over it!
...ack at
...n High...
BAM! BAM! BAM!
Who on earth is hammering on this--Mrs. Parker?!?
W-what can I do for you?
I've come for my daughter, Mr. Slattery.
B-but...
She is coming with me.
No ifs, ands or buts.
And, with all due respect, sir...
...if you ever dare to answer her cell phone again...
...I will sue this school and you, personally.

Wow! Way to go, mom! I've never seen Slattery go speechless before.

But I'm not blameless. He actually had a legitimate reason for giving me--

We can sort that out when we get home. I need to know if you're feeling any *tingles.*

Wha--**oh!** You mean *tingle* tingles.

No, we're alone. It's safe to talk.

Your father called. The detectives think someone may be targeting the teenage volunteers at **St. Andrew's.**

Ohmigosh!

Courtney's headed over there.

Then it's a good thing I brought *this--!*

Are... ...you... *serious?!*

This doesn't change **anything,** May.

I can't help the way I feel.

I still hate the idea of you risking your life.

But I could never forgive myself if some other girl were hurt--

--beca I preve *Spider-* from sa her.

One thi

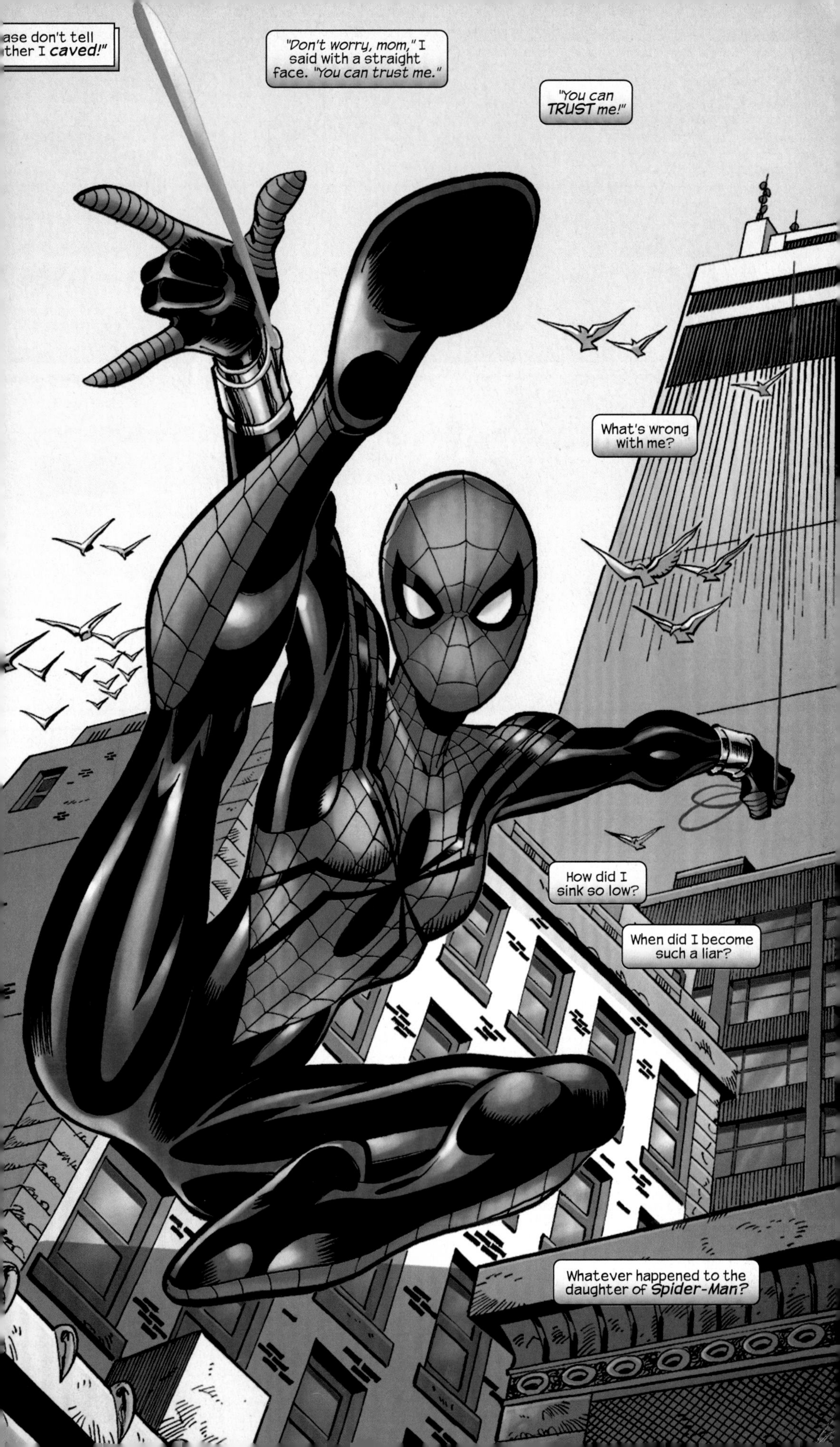
ase don't tell
ther I caved!"
"Don't worry, mom," I said with a straight face. "You can trust me."
"You can TRUST me!"
What's wrong with me?
How did I sink so low?
When did I become such a liar?
Whatever happened to the daughter of Spider-Man?

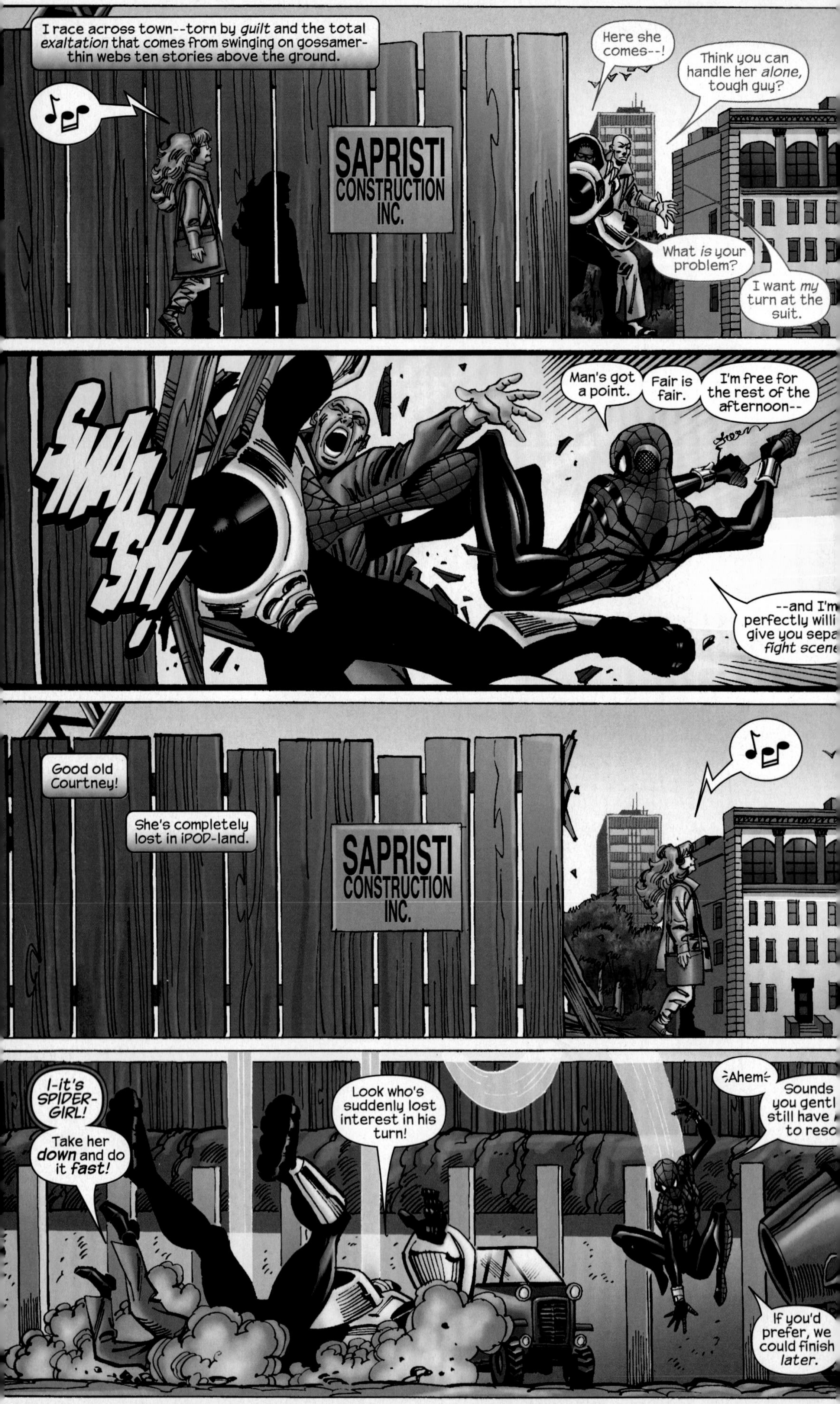

I race across town--torn by *guilt* and the total *exaltation* that comes from swinging on gossamer-thin webs ten stories above the ground.
Here she comes--!
Think you can handle her *alone*, tough guy?
SAPRISTI CONSTRUCTION INC.
What *is* your problem?
I want *my* turn at the suit.
SMASH!
Man's got a point.
Fair is fair.
I'm free for the rest of the afternoon--
--and I'm perfectly willi give you sepa *fight scene*
Good old Courtney!
She's completely lost in iPOD-land.
SAPRISTI CONSTRUCTION INC.
I-it's SPIDER-GIRL!
Take her *down* and do it *fast!*
Look who's suddenly lost interest in his turn!
Ahem
Sounds you gentl still have to reso
If you'd prefer, we could finish *later*.

--but there's no time like the present.

This won't take long, anyway.

Stay down, Barney--*and* watch me WORK!

W-whatever you say, pal.

Balance is still off. I barely managed to dodge that blast.

At least I can maneuver out here.

WHAAM!

Mind if I ask about your interest in *St. Andrew's*?

There's a huge *reward* for one of the former residents.

Why? What's so special about her?

Don't know. Don't care.

Haven't you ever heard *knowledge is power?*

What the--?!

WAP!

Oops! Is my impact webbing clogging your blasters?

WAP!

Clumsy me! I also gunked your main speaker.

You think this stupid webbing can stop me?

I'll just crank UP the volume--

--and blow it AWAY!

MMMMMMMM

Careful! This is a peaceful neighborhood.

You don't want to disturb anyone.

MMMMMMMMMMMM

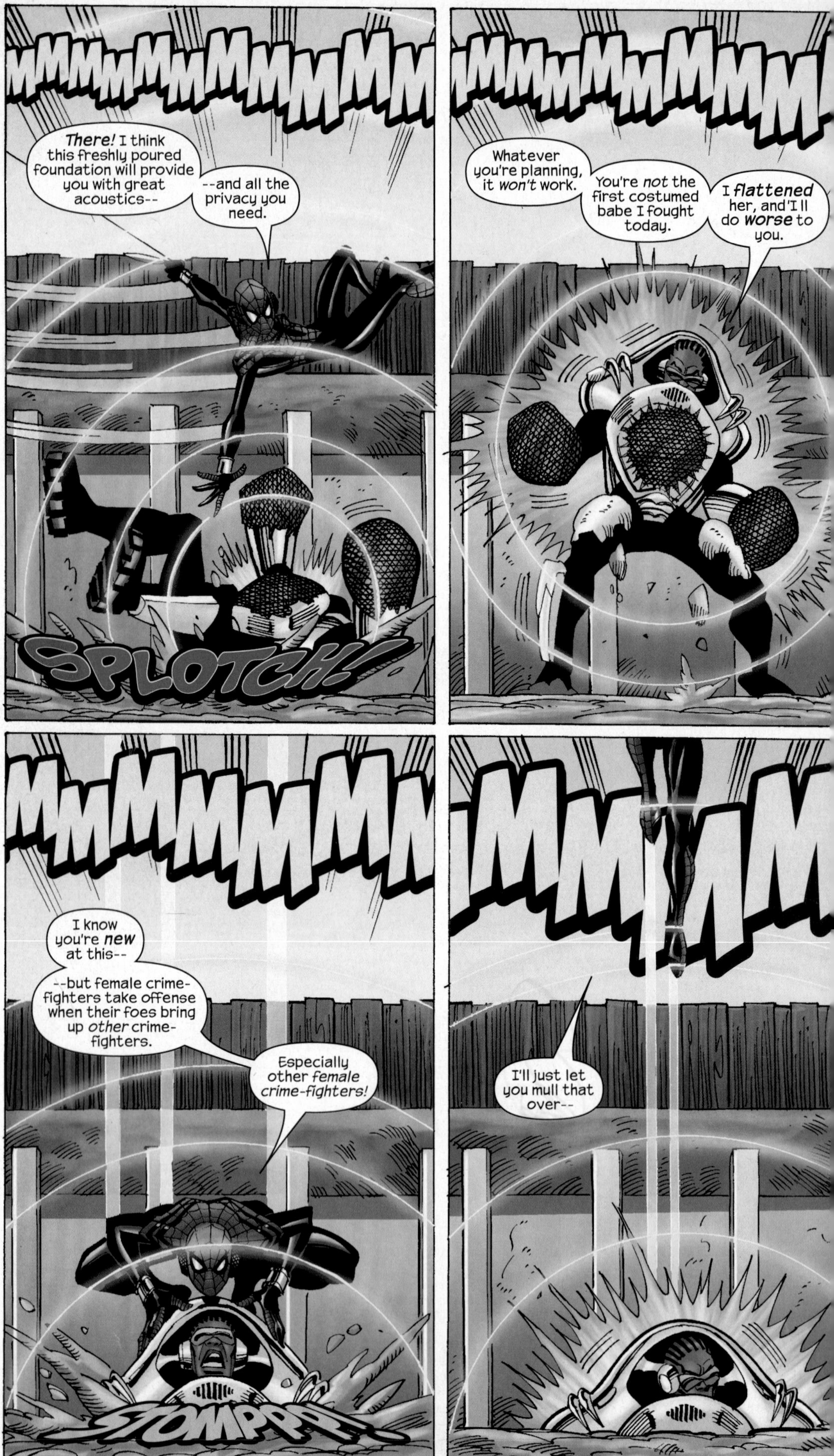
MMMMMMMMMMMMMM
There! I think this freshly poured foundation will provide you with great acoustics--
--and all the privacy you need.
SPLOTCH!
MMMMMMMMMMMMM
Whatever you're planning, it won't work.
You're not the first costumed babe I fought today.
I flattened her, and I'll do worse to you.
MMMMMMMMMM
I know you're new at this--
--but female crime-fighters take offense when their foes bring up other crime-fighters.
Especially other female crime-fighters!
STOMPPP!
MMMMM
I'll just let you mull that over--

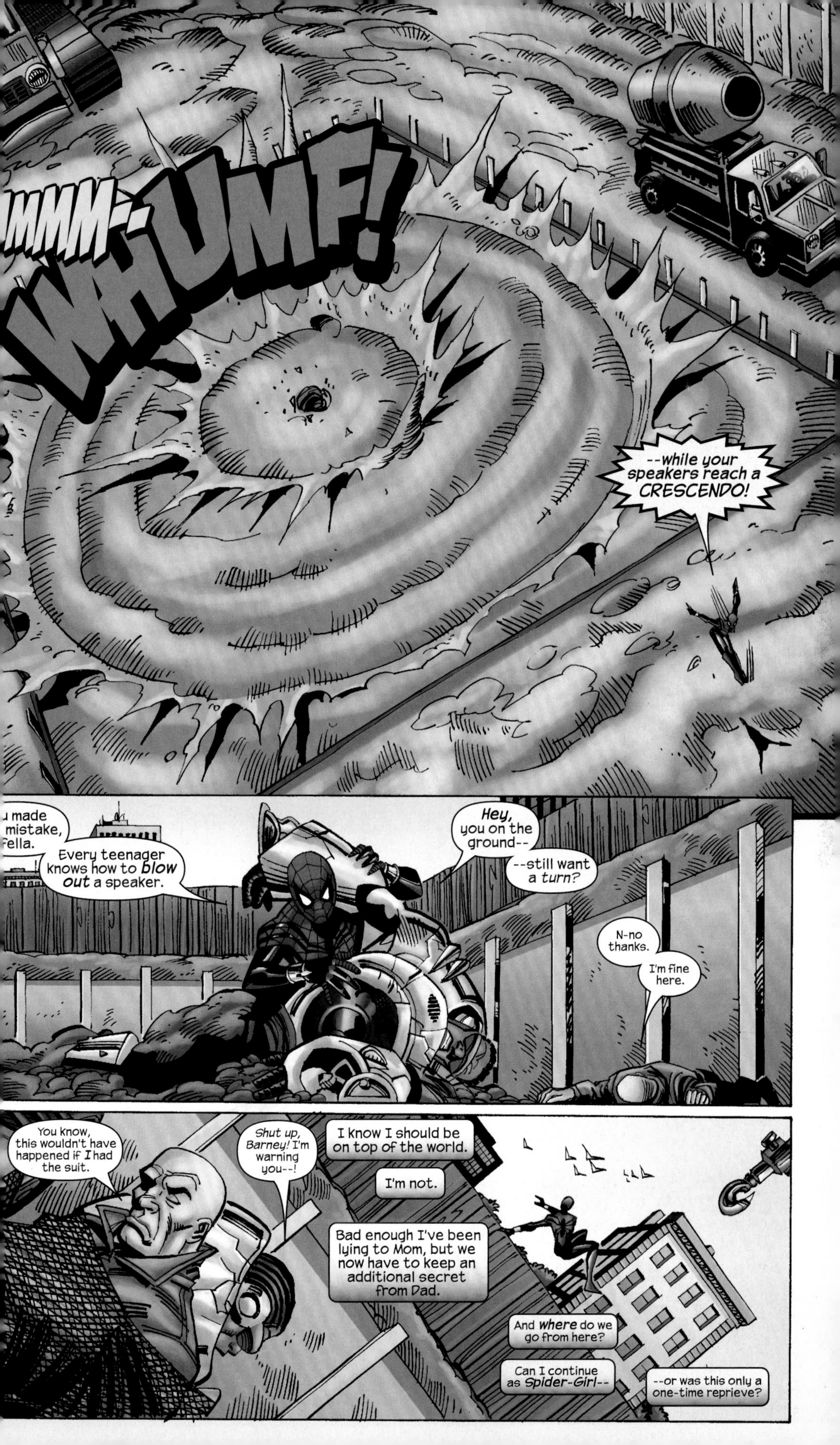
MMMM-
WHUMF!
--while your speakers reach a CRESCENDO!
u made mistake, fella.
Every teenager knows how to blow out a speaker.
Hey, you on the ground--
--still want a turn?
N-no thanks.
I'm fine here.
You know, this wouldn't have happened if I had the suit.
Shut up, Barney! I'm warning you--!
I know I should be on top of the world.
I'm not.
Bad enough I've been lying to Mom, but we now have to keep an additional secret from Dad.
And where do we go from here?
Can I continue as Spider-Girl--
--or was this only a one-time reprieve?

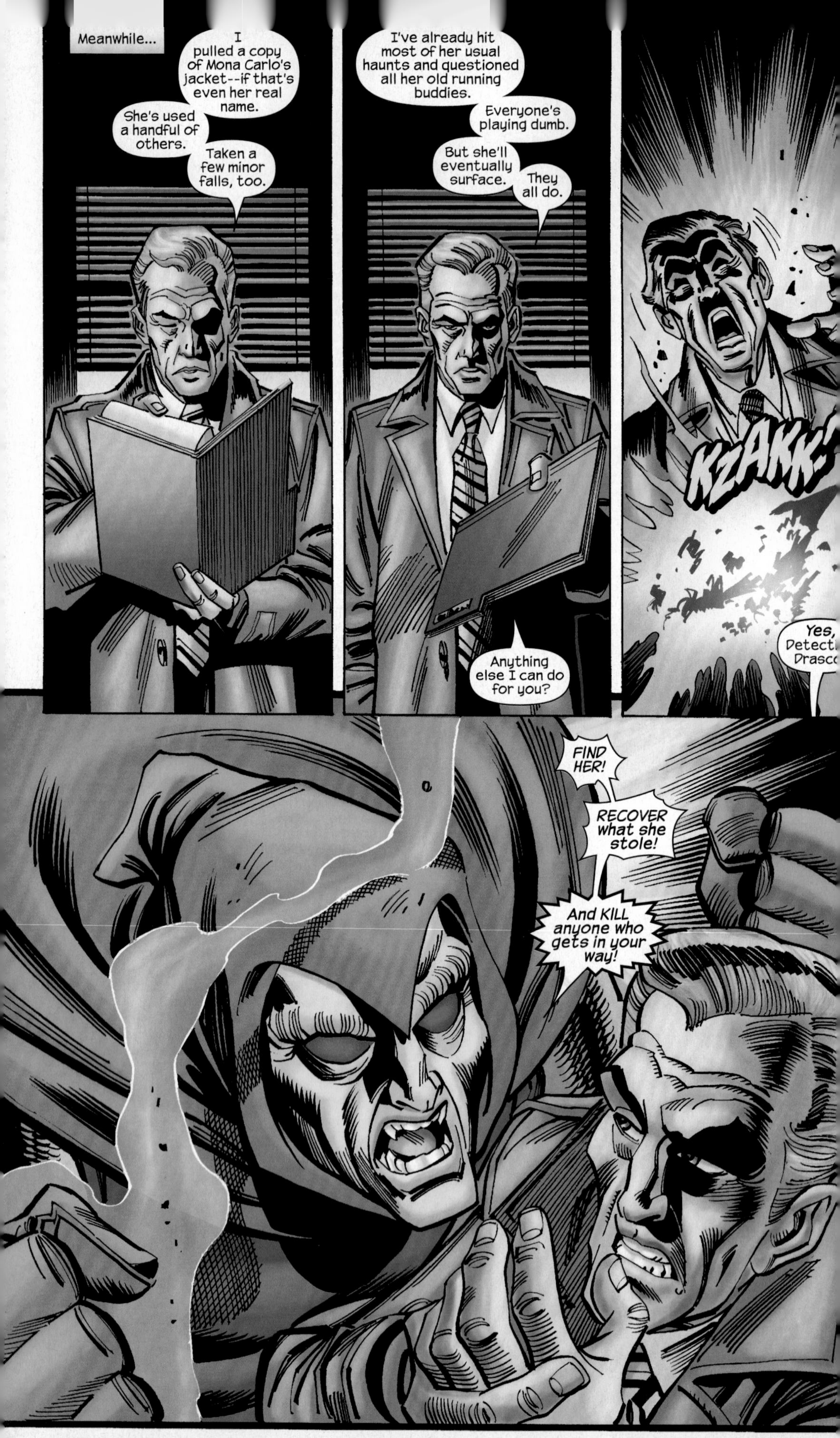

Meanwhile...
I pulled a copy of Mona Carlo's jacket--if that's even her real name.
She's used a handful of others.
Taken a few minor falls, too.
I've already hit most of her usual haunts and questioned all her old running buddies.
Everyone's playing dumb.
But she'll eventually surface.
They all do.
Anything else I can do for you?
KZAKK!
FIND HER!
RECOVER what she stole!
And KILL anyone who gets in your way!

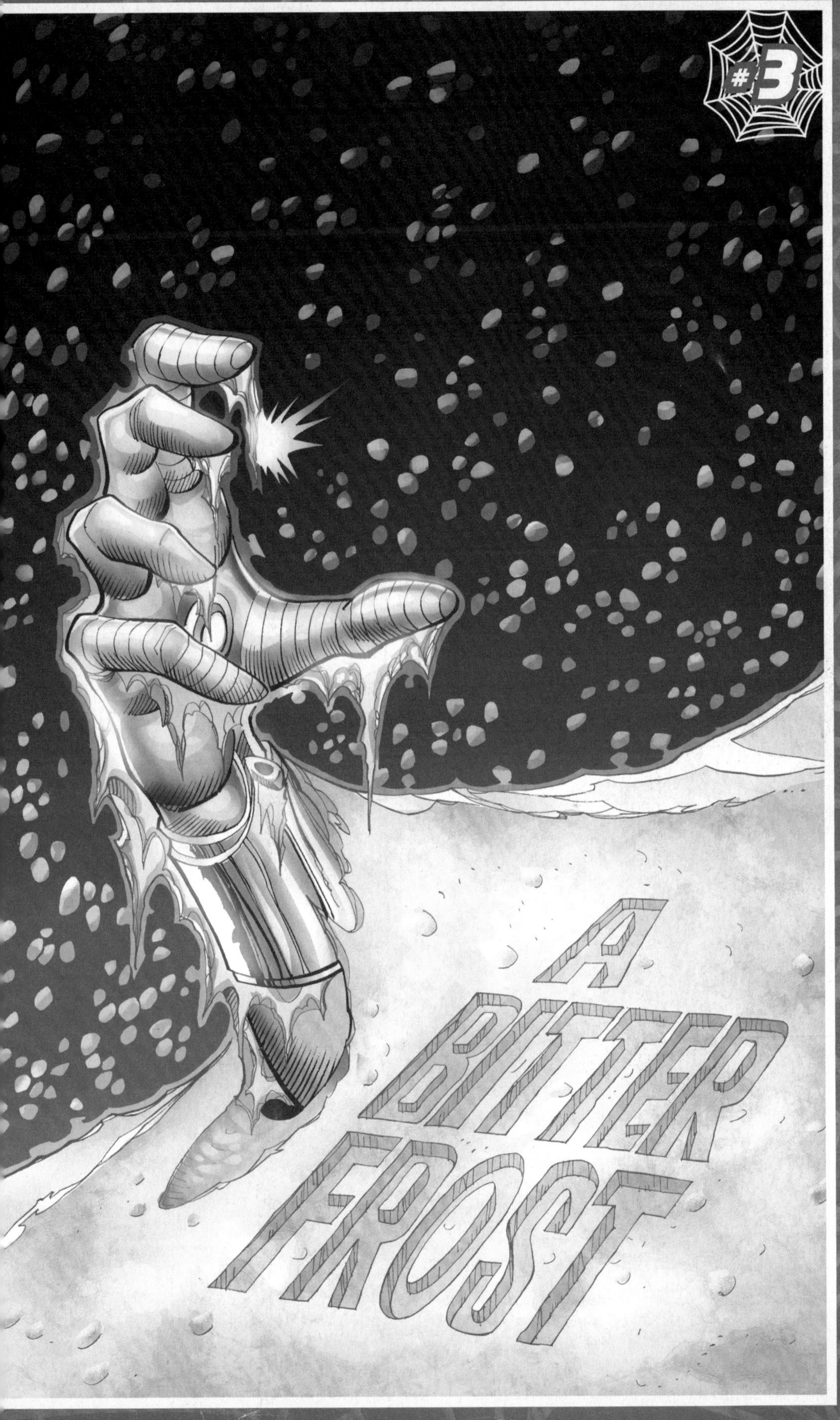
#3
A BITTER FROST

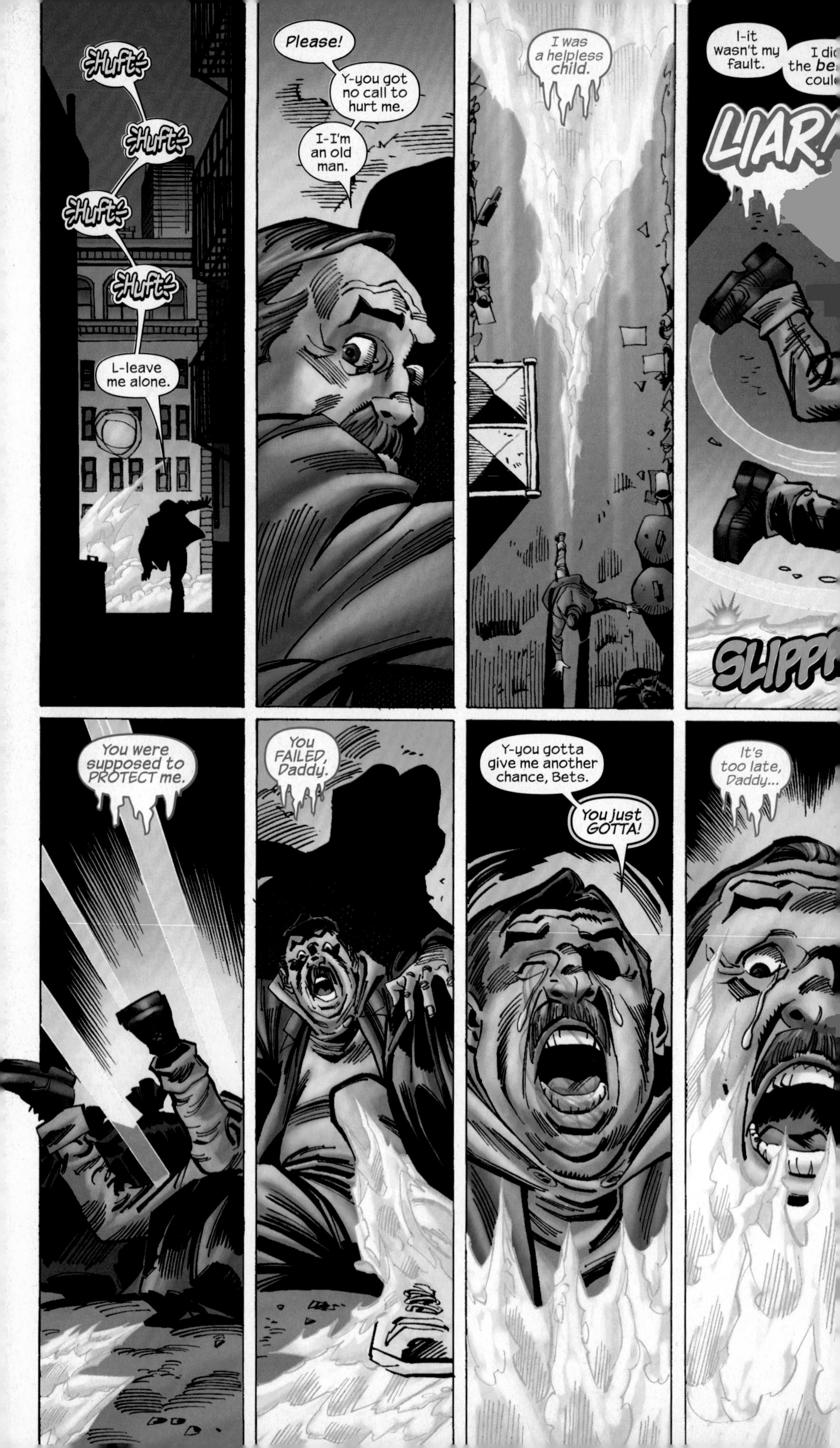
Huft
Huft
Huft
Huft
L-leave me alone.
Please!
Y-you got no call to hurt me.
I-I'm an old man.
I was a helpless child.
I-it wasn't my fault.
I di the be coul
LIAR
SLIPP
You were supposed to PROTECT me.
You FAILED, Daddy.
Y-you gotta give me another chance, Bets.
You just GOTTA!
It's too late, Daddy...

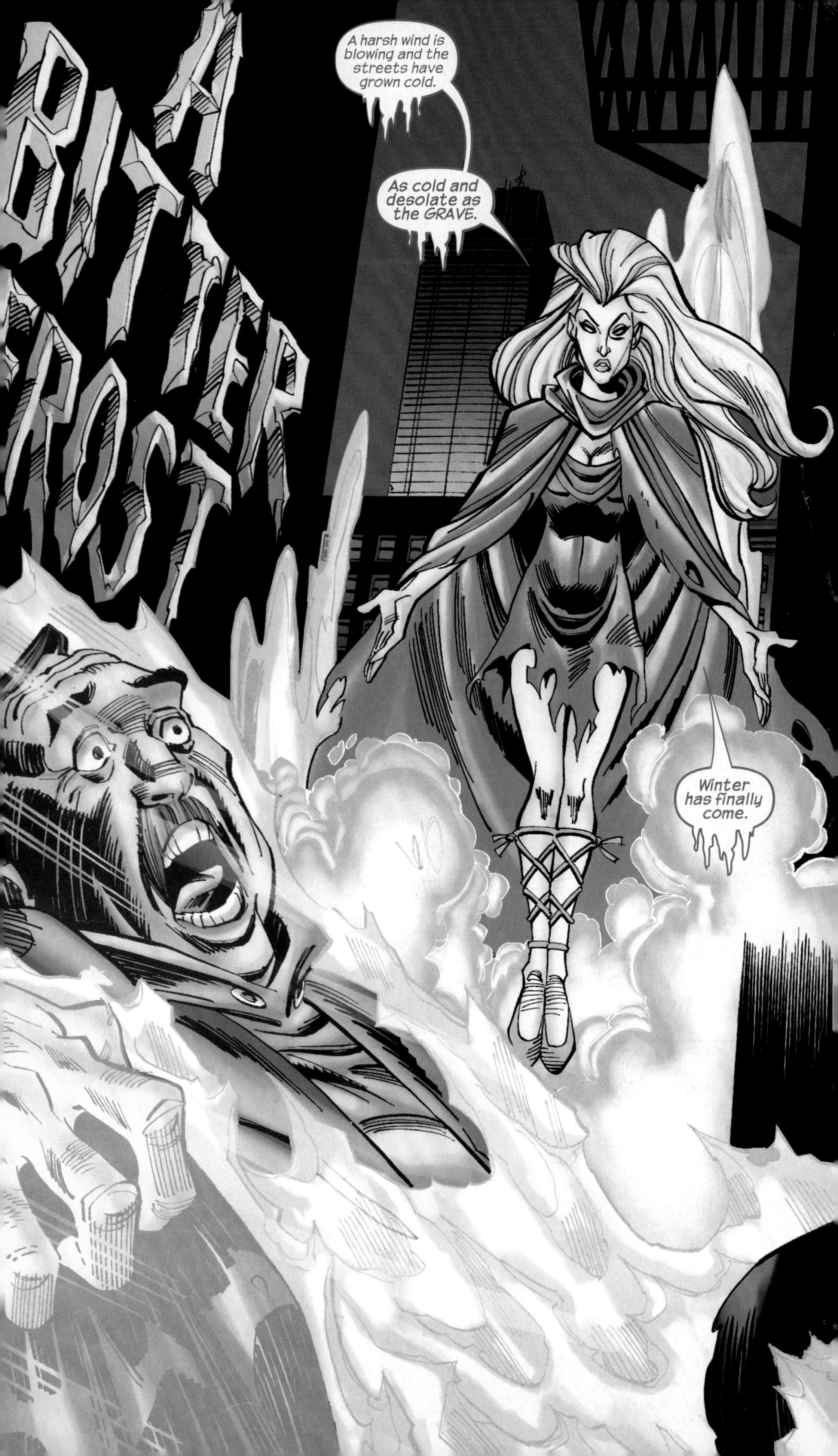
A harsh wind is blowing and the streets have grown cold.
As cold and desolate as the GRAVE.
Winter has finally come.

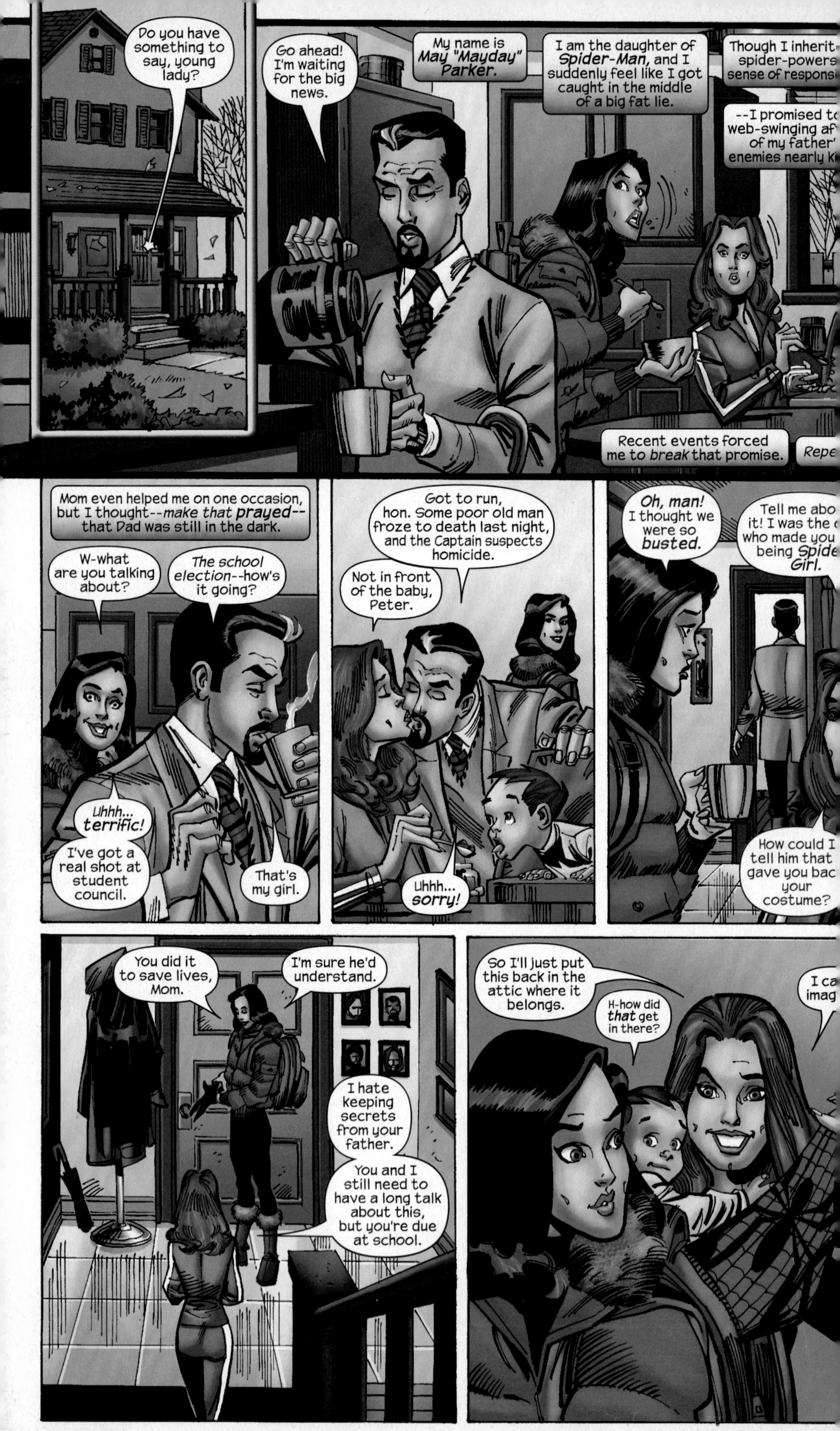

Do you have something to say, young lady?
Go ahead! I'm waiting for the big news.
My name is May "Mayday" Parker.
I am the daughter of Spider-Man, and I suddenly feel like I got caught in the middle of a big fat lie.
Though I inherit spider-powers sense of respons
--I promised t web-swinging af of my father' enemies nearly k
Recent events forced me to break that promise.
Repe
Mom even helped me on one occasion, but I thought--make that prayed--that Dad was still in the dark.
W-what are you talking about?
The school election--how's it going?
Uhhh... terrific!
I've got a real shot at student council.
That's my girl.
Got to run, hon. Some poor old man froze to death last night, and the Captain suspects homicide.
Not in front of the baby, Peter.
Uhhh... sorry!
Oh, man! I thought we were so busted.
Tell me abo it! I was the who made you being Spide Girl.
How could I tell him that gave you bac your costume?
You did it to save lives, Mom.
I'm sure he'd understand.
I hate keeping secrets from your father.
You and I still need to have a long talk about this, but you're due at school.
So I'll just put this back in the attic where it belongs.
H-how did that get in there?
I ca imag

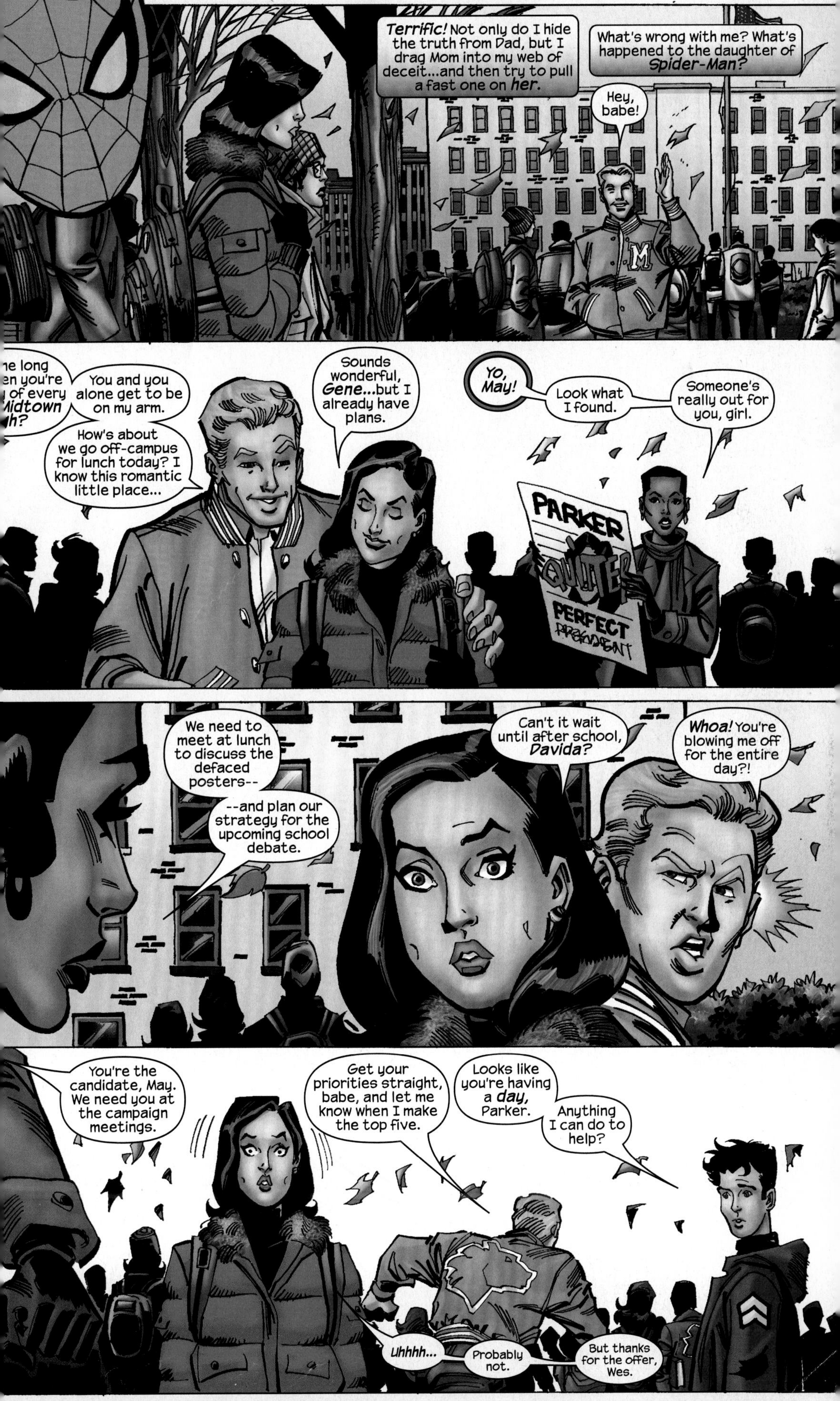
Terrific! Not only do I hide the truth from Dad, but I drag Mom into my web of deceit...and then try to pull a fast one on her.
What's wrong with me? What's happened to the daughter of Spider-Man?
Hey, babe!
You and you alone get to be on my arm.
How's about we go off-campus for lunch today? I know this romantic little place...
Sounds wonderful, Gene...but I already have plans.
Yo, May!
Look what I found.
Someone's really out for you, girl.
PARKER
QUITTER
PERFECT
We need to meet at lunch to discuss the defaced posters--
--and plan our strategy for the upcoming school debate.
Can't it wait until after school, Davida?
Whoa! You're blowing me off for the entire day?!
You're the candidate, May. We need you at the campaign meetings.
Get your priorities straight, babe, and let me know when I make the top five.
Looks like you're having a day, Parker.
Anything I can do to help?
Uhhhh...
Probably not.
But thanks for the offer, Wes.

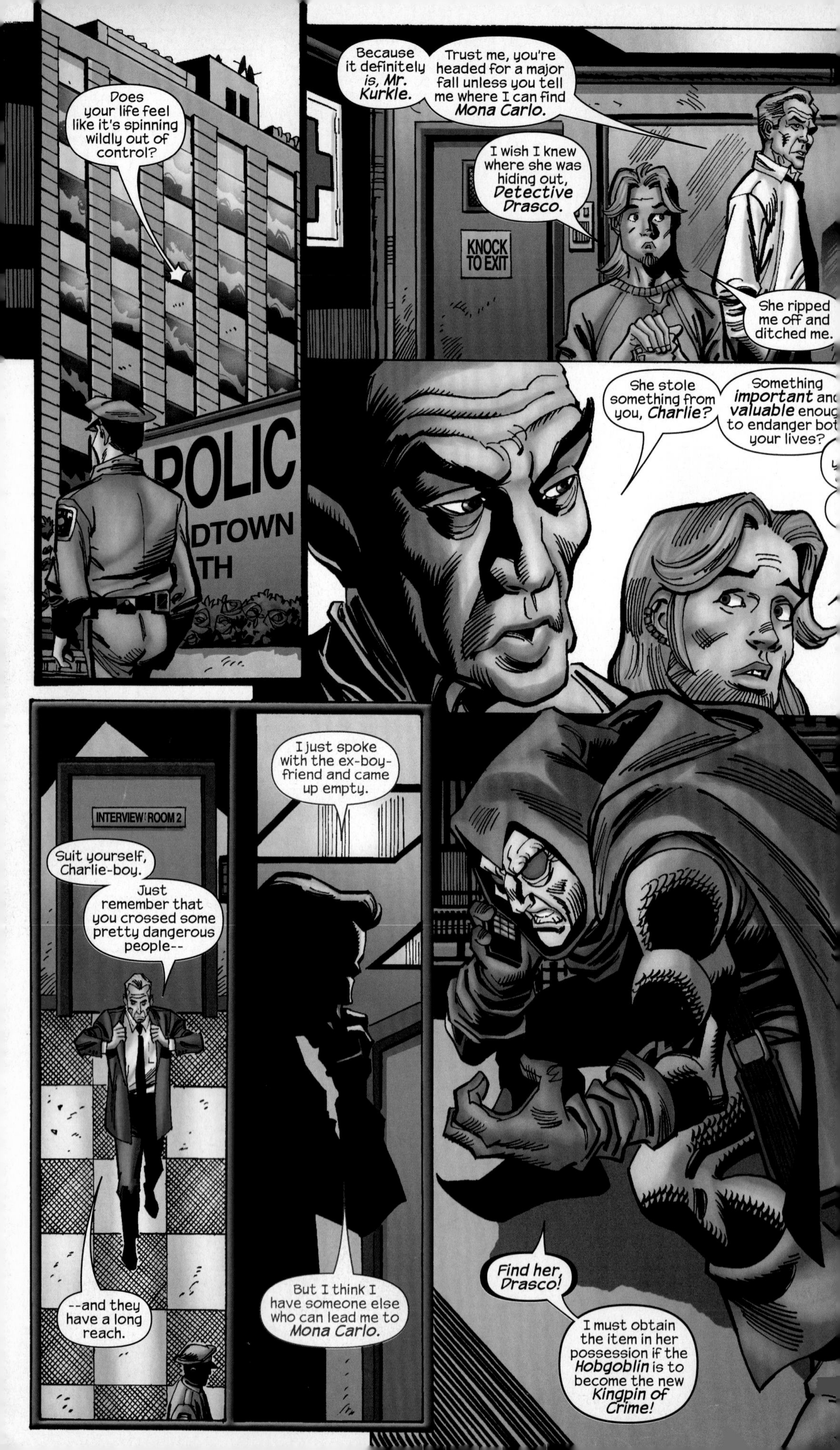
Does your life feel like it's spinning wildly out of control?
POLIC
DTOWN
TH
Because it definitely *is, Mr. Kurkle.*
Trust me, you're headed for a major fall unless you tell me where I can find *Mona Carlo.*
KNOCK TO EXIT
I wish I knew where she was hiding out, *Detective Drasco.*
She ripped me off and ditched me.
She stole something from you, *Charlie?*
Something *important* and *valuable* enoug to endanger bot your lives?
INTERVIEW ROOM 2
Suit yourself, Charlie-boy.
Just remember that you crossed some pretty dangerous people--
--and they have a long reach.
I just spoke with the ex-boy-friend and came up empty.
But I think I have someone else who can lead me to *Mona Carlo.*
Find her, Drasco!
I must obtain the item in her possession if the *Hobgoblin* is to become the new *Kingpin of Crime!*

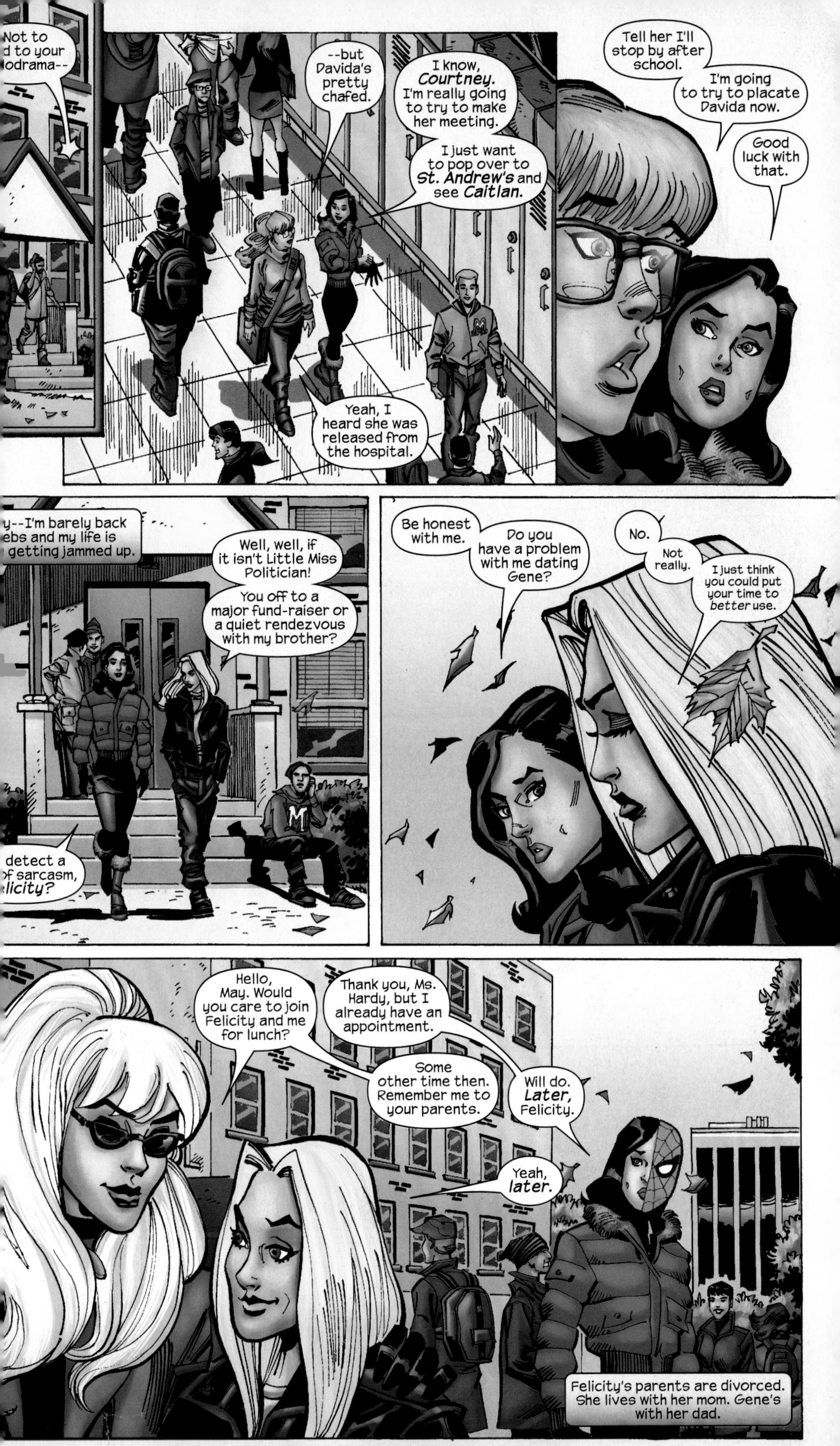

Not to
d to your
odrama--
--but Davida's pretty chafed.
I know, Courtney. I'm really going to try to make her meeting.
I just want to pop over to St. Andrew's and see Caitlan.
Yeah, I heard she was released from the hospital.
Tell her I'll stop by after school.
I'm going to try to placate Davida now.
Good luck with that.
y--I'm barely back
ebs and my life is
getting jammed up.
Well, well, if it isn't Little Miss Politician!
You off to a major fund-raiser or a quiet rendezvous with my brother?
detect a
of sarcasm,
licity?
Be honest with me.
Do you have a problem with me dating Gene?
No.
Not really.
I just think you could put your time to better use.
Hello, May. Would you care to join Felicity and me for lunch?
Thank you, Ms. Hardy, but I already have an appointment.
Some other time then. Remember me to your parents.
Will do. Later, Felicity.
Yeah, later.
Felicity's parents are divorced. She lives with her mom. Gene's with her dad.

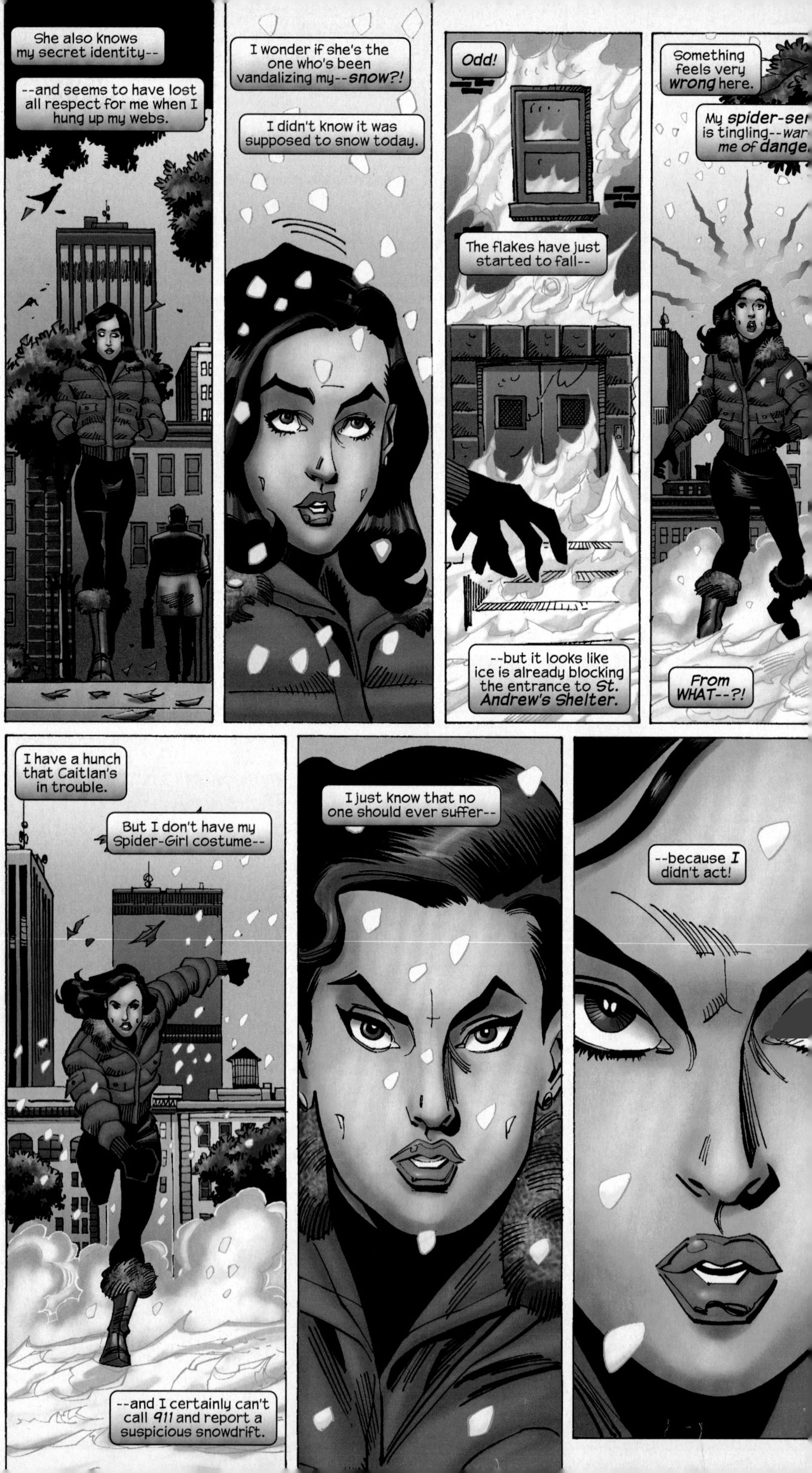

She also knows my secret identity--
--and seems to have lost all respect for me when I hung up my webs.
I wonder if she's the one who's been vandalizing my--snow?!
I didn't know it was supposed to snow today.
Odd!
The flakes have just started to fall--
--but it looks like ice is already blocking the entrance to St. Andrew's Shelter.
Something feels very wrong here.
My spider-se is tingling--war me of dange
From WHAT--?!
I have a hunch that Caitlan's in trouble.
But I don't have my Spider-Girl costume--
--and I certainly can't call 911 and report a suspicious snowdrift.
I just know that no one should ever suffer--
--because I didn't act!

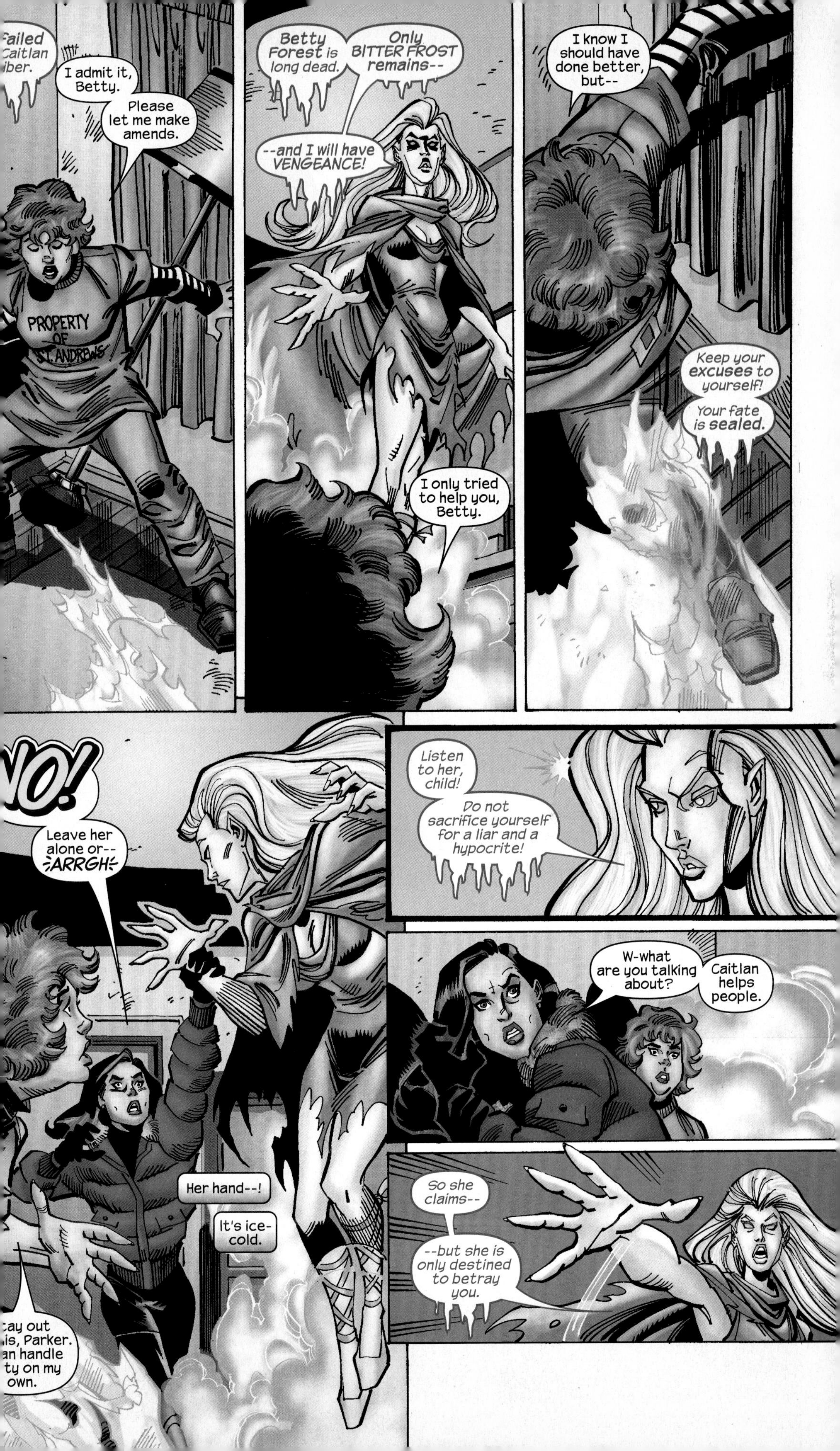

ailed Caitlan iber.
I admit it, Betty.
Please let me make amends.
Betty Forest is long dead.
Only BITTER FROST remains--
--and I will have VENGEANCE!
I only tried to help you, Betty.
I know I should have done better, but--
Keep your excuses to yourself!
Your fate is sealed.
PROPERTY OF ST. ANDREWS
NO!
Leave her alone or-- ARRGH!
Her hand--!
It's ice-cold.
tay out is, Parker. an handle ty on my own.
Listen to her, child!
Do not sacrifice yourself for a liar and a hypocrite!
W-what are you talking about?
Caitlan helps people.
So she claims--
--but she is only destined to betray you.

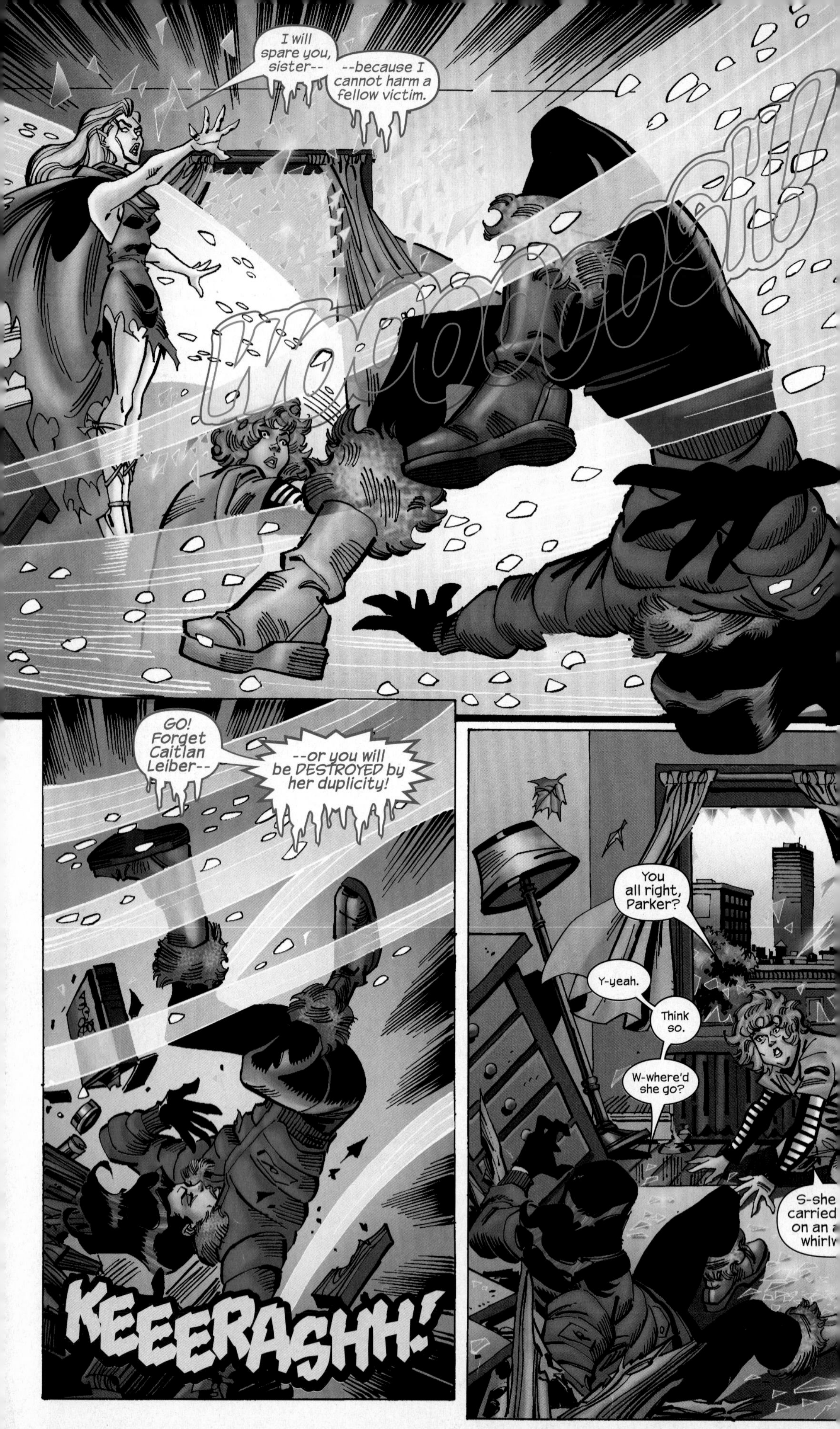
I will spare you, sister--
--because I cannot harm a fellow victim.
GO! Forget Caitlan Leiber--
--or you will be DESTROYED by her duplicity!
KEEERASHH!
You all right, Parker?
Y-yeah.
Think so.
W-where'd she go?
S-she carried on an

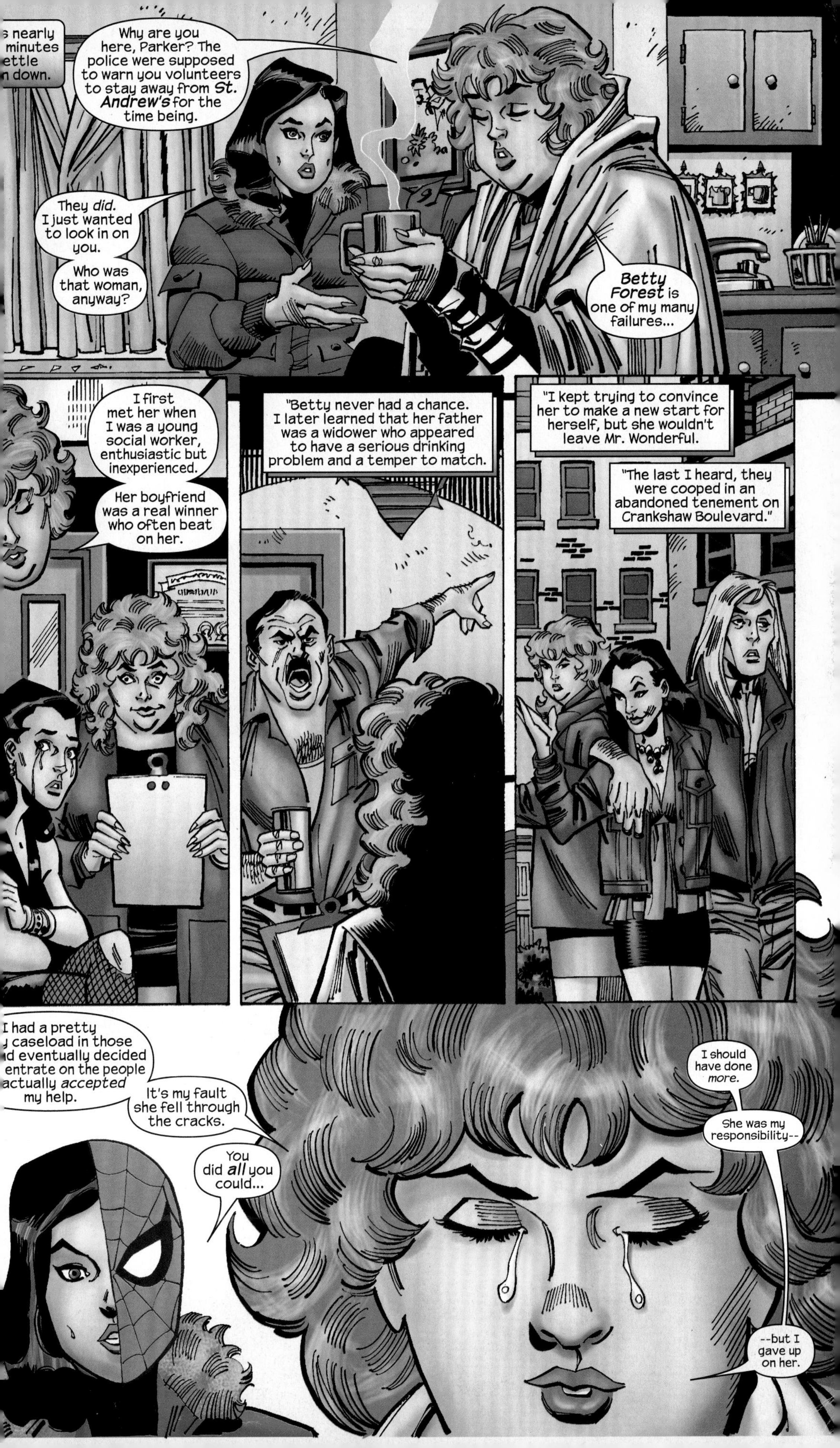
s nearly
minutes
ettle
n down.
Why are you here, Parker? The police were supposed to warn you volunteers to stay away from St. Andrew's for the time being.
They did. I just wanted to look in on you.
Who was that woman, anyway?
Betty Forest is one of my many failures...
I first met her when I was a young social worker, enthusiastic but inexperienced.
Her boyfriend was a real winner who often beat on her.
"Betty never had a chance. I later learned that her father was a widower who appeared to have a serious drinking problem and a temper to match.
"I kept trying to convince her to make a new start for herself, but she wouldn't leave Mr. Wonderful.
"The last I heard, they were cooped in an abandoned tenement on Crankshaw Boulevard."
I had a pretty
caseload in those
d eventually decided
entrate on the people
actually accepted
my help.
It's my fault she fell through the cracks.
You did all you could...
I should have done more.
She was my responsibility--
--but I gave up on her.

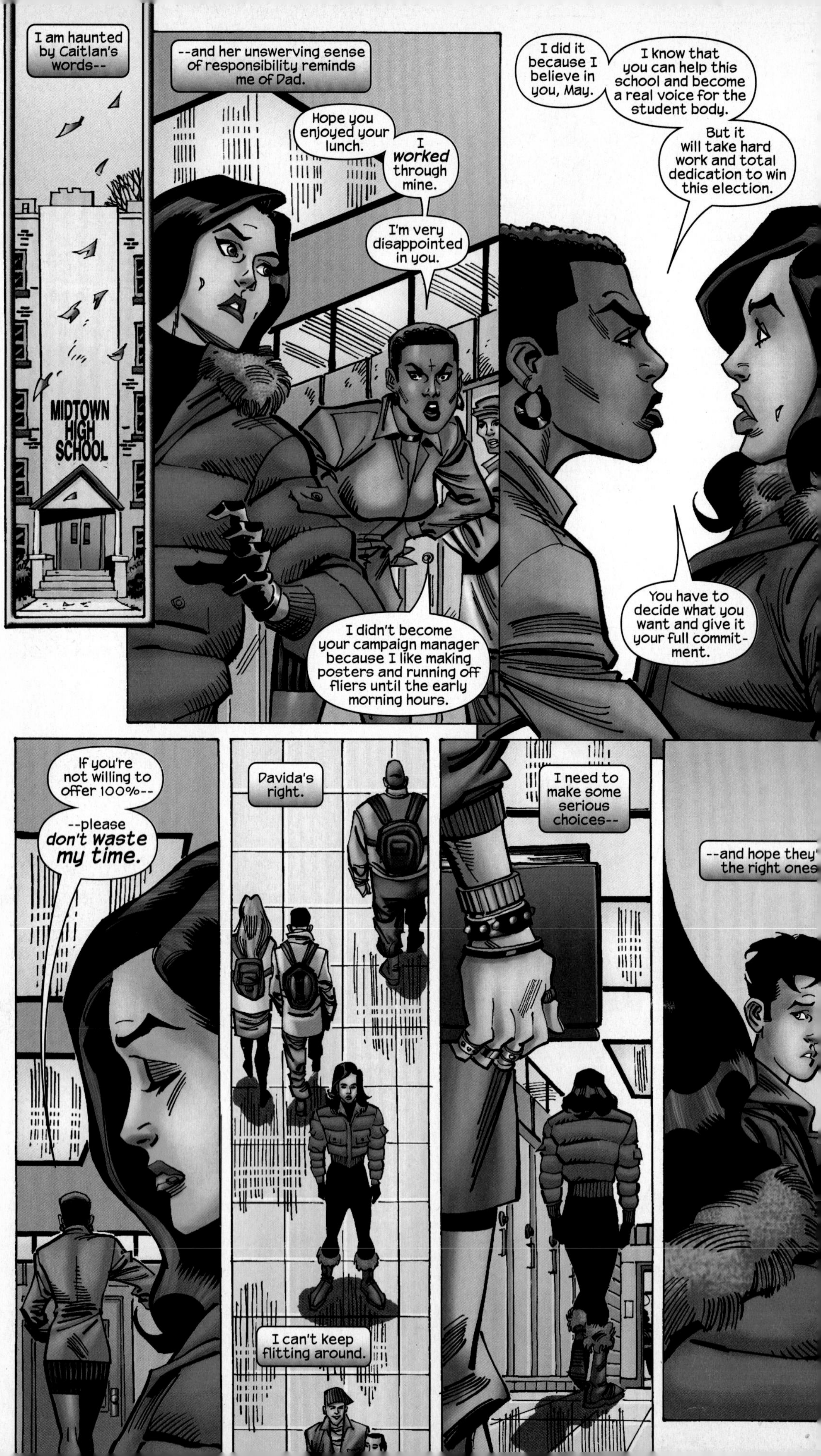
I am haunted by Caitlan's words--
--and her unswerving sense of responsibility reminds me of Dad.
MIDTOWN HIGH SCHOOL
Hope you enjoyed your lunch.
I *worked* through mine.
I'm very disappointed in you.
I didn't become your campaign manager because I like making posters and running off fliers until the early morning hours.
I did it because I believe in you, May.
I know that you can help this school and become a real voice for the student body.
But it will take hard work and total dedication to win this election.
You have to decide what you want and give it your full commitment.
If you're not willing to offer 100%--
--please *don't waste my time.*
Davida's right.
I can't keep flitting around.
I need to make some serious choices--
--and hope they' the right ones

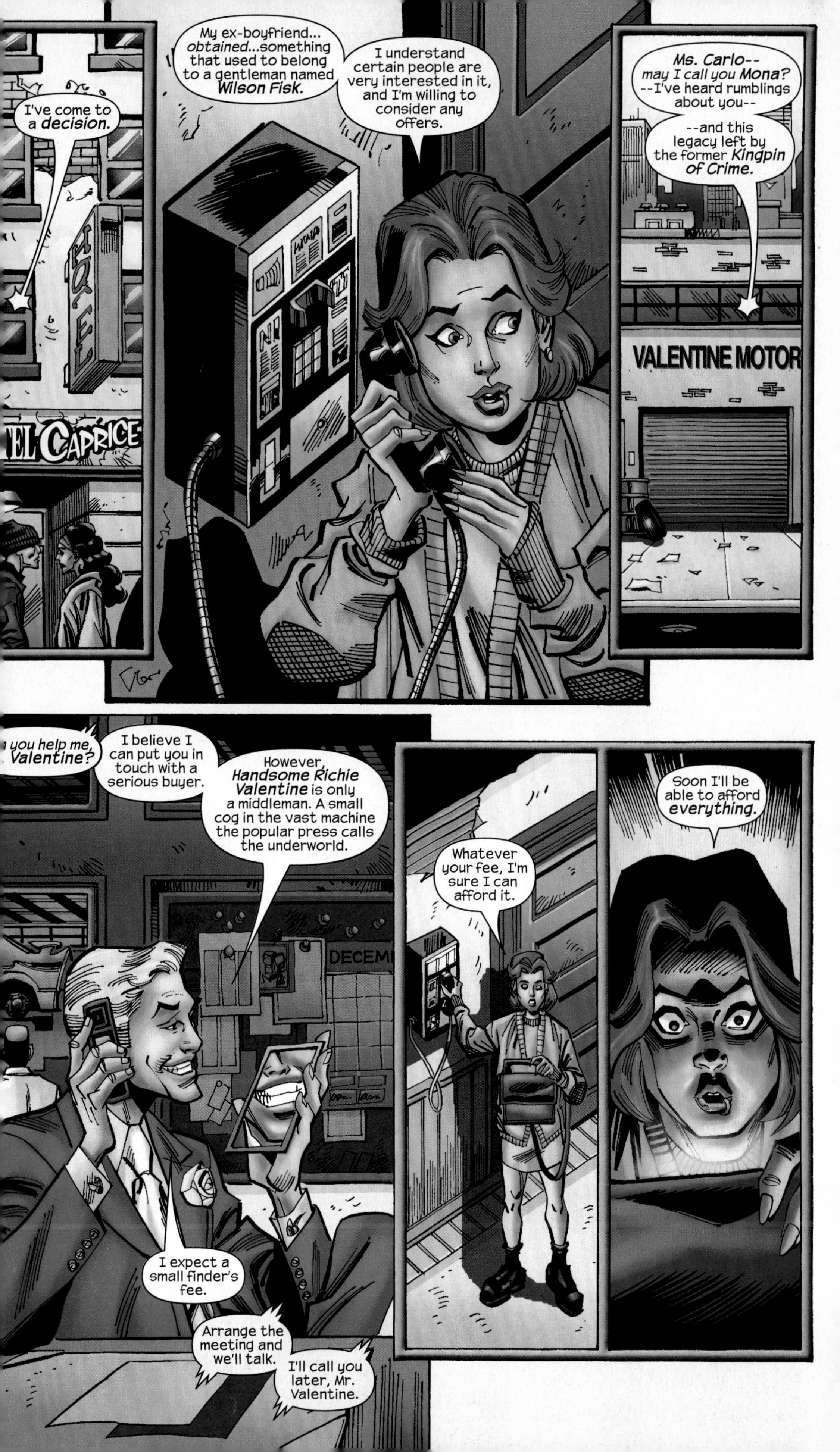

I've come to a *decision.*
HOTEL
EL CAPRICE
My ex-boyfriend... *obtained*...something that used to belong to a gentleman named *Wilson Fisk.*
I understand certain people are very interested in it, and I'm willing to consider any offers.
Ms. Carlo-- may I call you *Mona?* --I've heard rumblings about you--
--and this legacy left by the former *Kingpin of Crime.*
VALENTINE MOTOR
you help me, *Valentine?*
I believe I can put you in touch with a serious buyer.
However, *Handsome Richie Valentine* is only a middleman. A small cog in the vast machine the popular press calls the underworld.
DECEM
I expect a small finder's fee.
Arrange the meeting and we'll talk.
I'll call you later, Mr. Valentine.
Whatever your fee, I'm sure I can afford it.
Soon I'll be able to afford *everything.*

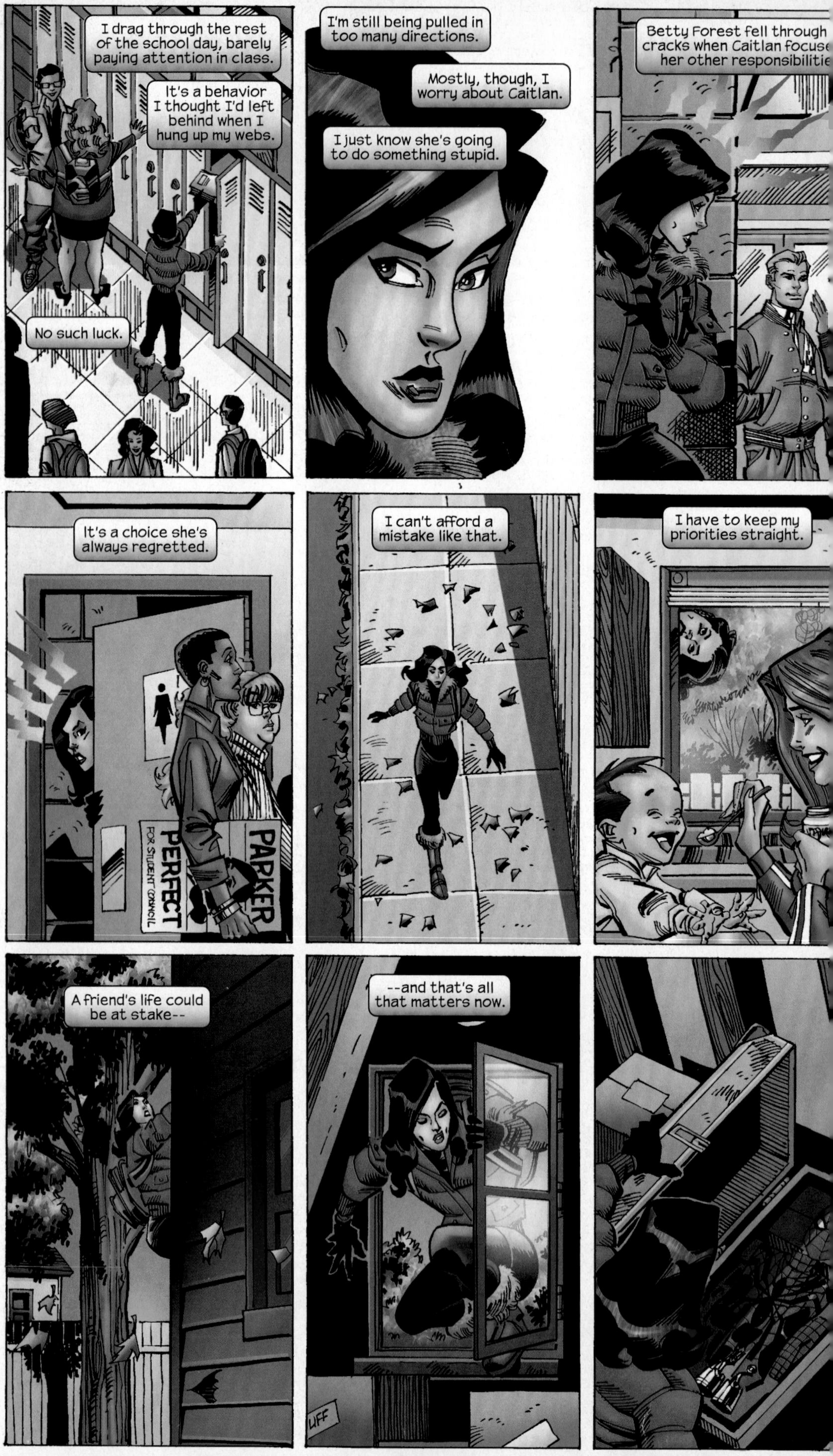
I drag through the rest of the school day, barely paying attention in class.
It's a behavior I thought I'd left behind when I hung up my webs.
No such luck.
I'm still being pulled in too many directions.
Mostly, though, I worry about Caitlan.
I just know she's going to do something stupid.
Betty Forest fell through cracks when Caitlan focuse her other responsibilitie
It's a choice she's always regretted.
PARKER
PERFECT
FOR STUDENT COUNCIL
I can't afford a mistake like that.
I have to keep my priorities straight.
A friend's life could be at stake--
--and that's all that matters now.

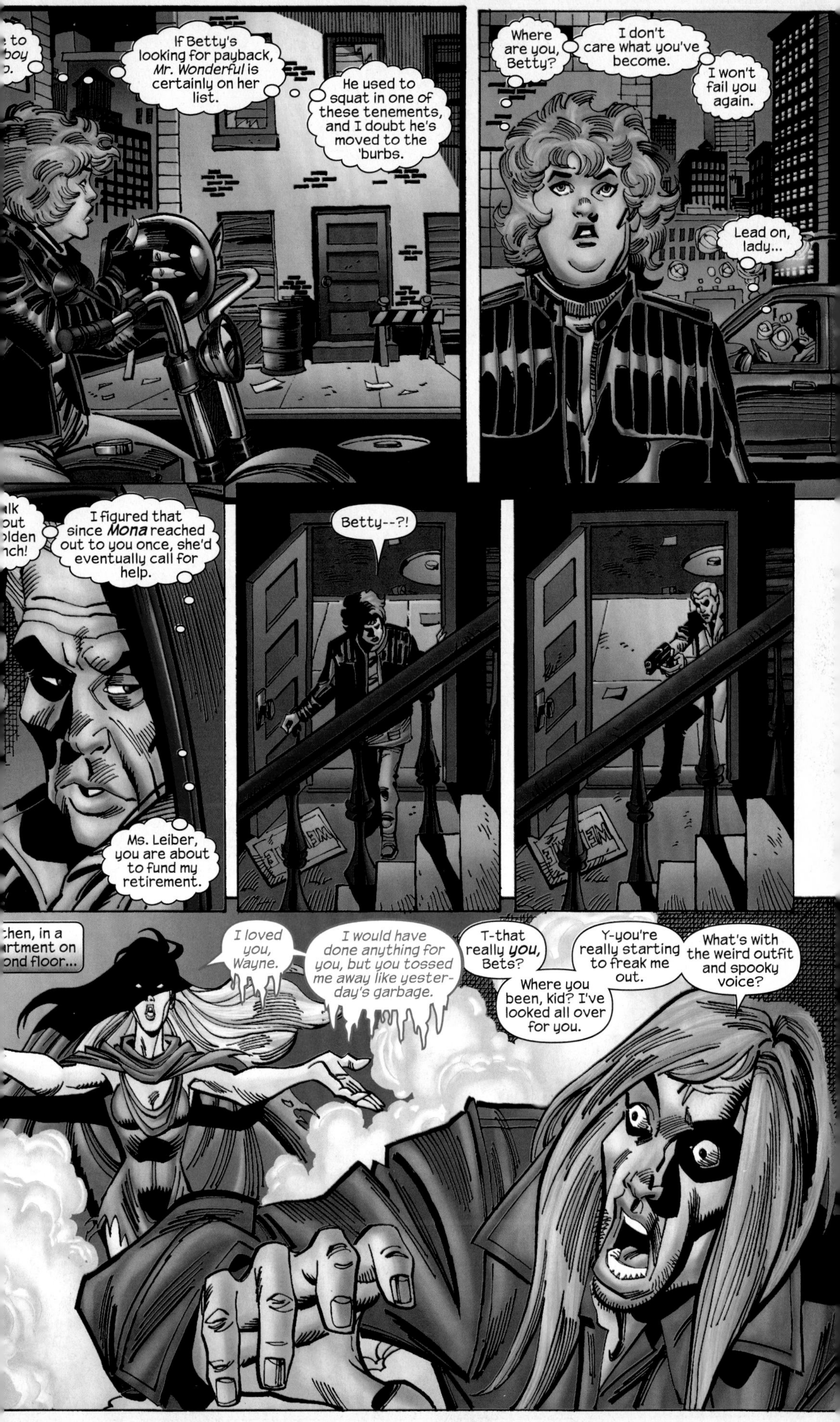

If Betty's looking for payback, *Mr. Wonderful* is certainly on her list.
He used to squat in one of these tenements, and I doubt he's moved to the 'burbs.
Where are you, Betty?
I don't care what you've become.
I won't fail you again.
Lead on, lady...
I figured that since ***Mona*** reached out to you once, she'd eventually call for help.
Ms. Leiber, you are about to fund my retirement.
Betty--?!
I loved you, Wayne.
I would have done anything for you, but you tossed me away like yesterday's garbage.
T-that really ***you,*** Bets?
Where you been, kid? I've looked all over for you.
Y-you're really starting to freak me out.
What's with the weird outfit and spooky voice?

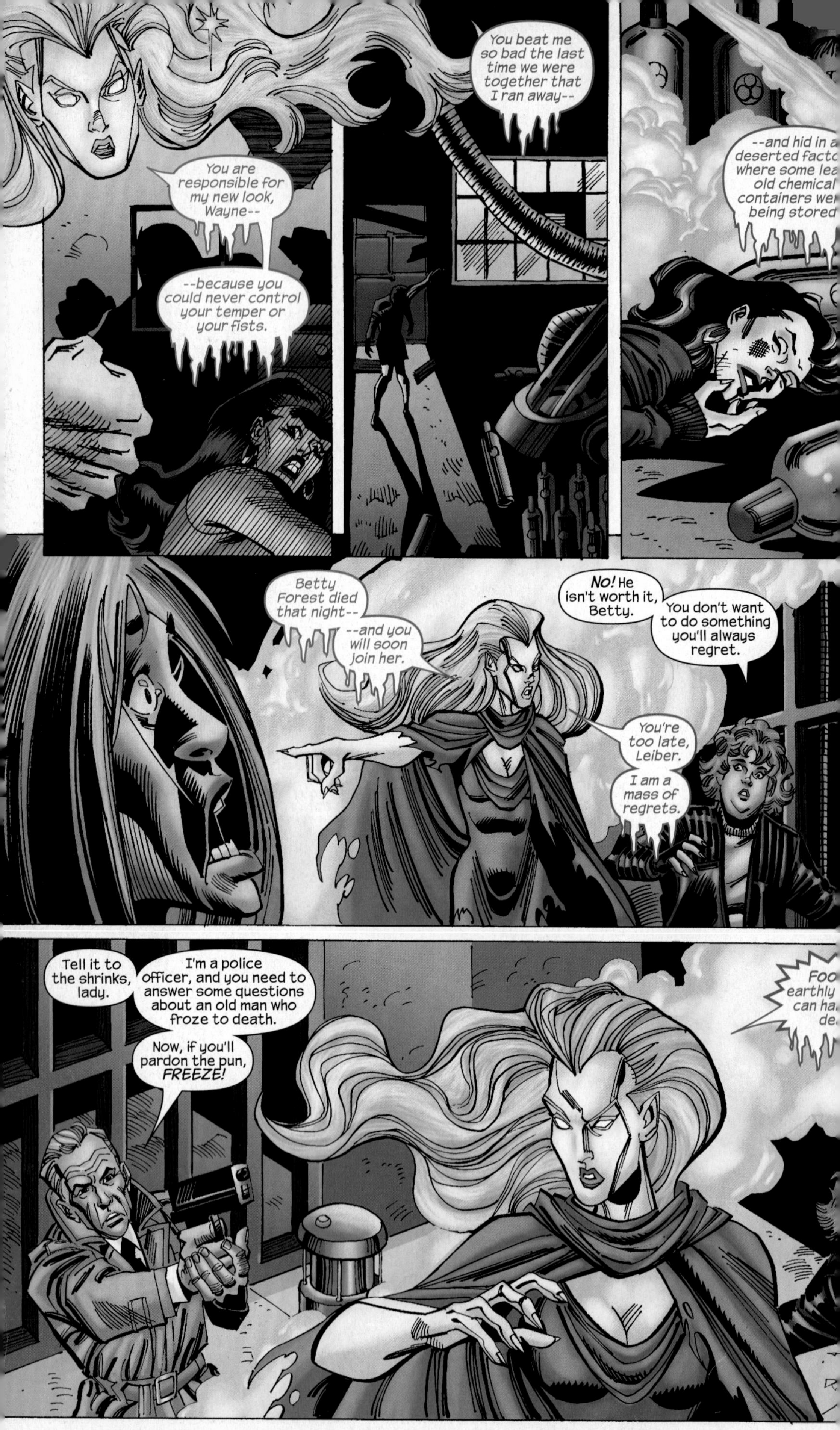
You are responsible for my new look, Wayne--
--because you could never control your temper or your fists.
You beat me so bad the last time we were together that I ran away--
--and hid in a deserted facto where some lea old chemical containers wer being stored
Betty Forest died that night--
--and you will soon join her.
NO! He isn't worth it, Betty.
You don't want to do something you'll always regret.
You're too late, Leiber.
I am a mass of regrets.
Tell it to the shrinks, lady.
I'm a police officer, and you need to answer some questions about an old man who froze to death.
Now, if you'll pardon the pun, FREEZE!
Foo earthly can ha de

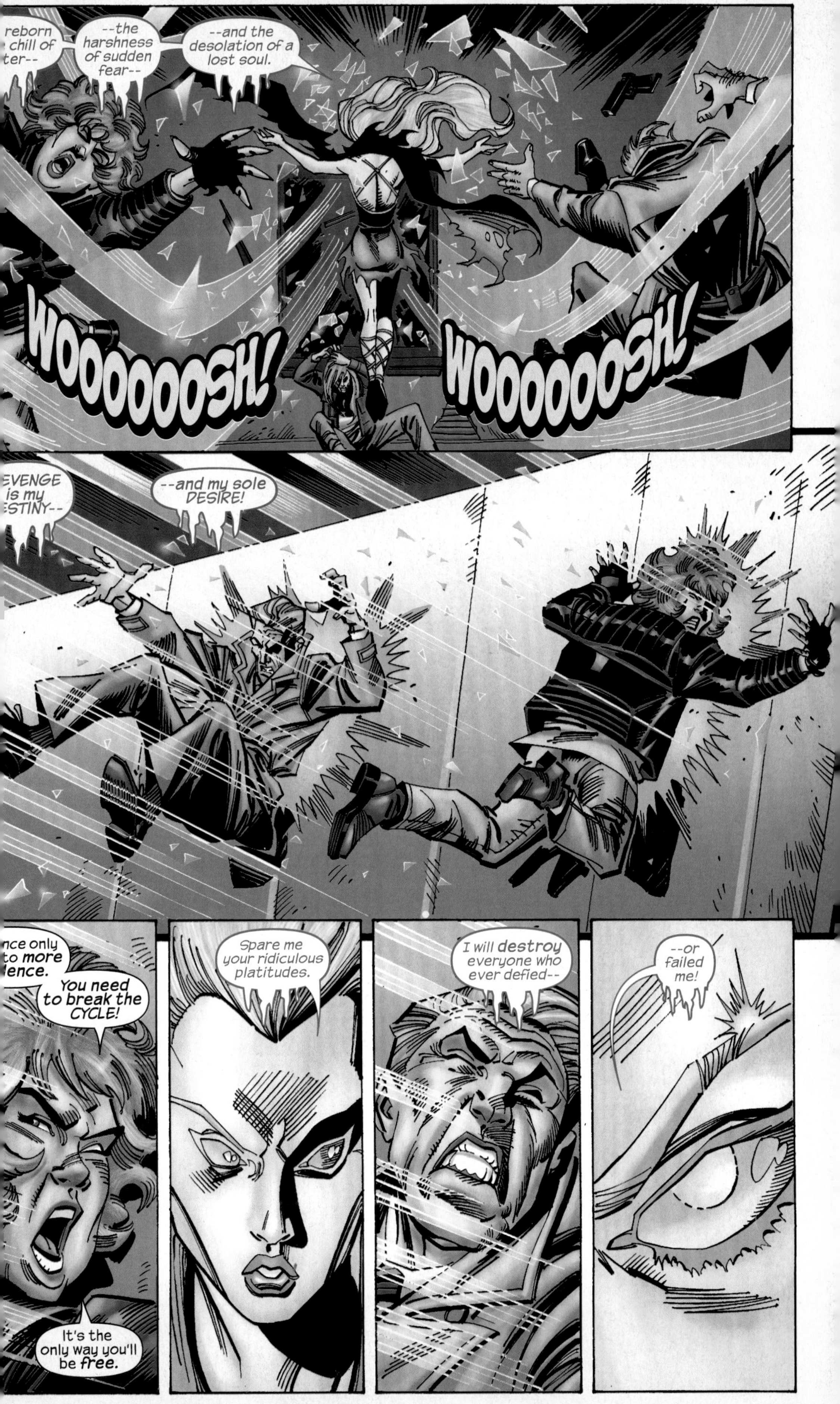
reborn chill of ter--
--the harshness of sudden fear--
--and the desolation of a lost soul.
WOOOOOOSH!
WOOOOOOSH!
EVENGE is my ESTINY--
--and my sole DESIRE!
nce only to more lence.
You need to break the CYCLE!
It's the only way you'll be free.
Spare me your ridiculous platitudes.
I will destroy everyone who ever defied--
--or failed me!

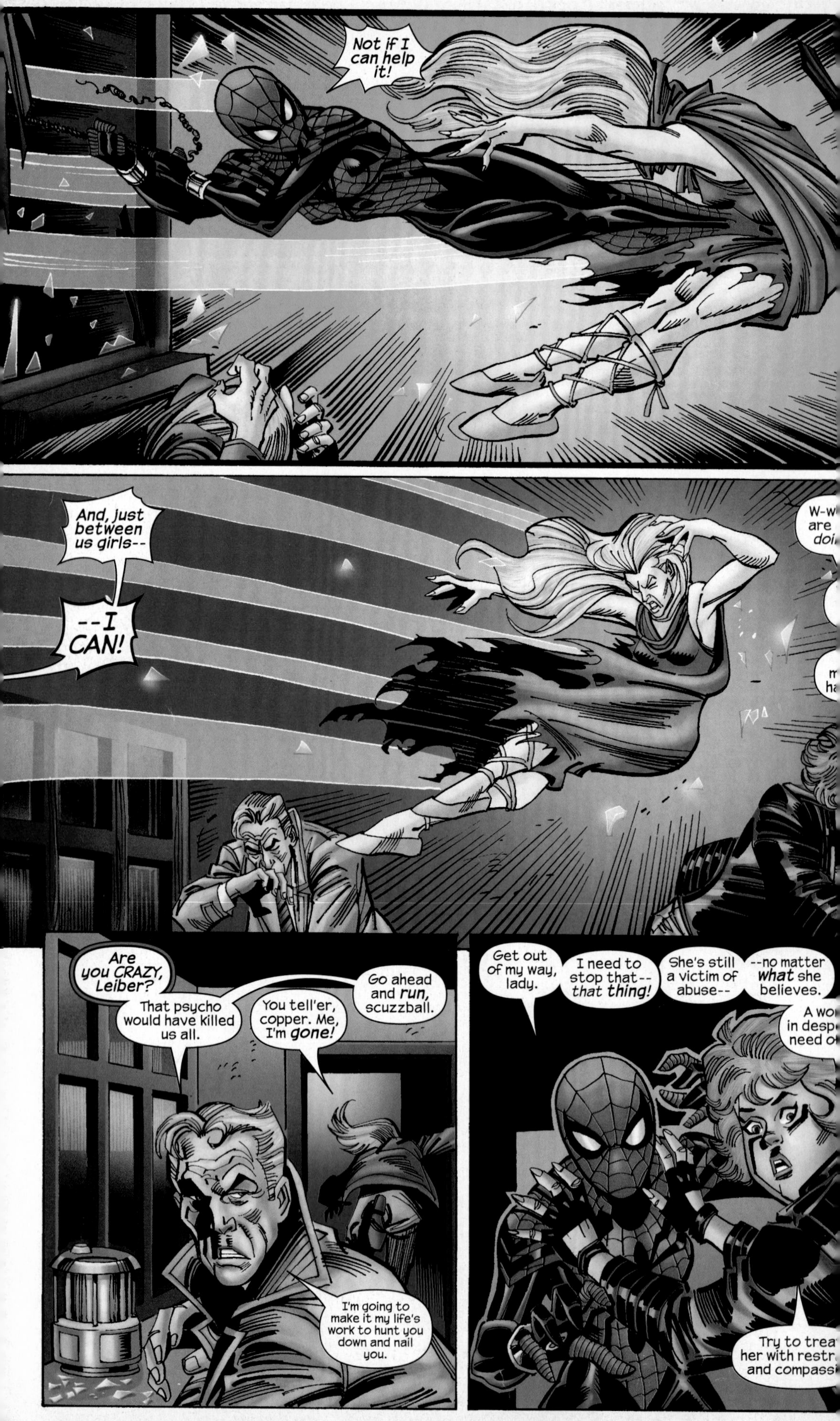

Not if I can help it!
And, just between us girls--
--I CAN!
Are you CRAZY, Leiber?
That psycho would have killed us all.
Go ahead and run, scuzzball.
You tell'er, copper. Me, I'm gone!
I'm going to make it my life's work to hunt you down and nail you.
Get out of my way, lady.
I need to stop that-- that thing!
She's still a victim of abuse--
--no matter what she believes.

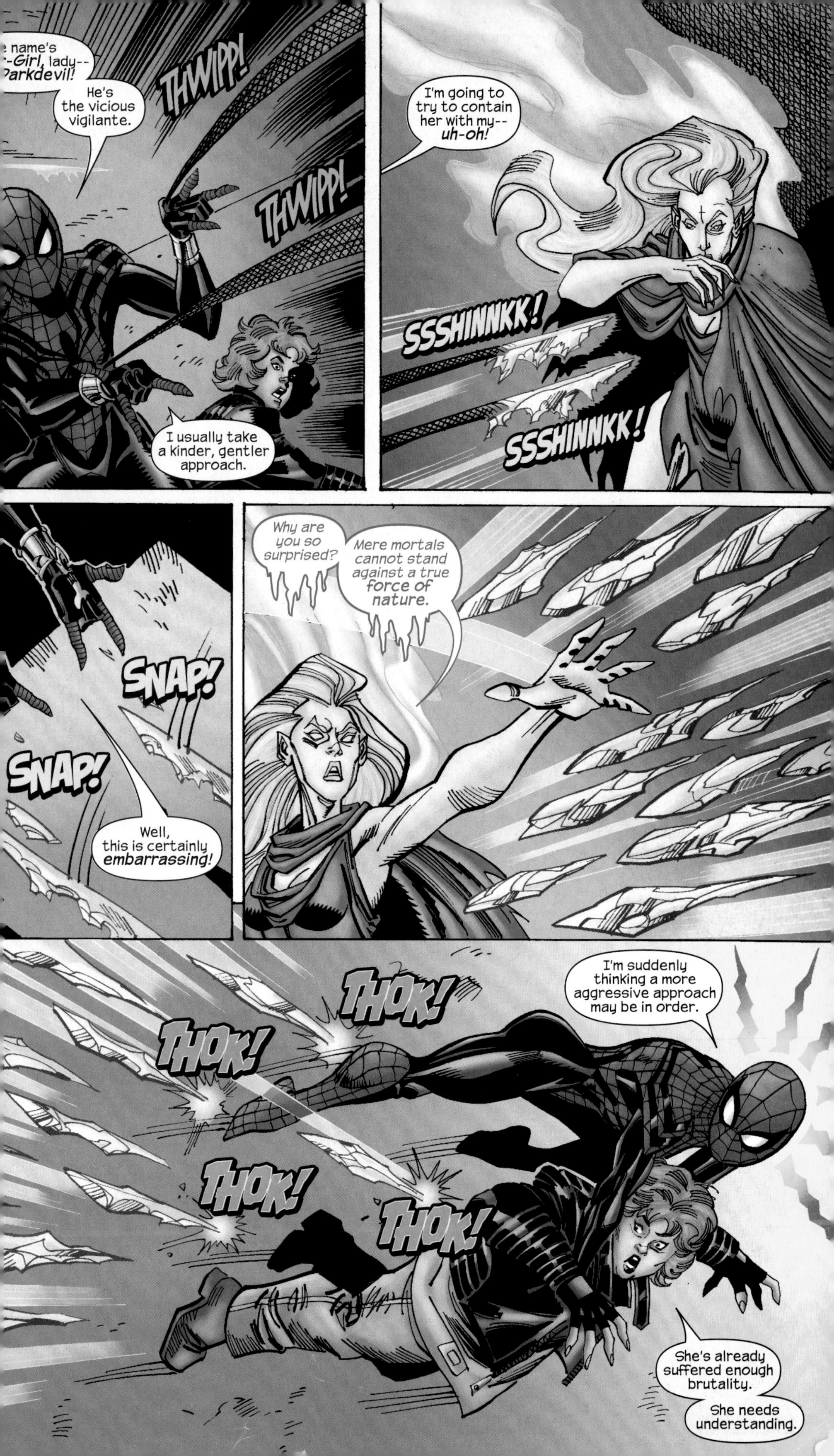

name's
-Girl, lady--
Parkdevil!
He's the vicious vigilante.
THWIPP!
THWIPP!
I usually take a kinder, gentler approach.
I'm going to try to contain her with my-- uh-oh!
SSSHINNKK!
SSSHINNKK!
SNAP!
SNAP!
Well, this is certainly embarrassing!
Why are you so surprised?
Mere mortals cannot stand against a true force of nature.
THOK!
THOK!
THOK!
THOK!
I'm suddenly thinking a more aggressive approach may be in order.
She's already suffered enough brutality.
She needs understanding.

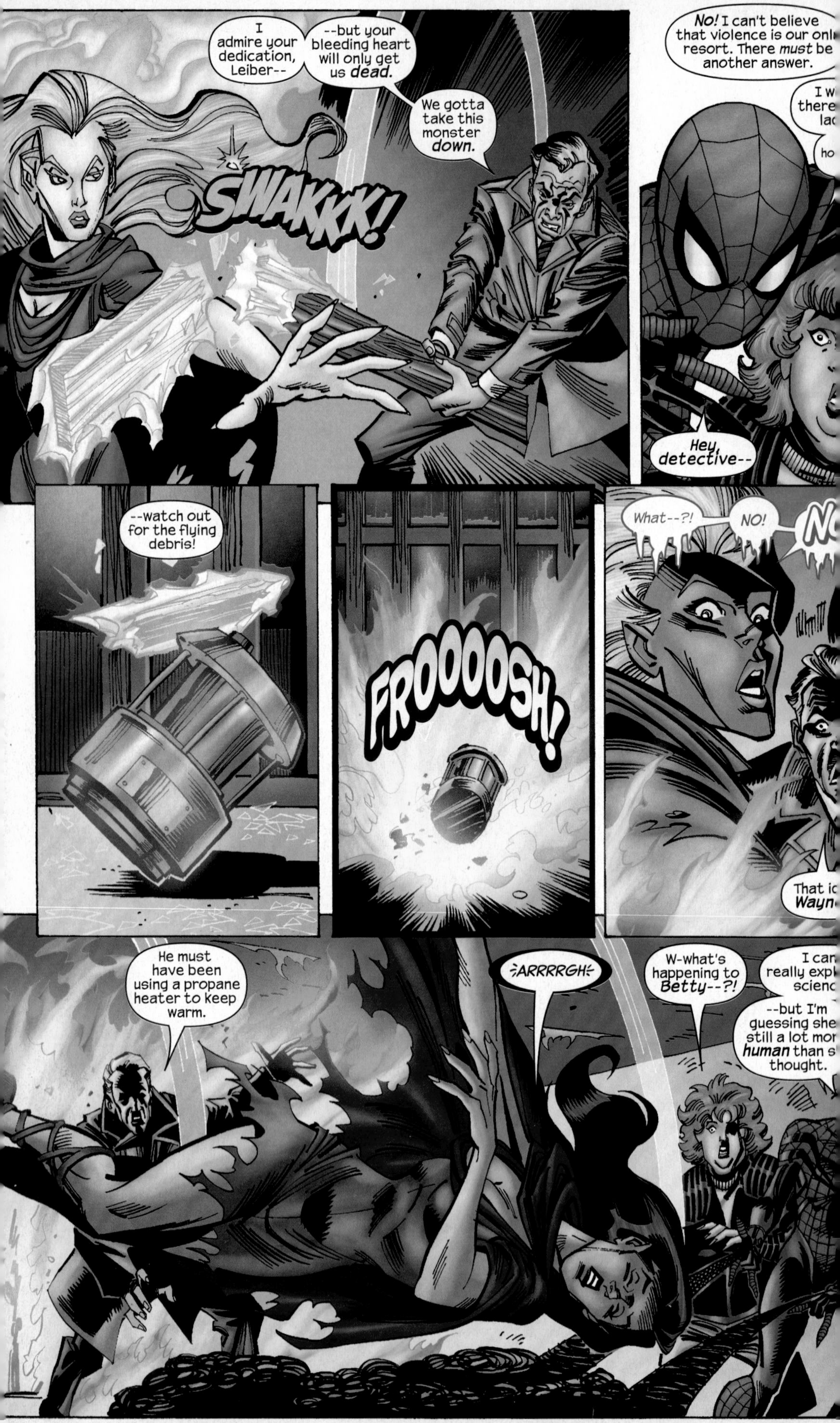
I admire your dedication, Leiber--
--but your bleeding heart will only get us *dead.*
We gotta take this monster *down.*
SWAKKK!
No! I can't believe that violence is our onl
resort. There *must* be another answer.
Hey, detective--
--watch out for the flying debris!
FROOOOSH!
What--?!
NO!
That i
Wayn
He must have been using a propane heater to keep warm.
ARRRRGH
W-what's happening to *Betty*--?!
--but I'm guessing she
still a lot mor
human than s
thought.

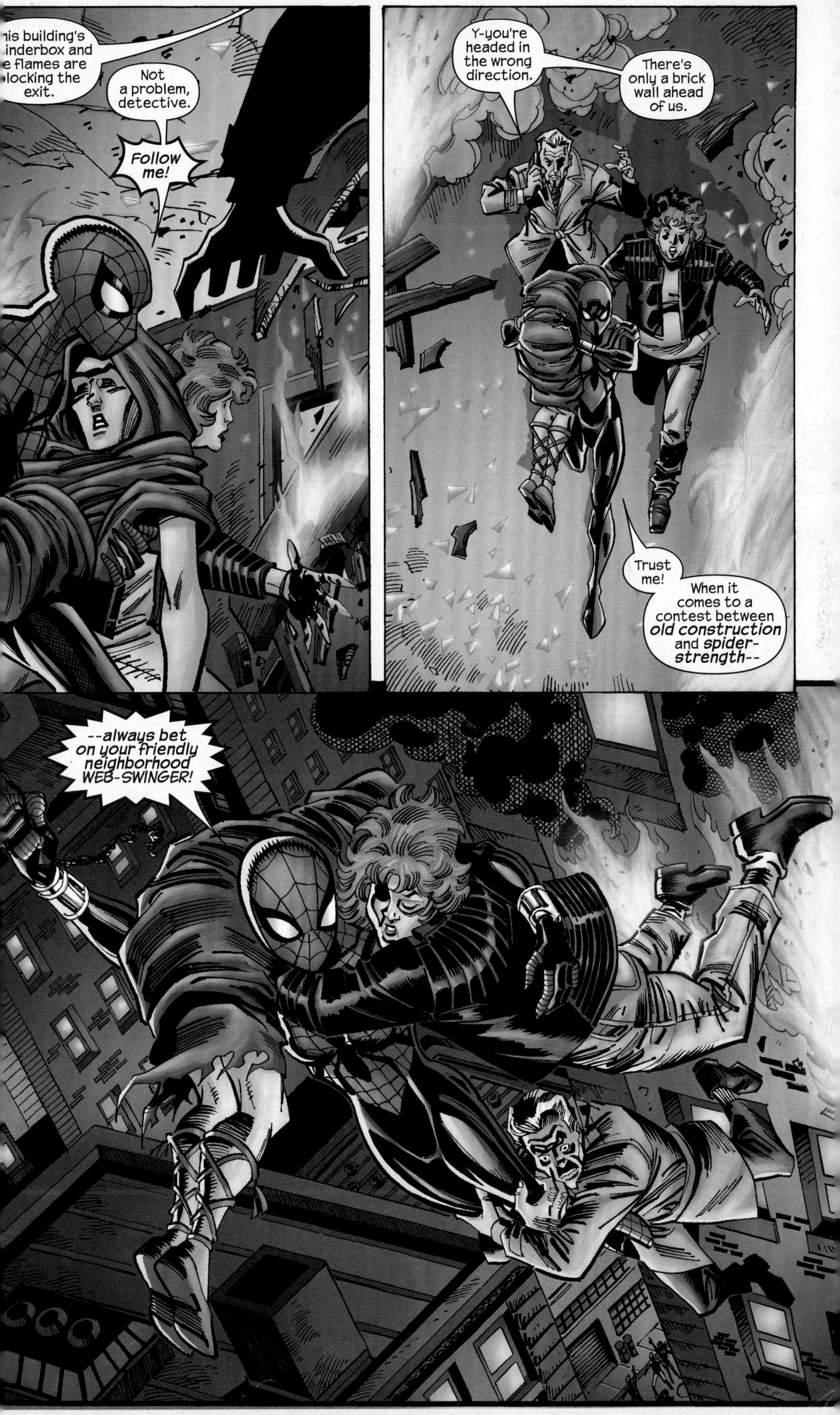

his building's
inderbox and
e flames are
locking the
exit.
Not a problem, detective.
Follow me!
Y-you're headed in the wrong direction.
There's only a brick wall ahead of us.
Trust me!
When it comes to a contest between old construction and spider-strength--
--always bet on your friendly neighborhood WEB-SWINGER!

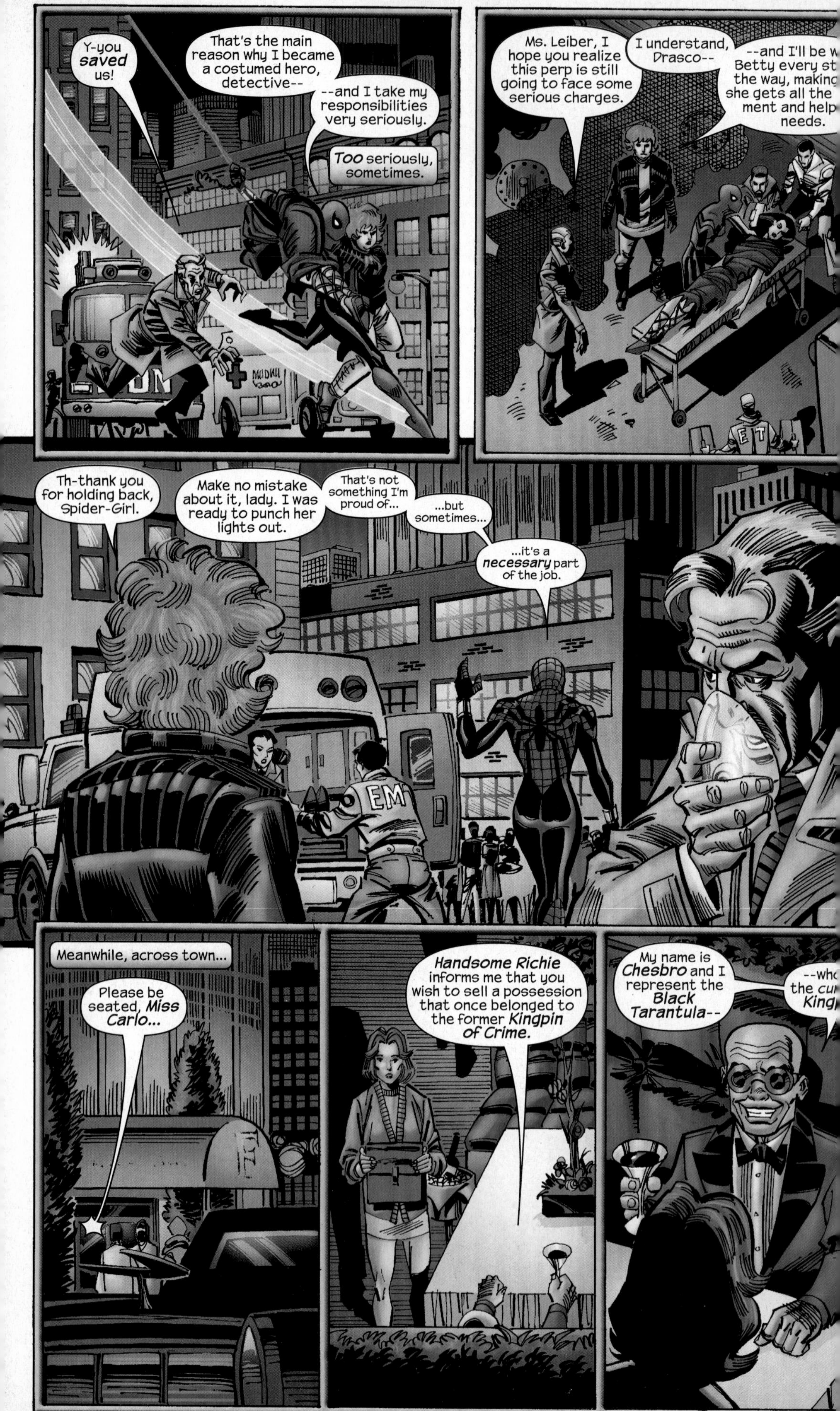

Y-you saved us!
That's the main reason why I became a costumed hero, detective--
--and I take my responsibilities very seriously.
Too seriously, sometimes.
Ms. Leiber, I hope you realize this perp is still going to face some serious charges.
I understand, Drasco--
--and I'll be w Betty every st the way, makin she gets all the ment and help needs.
Th-thank you for holding back, Spider-Girl.
Make no mistake about it, lady. I was ready to punch her lights out.
That's not something I'm proud of...
...but sometimes...
...it's a necessary part of the job.
Meanwhile, across town...
Please be seated, Miss Carlo...
Handsome Richie informs me that you wish to sell a possession that once belonged to the former Kingpin of Crime.
My name is Chesbro and I represent the Black Tarantula--
--wh the cu King

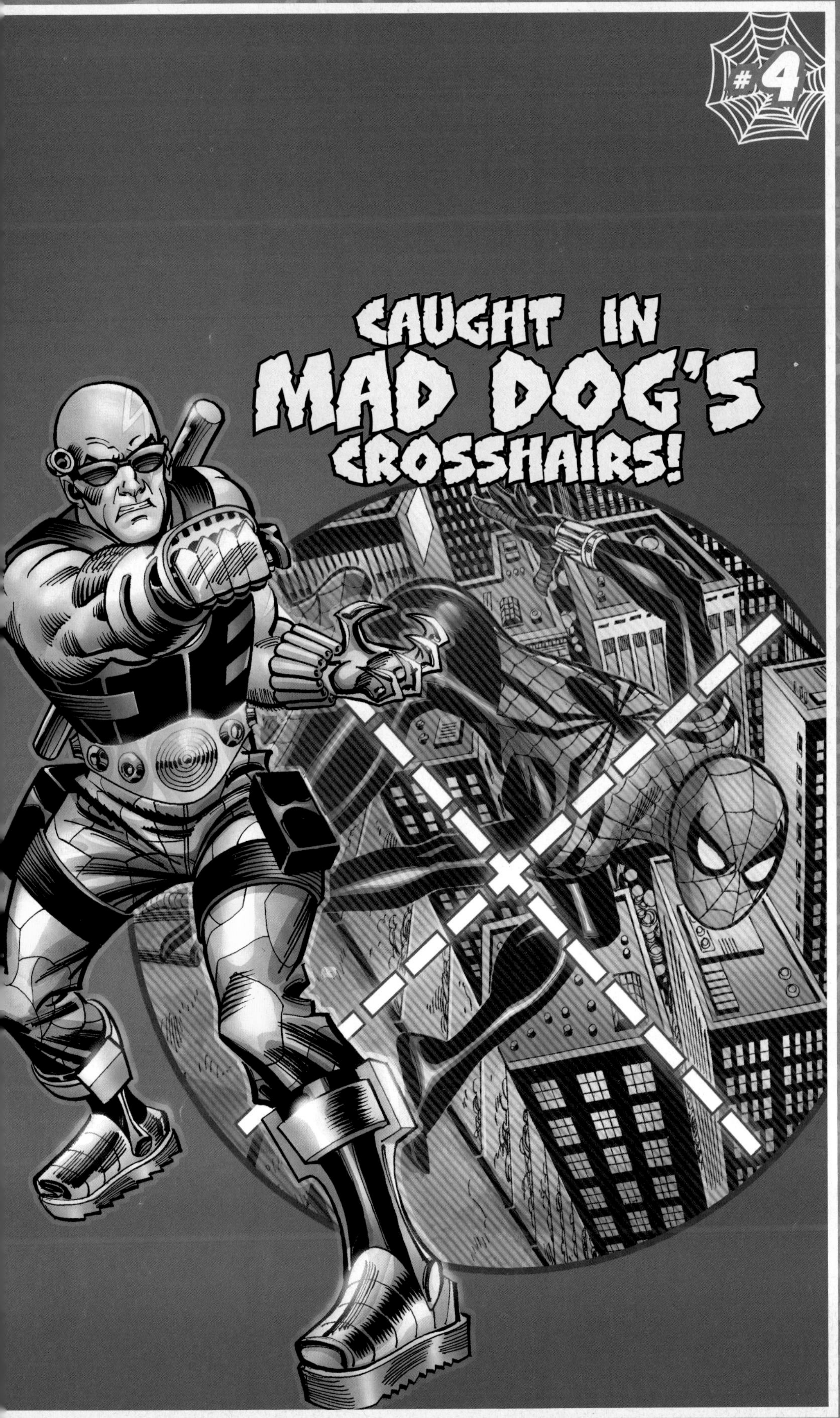
#4
CAUGHT IN
MAD DOG'S
CROSSHAIRS!

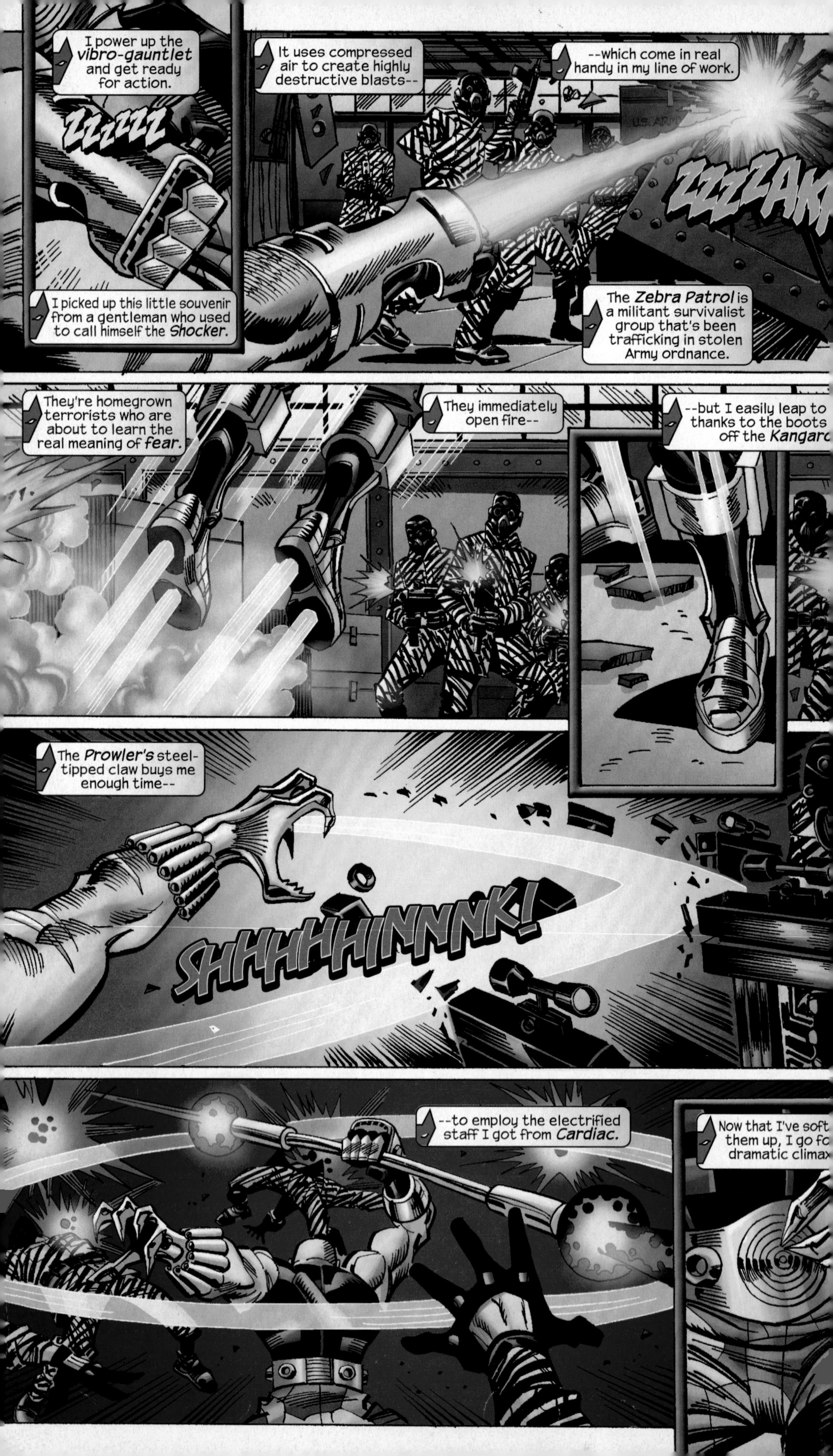
I power up the vibro-gauntlet and get ready for action.
ZZZZZZ
I picked up this little souvenir from a gentleman who used to call himself the Shocker.
It uses compressed air to create highly destructive blasts--
--which come in real handy in my line of work.
ZZZZAK
The Zebra Patrol is a militant survivalist group that's been trafficking in stolen Army ordnance.
They're homegrown terrorists who are about to learn the real meaning of fear.
They immediately open fire--
--but I easily leap to
thanks to the boots
off the
The Prowler's steel-tipped claw buys me enough time--
SHHHHHINNNNK!
--to employ the electrified staff I got from Cardiac.
Now that I've soft
them up, I go fo
dramatic climax

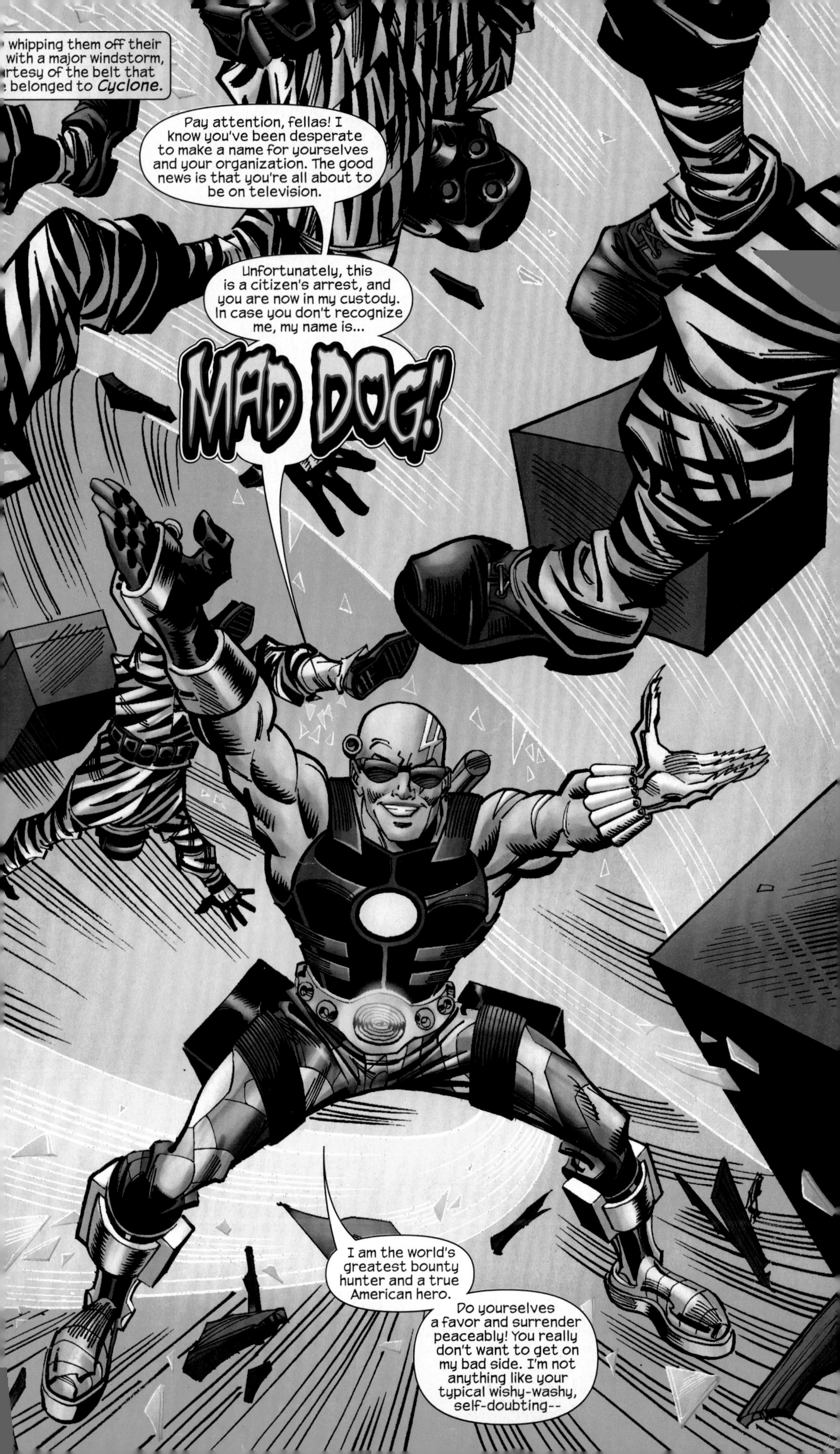
whipping them off their
with a major windstorm,
rtesy of the belt that
belonged to Cyclone.
Pay attention, fellas! I know you've been desperate to make a name for yourselves and your organization. The good news is that you're all about to be on television.
Unfortunately, this is a citizen's arrest, and you are now in my custody. In case you don't recognize me, my name is...
MAD DOG!
I am the world's greatest bounty hunter and a true American hero.
Do yourselves a favor and surrender peaceably! You really don't want to get on my bad side. I'm not anything like your typical wishy-washy, self-doubting--

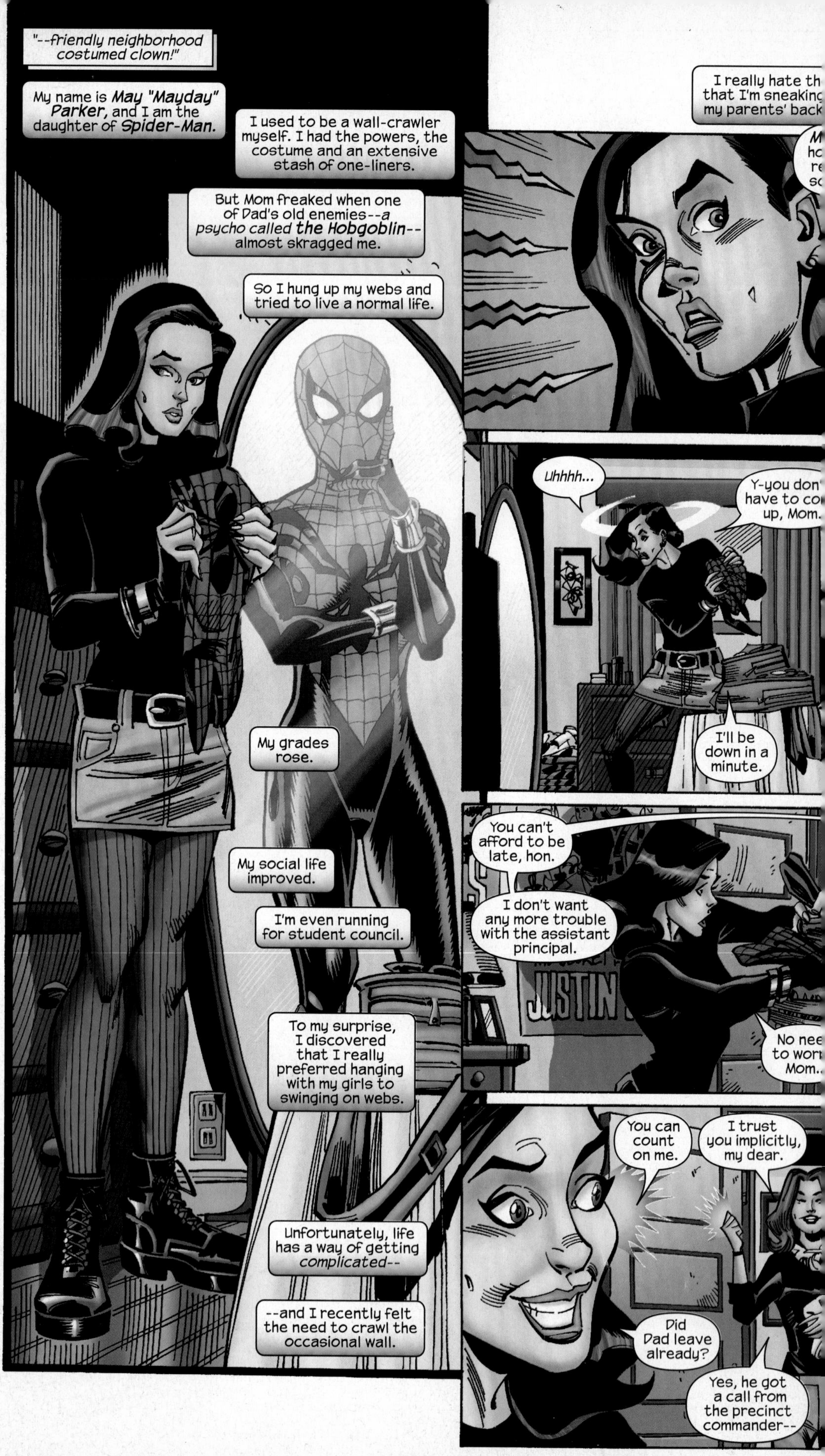
"--friendly neighborhood costumed clown!"
My name is *May "Mayday" Parker,* and I am the daughter of *Spider-Man.*
I used to be a wall-crawler myself. I had the powers, the costume and an extensive stash of one-liners.
But Mom freaked when one of Dad's old enemies--*a psycho called the Hobgoblin*--almost skragged me.
So I hung up my webs and tried to live a normal life.
My grades rose.
My social life improved.
I'm even running for student council.
To my surprise, I discovered that I really preferred hanging with my girls to swinging on webs.
Unfortunately, life has a way of getting *complicated*--
--and I recently felt the need to crawl the occasional wall.
I really hate th
that I'm sneakin
my parents' back
Uhhhh...
Y-you don'
have to co
up, Mom.
I'll be down in a minute.
You can't afford to be late, hon.
I don't want any more trouble with the assistant principal.
JUSTIN
No nee
to wor
Mom..
You can count on me.
I trust you implicitly, my dear.
Did Dad leave already?
Yes, he got a call from the precinct commander--

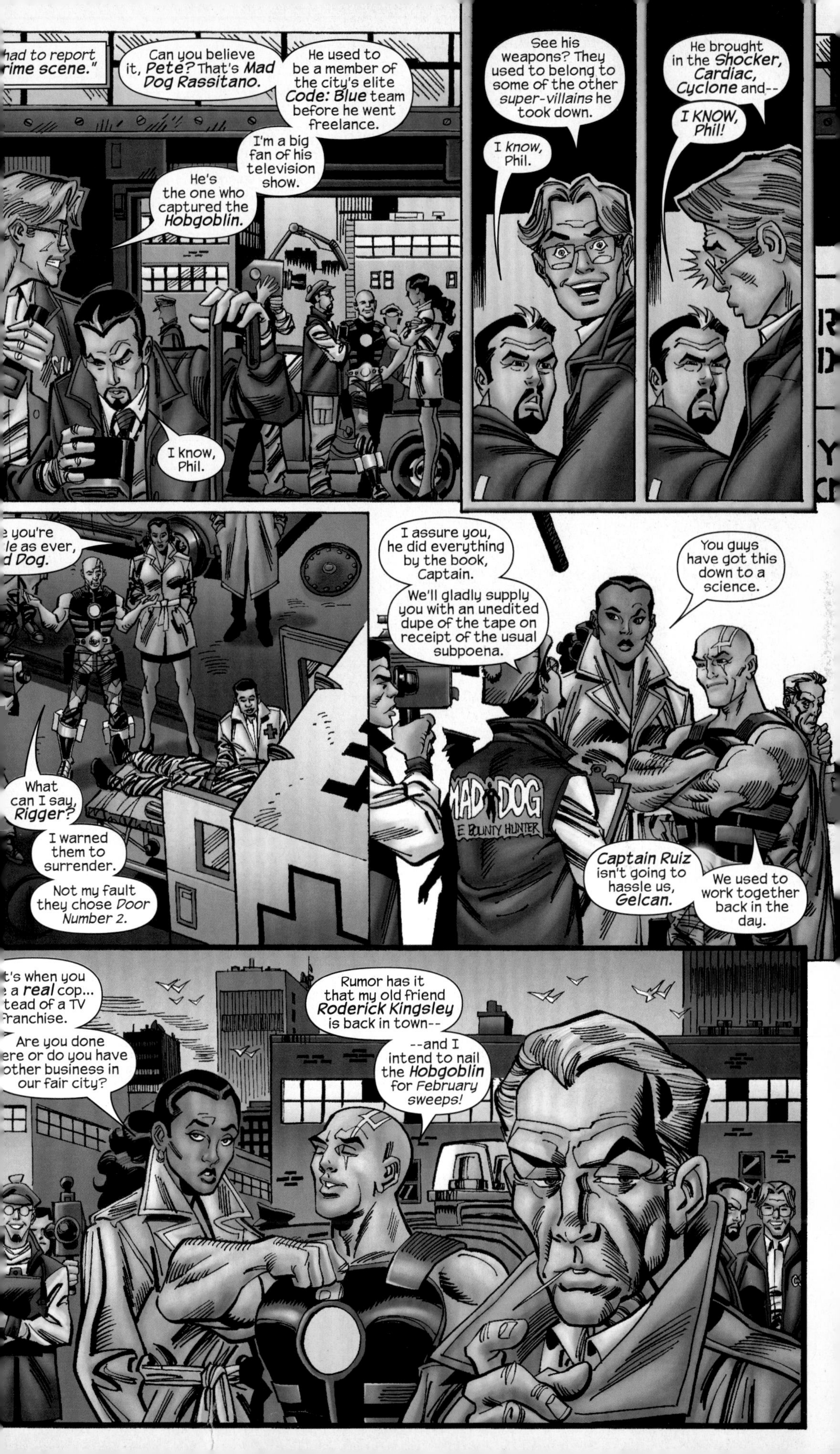
had to report rime scene."
Can you believe it, Pete? That's Mad Dog Rassitano.
He used to be a member of the city's elite Code: Blue team before he went freelance.
I'm a big fan of his television show.
He's the one who captured the Hobgoblin.
I know, Phil.
See his weapons? They used to belong to some of the other super-villains he took down.
I know, Phil.
He brought in the Shocker, Cardiac, Cyclone and--
I KNOW, Phil!
you're le as ever, d Dog.
What can I say, Rigger?
I warned them to surrender.
Not my fault they chose Door Number 2.
I assure you, he did everything by the book, Captain.
We'll gladly supply you with an unedited dupe of the tape on receipt of the usual subpoena.
You guys have got this down to a science.
MAD DOG
E BOUNTY HUNTER
Captain Ruiz isn't going to hassle us, Gelcan.
We used to work together back in the day.
t's when you a real cop... tead of a TV ranchise.
Are you done ere or do you have other business in our fair city?
Rumor has it that my old friend Roderick Kingsley is back in town--
--and I intend to nail the Hobgoblin for February sweeps!

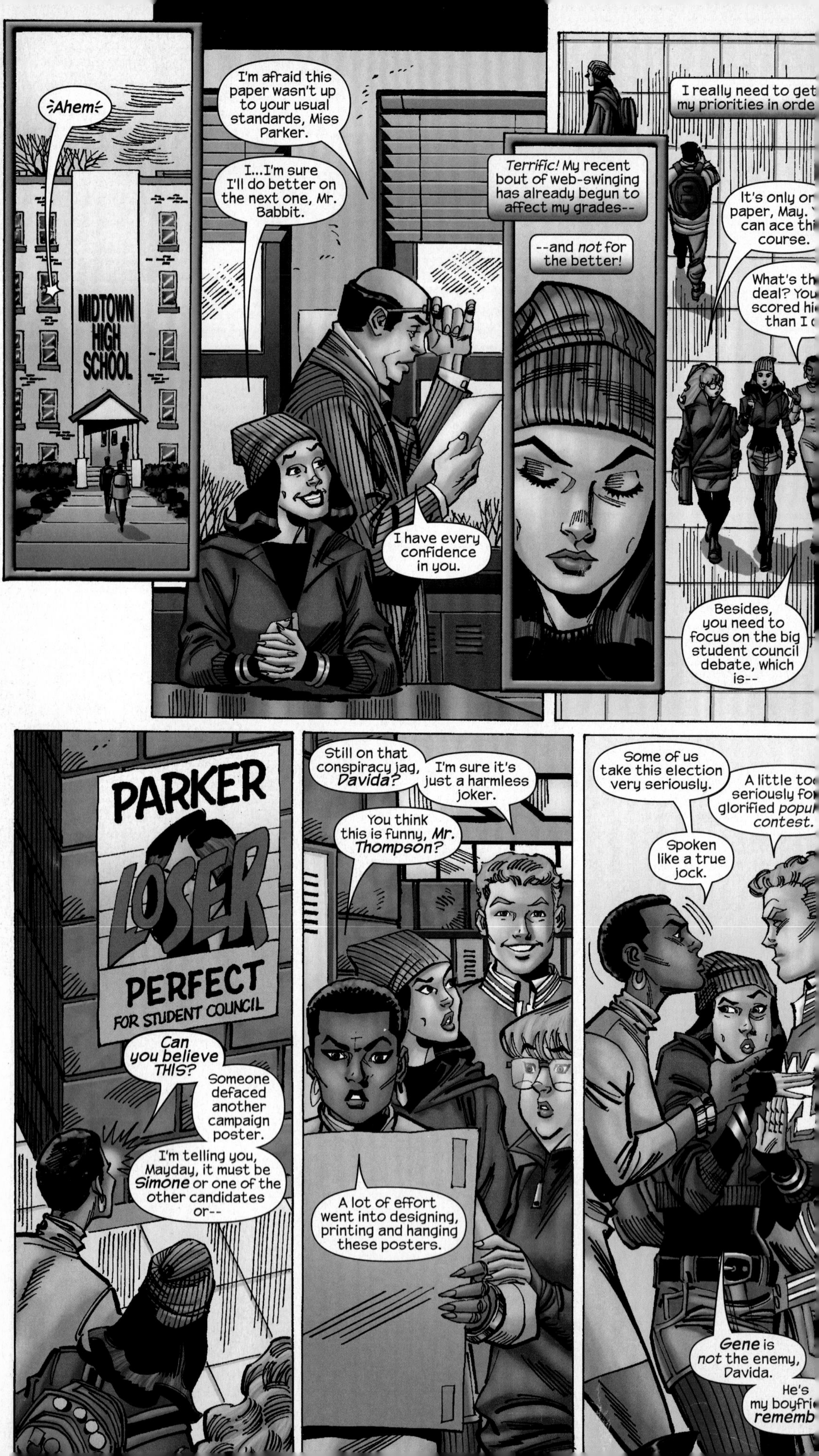

Ahem
MIDTOWN HIGH SCHOOL
I'm afraid this paper wasn't up to your usual standards, Miss Parker.
I...I'm sure I'll do better on the next one, Mr. Babbit.
I have every confidence in you.
Terrific! My recent bout of web-swinging has already begun to affect my grades--
--and not for the better!
I really need to get my priorities in orde
It's only or paper, May.
can ace th course.
What's th deal? You scored hi than I
Besides, you need to focus on the big student council debate, which is--
PARKER LOSER PERFECT FOR STUDENT COUNCIL
Can you believe THIS?
Someone defaced another campaign poster.
I'm telling you, Mayday, it must be Simone or one of the other candidates or--
Still on that conspiracy jag, Davida?
I'm sure it's just a harmless joker.
You think this is funny, Mr. Thompson?
A lot of effort went into designing, printing and hanging these posters.
Some of us take this election very seriously.
A little to seriously fo glorified popu contest.
Spoken like a true jock.
Gene is not the enemy, Davida.
He's my boyfri remem

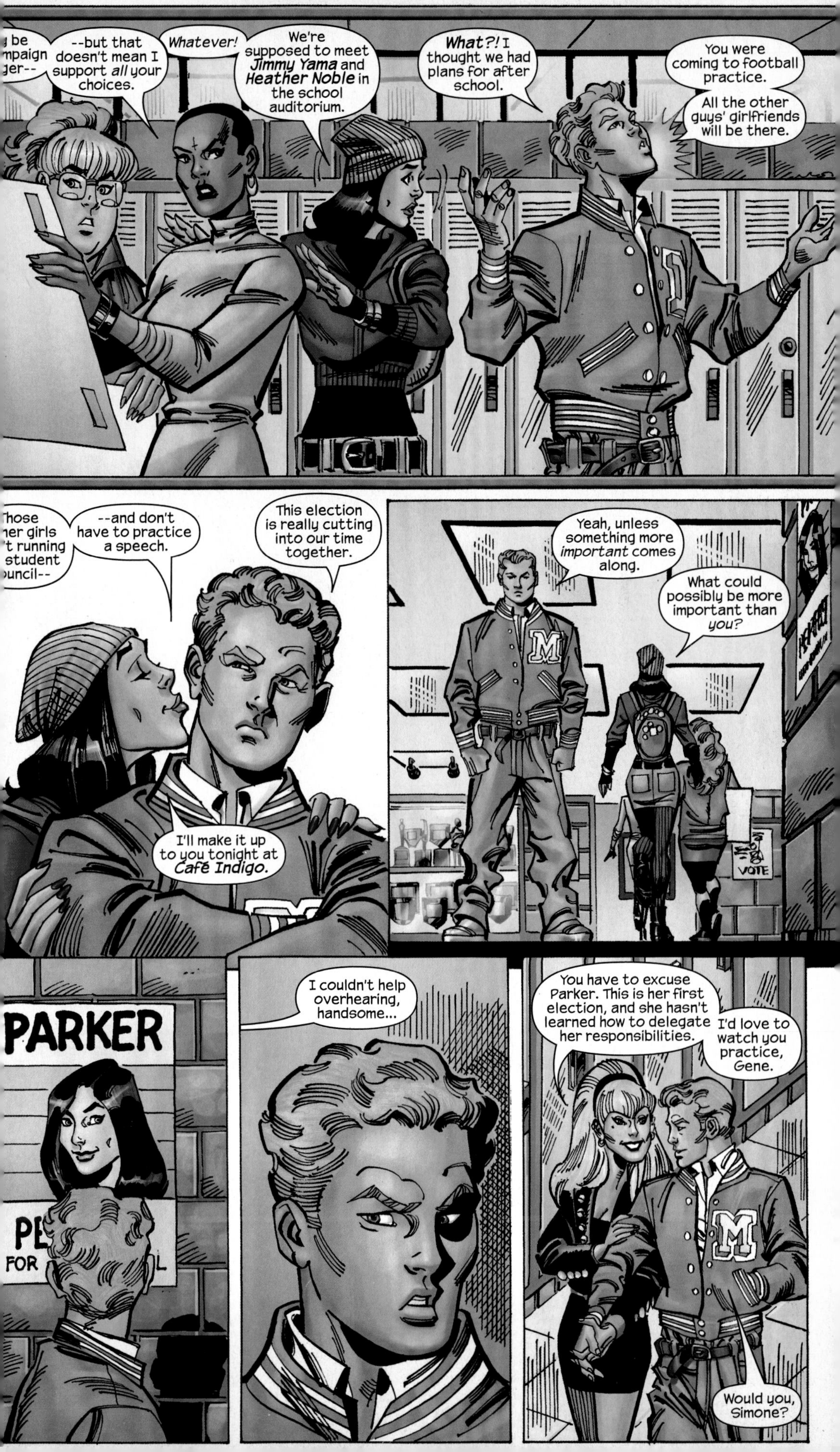

be
mpaign
ger--
--but that doesn't mean I support *all* your choices.
Whatever!
We're supposed to meet *Jimmy Yama* and *Heather Noble* in the school auditorium.
What?! I thought we had plans for after school.
You were coming to football practice.
All the other guys' girlfriends will be there.
hose
er girls
't running
student
uncil--
--and don't have to practice a speech.
This election is really cutting into our time together.
I'll make it up to you tonight at *Café Indigo.*
Yeah, unless something more *important* comes along.
What could possibly be more important than *you?*
VOTE
PARKER
PE
FOR
L
I couldn't help overhearing, handsome...
You have to excuse Parker. This is her first election, and she hasn't learned how to delegate her responsibilities.
I'd love to watch you practice, Gene.
Would you, Simone?

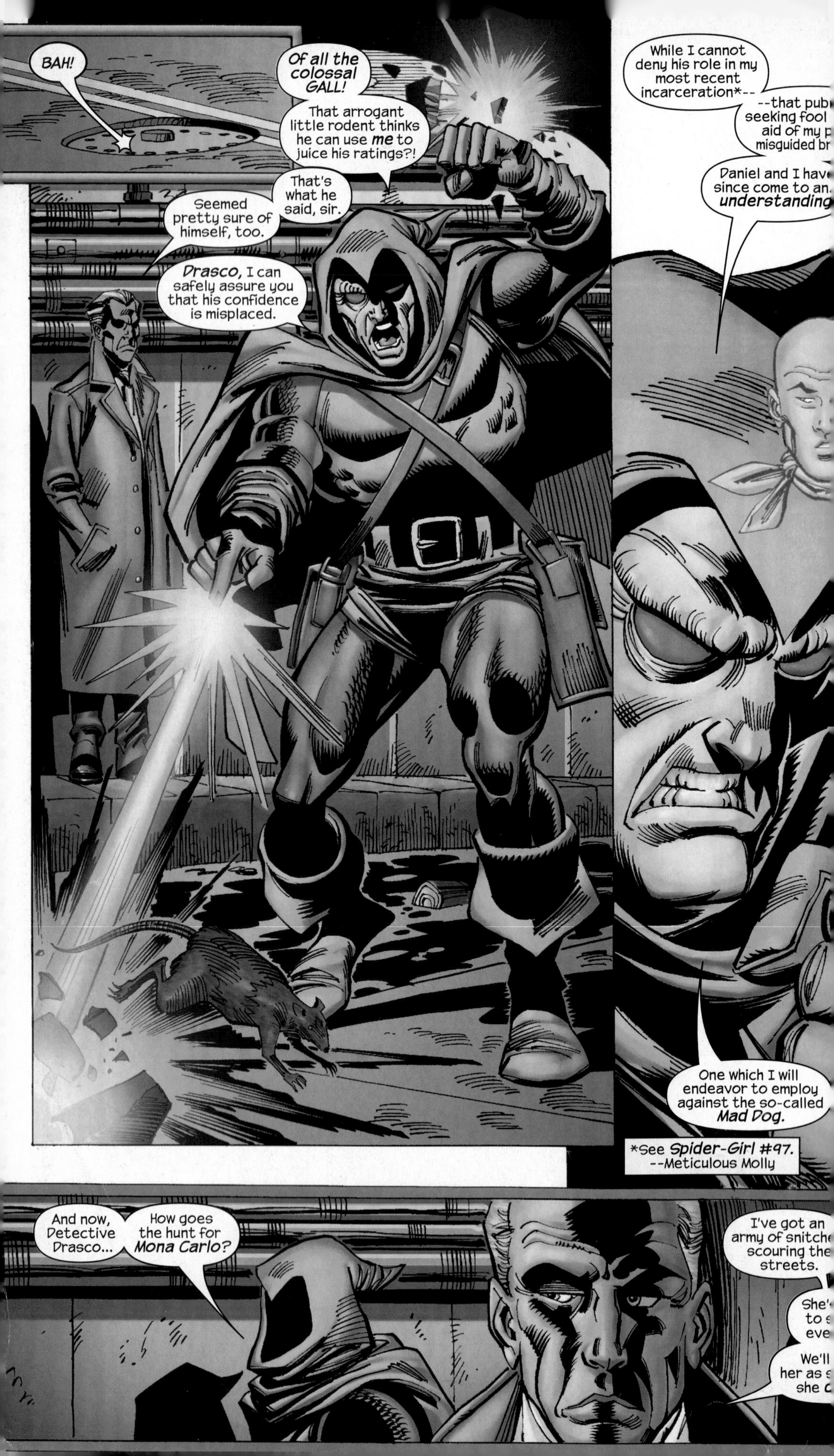
BAH!
Of all the colossal GALL!
That arrogant little rodent thinks he can use me to juice his ratings?!
That's what he said, sir.
Seemed pretty sure of himself, too.
Drasco, I can safely assure you that his confidence is misplaced.
While I cannot deny his role in my most recent incarceration*--
Daniel and I have since come to an understanding
One which I will endeavor to employ against the so-called Mad Dog.
*See Spider-Girl #97. --Meticulous Molly
And now, Detective Drasco...
How goes the hunt for Mona Carlo?
I've got an army of snitch scouring the streets.

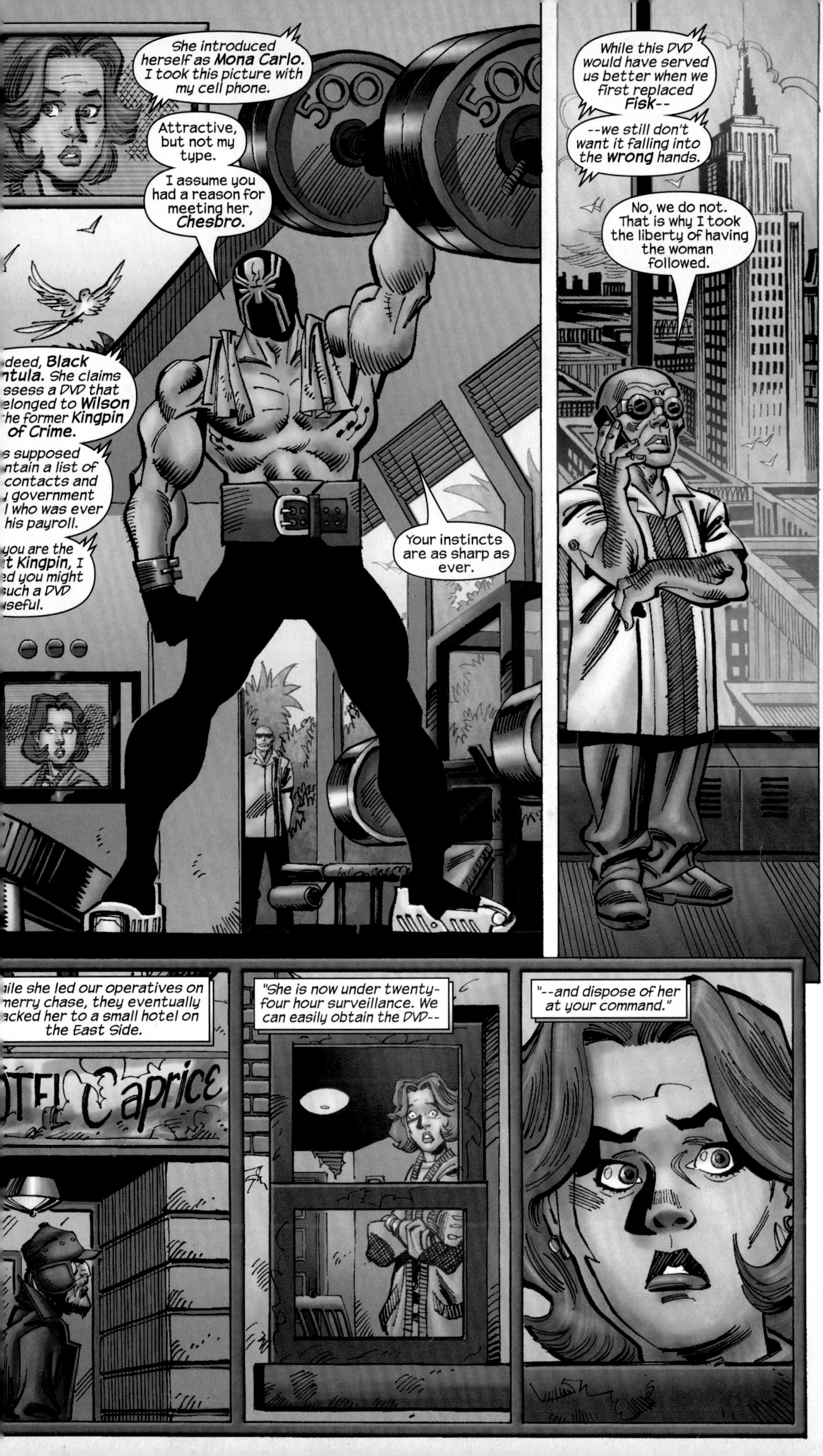
She introduced herself as Mona Carlo. I took this picture with my cell phone.
Attractive, but not my type.
I assume you had a reason for meeting her, Chesbro.
deed, Black ntula. She claims ssess a DVD that elonged to Wilson he former Kingpin of Crime.
s supposed ntain a list of contacts and government l who was ever his payroll.
you are the t Kingpin, I ed you might such a DVD seful.
Your instincts are as sharp as ever.
While this DVD would have served us better when we first replaced Fisk--
--we still don't want it falling into the wrong hands.
No, we do not. That is why I took the liberty of having the woman followed.
ile she led our operatives on merry chase, they eventually acked her to a small hotel on the East Side.
OTEL Caprice
"She is now under twenty-four hour surveillance. We can easily obtain the DVD--
"--and dispose of her at your command."

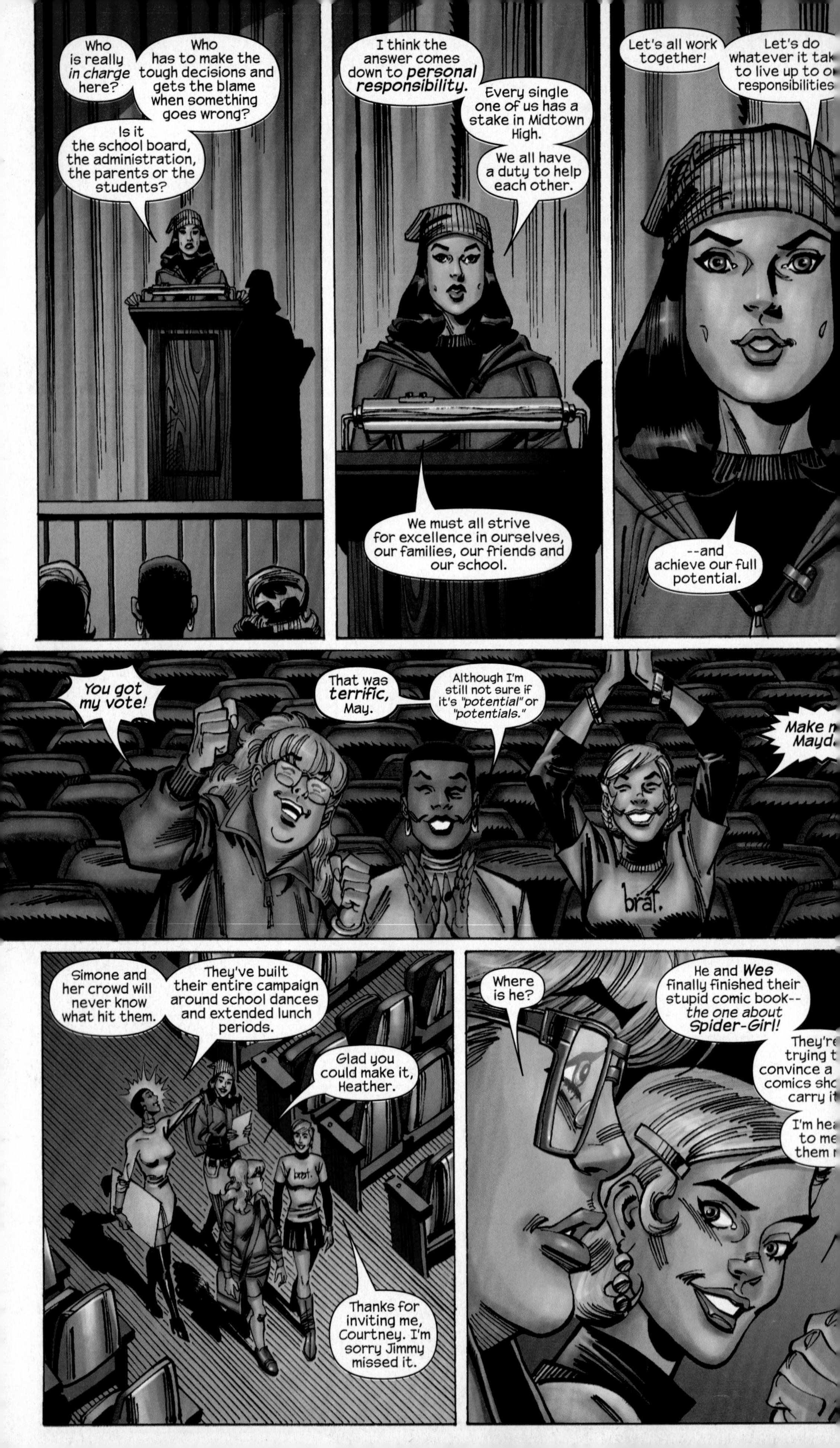

Who is really *in charge* here?
Who has to make the tough decisions and gets the blame when something goes wrong?
Is it the school board, the administration, the parents or the students?
I think the answer comes down to ***personal responsibility.***
Every single one of us has a stake in Midtown High.
We all have a duty to help each other.
We must all strive for excellence in ourselves, our families, our friends and our school.
Let's all work together!
Let's do whatever it tak to live up to o responsibilities
--and achieve our full potential.
You got my vote!
That was ***terrific,*** May.
Although I'm still not sure if it's *"potential"* or *"potentials."*
Make m Mayd
Simone and her crowd will never know what hit them.
They've built their entire campaign around school dances and extended lunch periods.
Glad you could make it, Heather.
Thanks for inviting me, Courtney. I'm sorry Jimmy missed it.
Where is he?
He and ***Wes*** finally finished their stupid comic book-- *the one about* ***Spider-Girl!***
They'r trying t convince a comics sho carry it
I'm hea to me them

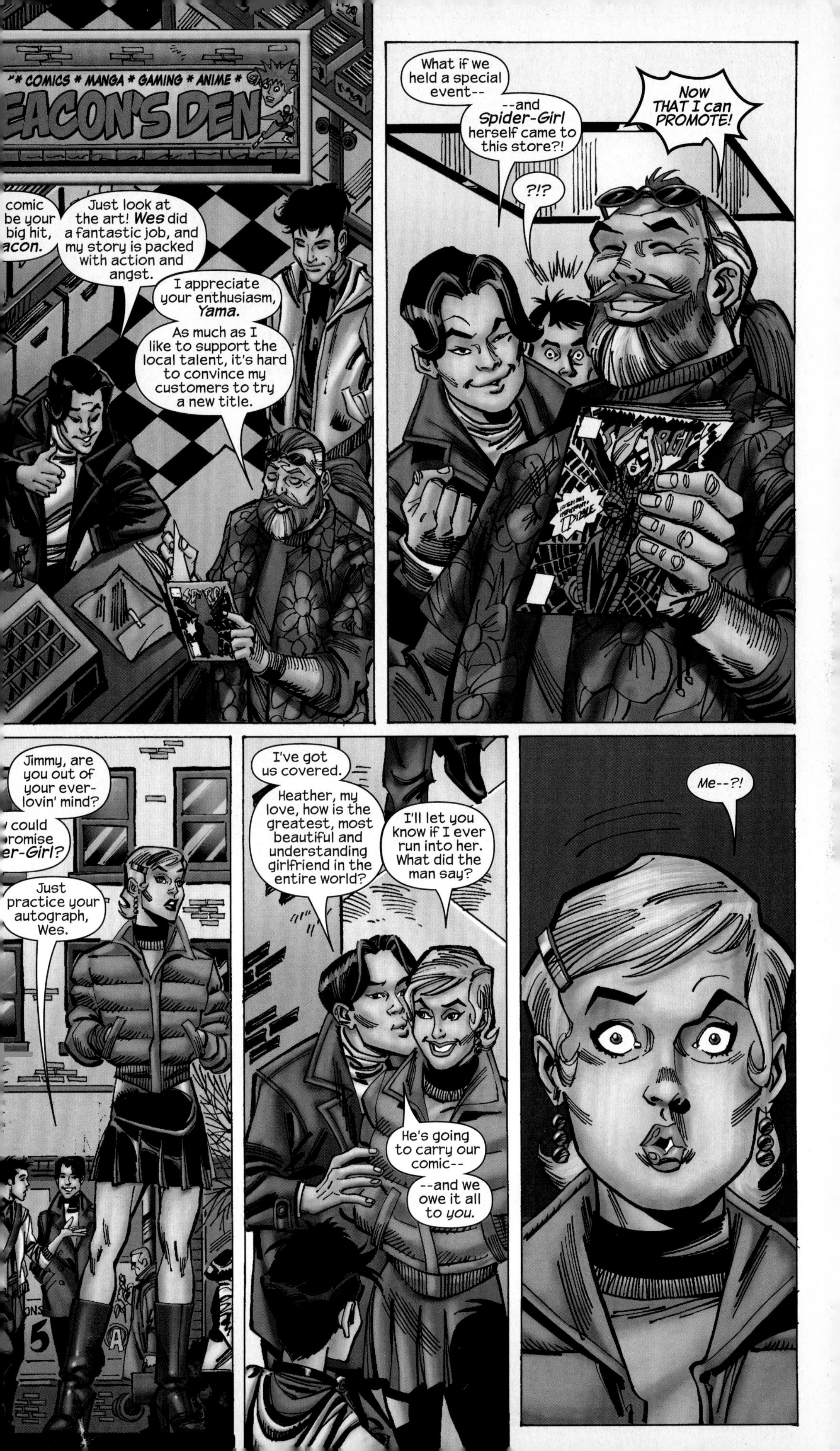
* COMICS * MANGA * GAMING * ANIME *
EACON'S DEN
comic be your big hit, acon.
Just look at the art! Wes did a fantastic job, and my story is packed with action and angst.
I appreciate your enthusiasm, Yama.
As much as I like to support the local talent, it's hard to convince my customers to try a new title.
What if we held a special event--
--and Spider-Girl herself came to this store?!
?!?
Now THAT I can PROMOTE!
Jimmy, are you out of your ever-lovin' mind?
could romise er-Girl?
Just practice your autograph, Wes.
I've got us covered.
Heather, my love, how is the greatest, most beautiful and understanding girlfriend in the entire world?
I'll let you know if I ever run into her. What did the man say?
He's going to carry our comic--
--and we owe it all to you.
Me--?!

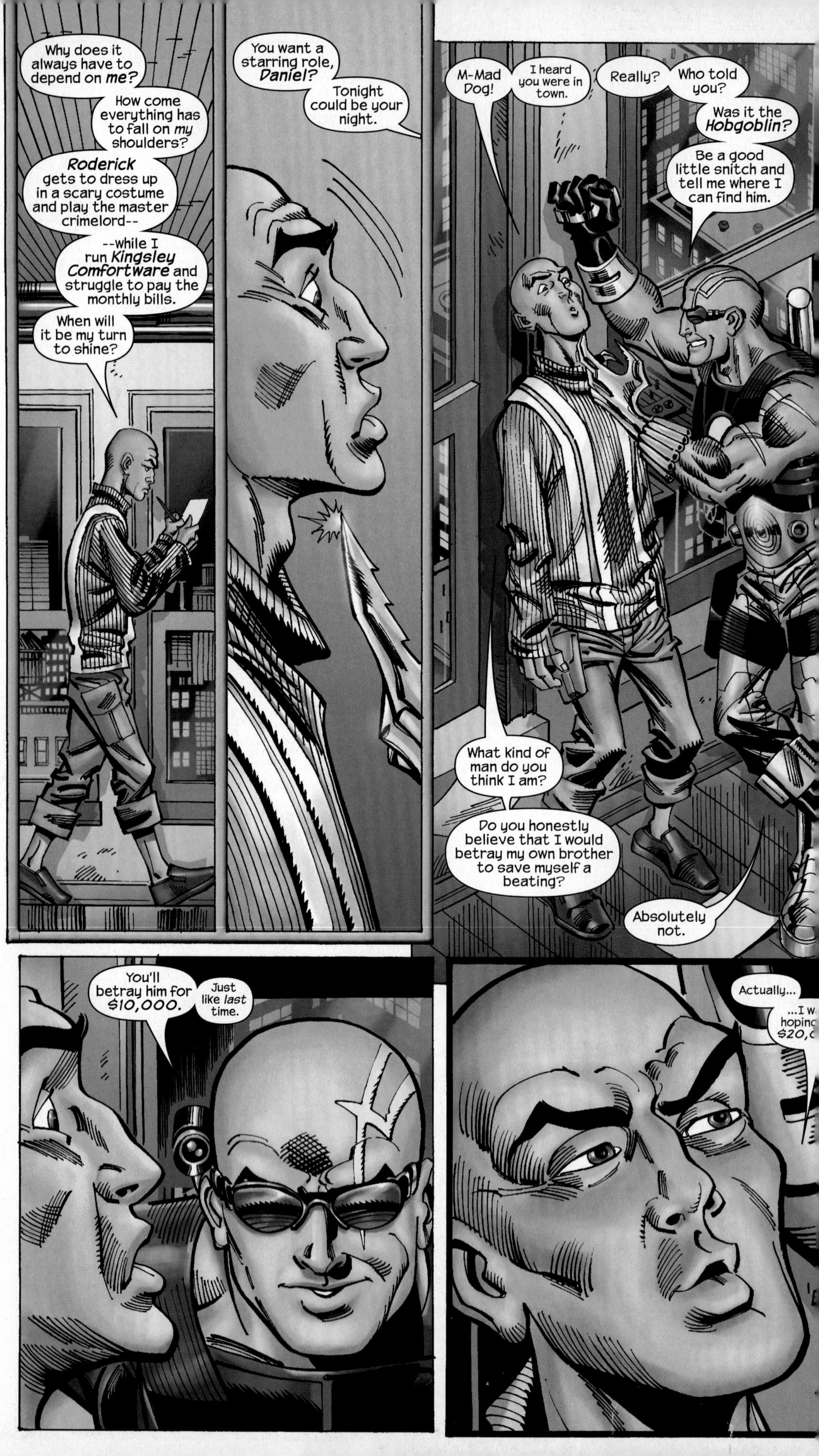

Why does it always have to depend on *me?*
How come everything has to fall on *my* shoulders?
Roderick gets to dress up in a scary costume and play the master crimelord--
--while I run ***Kingsley Comfortware*** and struggle to pay the monthly bills.
When will it be my turn to shine?
You want a starring role, *Daniel?*
Tonight could be your night.
M-Mad Dog!
I heard you were in town.
Really?
Who told you?
Was it the ***Hobgoblin?***
Be a good little snitch and tell me where I can find him.
What kind of man do you think I am?
Do you honestly believe that I would betray my own brother to save myself a beating?
Absolutely not.
You'll betray him for *$10,000.*
Just like *last* time.
Actually...

Daniel has done his part.

[Ma]d Dog believes [to] be at the westside docks tonight.

I have arranged an appropriate reception committee, and I want you on hand in case things go awry.

Hold on, Hobgoblin! I'm still a cop. I can't be a party to murder.

I OWN you, Detective Drasco. You will do as I say and you will not question me!

Is that clear?

Y-yes sir.

It's a pity we cannot include Spider-Girl in tonight's festivities.

[A f]ew hours later...

[Th]e [Hob]goblin [is go]ing [do]wn. I personally guarantee it.

This is a job for the world's greatest bounty hunter and a true American hero.

The police don't have the firepower to go up against someone like Hobgoblin.

Even the original Spider-Man failed to beat him.

The only one who could capture him was Mad Dog!

What are you watching?

The end of civilization as we know it.

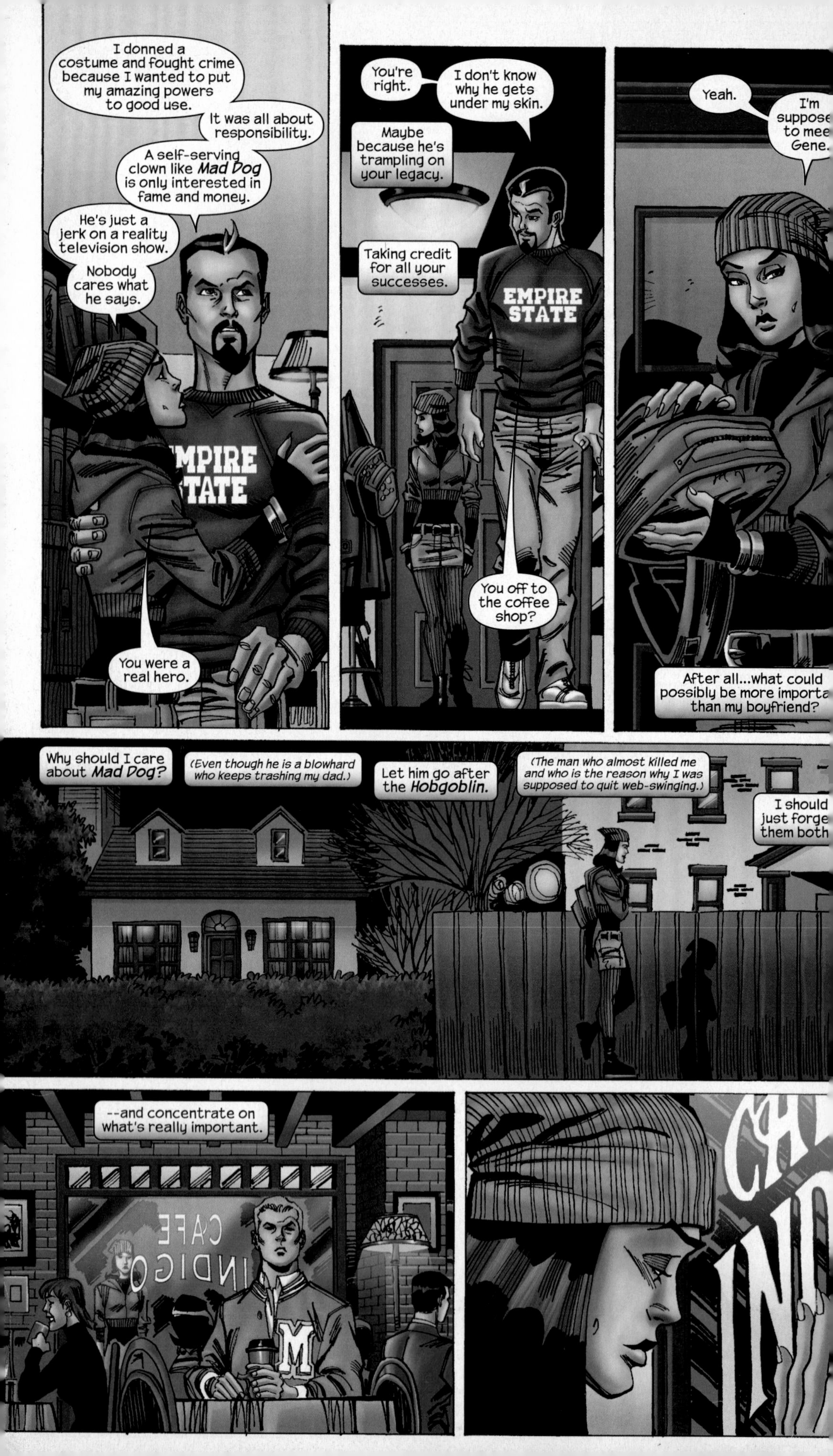
I donned a costume and fought crime because I wanted to put my amazing powers to good use.
It was all about responsibility.
A self-serving clown like *Mad Dog* is only interested in fame and money.
He's just a jerk on a reality television show.
Nobody cares what he says.
You were a real hero.
EMPIRE STATE
You're right.
I don't know why he gets under my skin.
Maybe because he's trampling on your legacy.
Taking credit for all your successes.
EMPIRE STATE
You off to the coffee shop?
Yeah.
I'm suppose to mee Gene.
After all...what could possibly be more importa than my boyfriend?
Why should I care about *Mad Dog?*
(Even though he is a blowhard who keeps trashing my dad.)
Let him go after the *Hobgoblin.*
(The man who almost killed me and who is the reason why I was supposed to quit web-swinging.)
I should just forge them both
--and concentrate on what's really important.
CAFE INDIGO

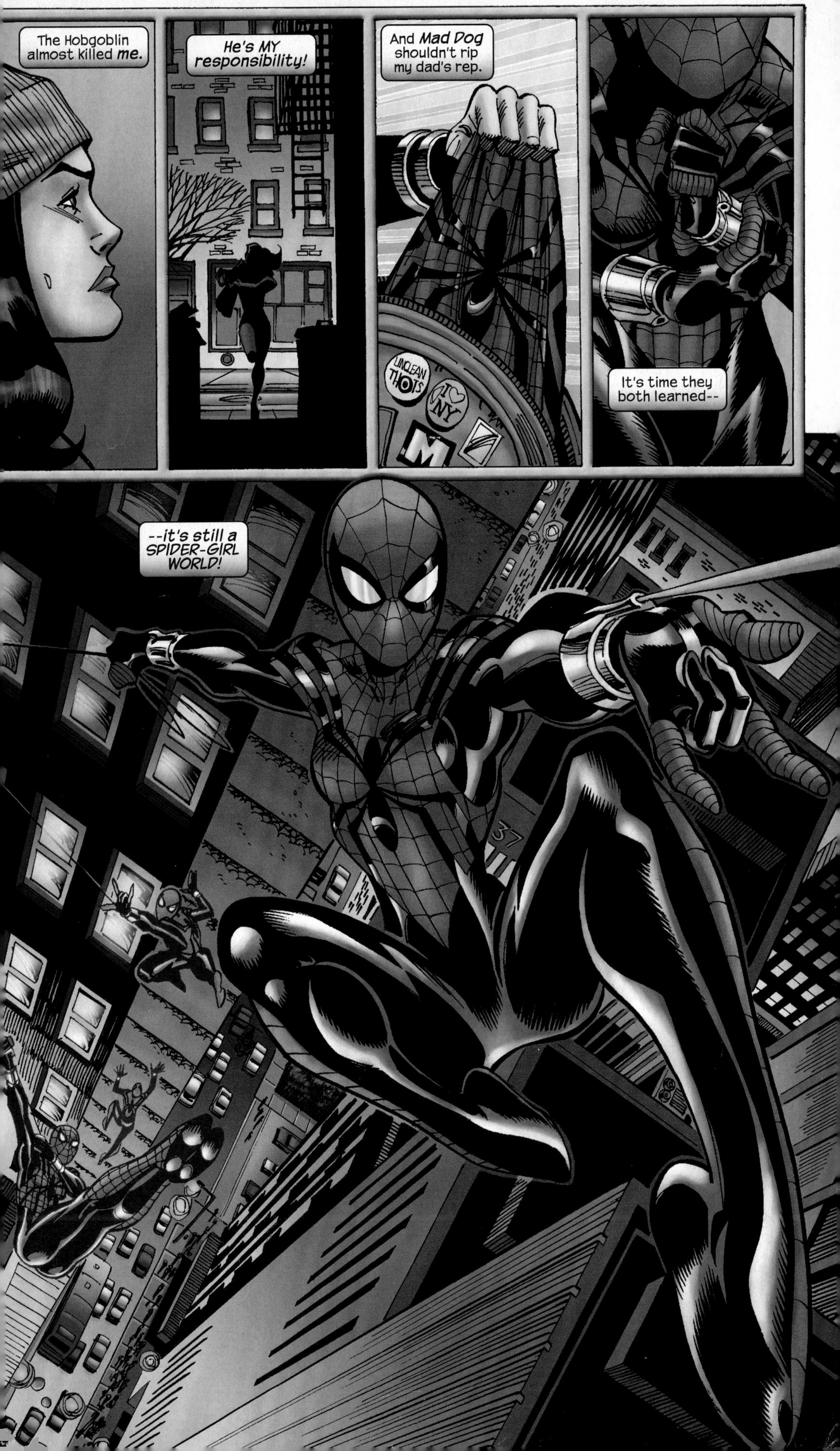

The Hobgoblin almost killed *me.*
He's MY responsibility!
And *Mad Dog* shouldn't rip my dad's rep.
UNCLEAN THOTS
I ♥ NY
M
It's time they both learned--
--it's still a SPIDER-GIRL WORLD!
37

Going on a little weekender, Mr. Kingsley?

Oh, no!

Not again.

already been around to ask about the Hobgoblin.

I'm guessing Mad Dog.

That means we don't have time for the usual *chit-chat*.

≶sigh≷

Y-you don't have *pockets* in that costume, do you?

No...a that's th questic get to

Shortly...

How's the reception, Gelcan?

Not bad--

--although your eye-cam could use a slight adjustment to the left.

WHIRR-KLIK

How's that?

You concentrate on the Hobgoblin. Our writers will handle the copy for your voice-over, and we'll dub it later.

But I like doing my own narration.

This suppos be rea televi

Yeah, and I got a brid to sell yo

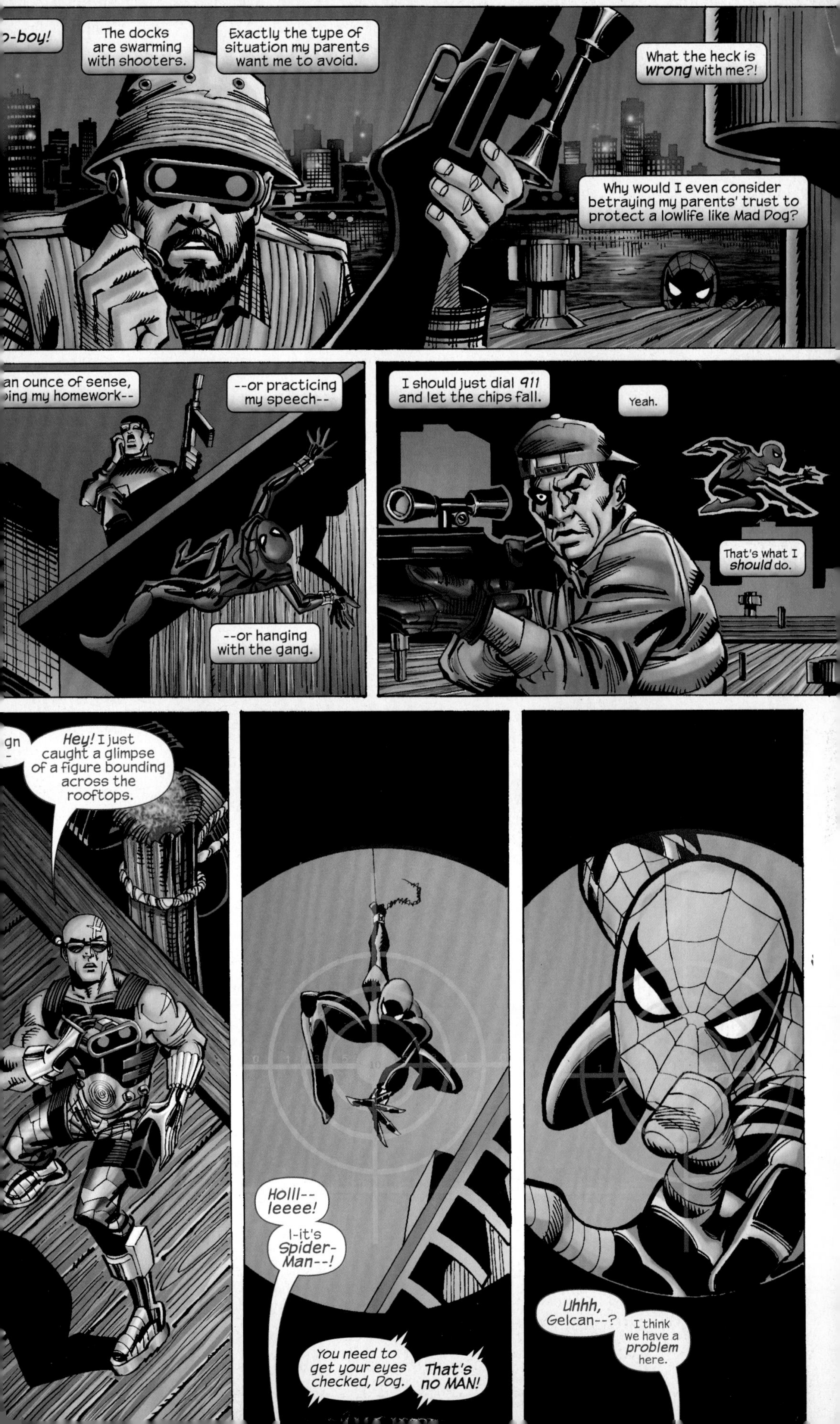
-boy!
The docks are swarming with shooters.
Exactly the type of situation my parents want me to avoid.
What the heck is wrong with me?!
Why would I even consider betraying my parents' trust to protect a lowlife like Mad Dog?
an ounce of sense,
oing my homework--
--or practicing my speech--
--or hanging with the gang.
I should just dial 911 and let the chips fall.
Yeah.
That's what I should do.
gn
Hey! I just caught a glimpse of a figure bounding across the rooftops.
Holll-- leeee!
I-it's Spider-Man--!
You need to get your eyes checked, Dog.
That's no MAN!
Uhhh, Gelcan--?
I think we have a problem here.

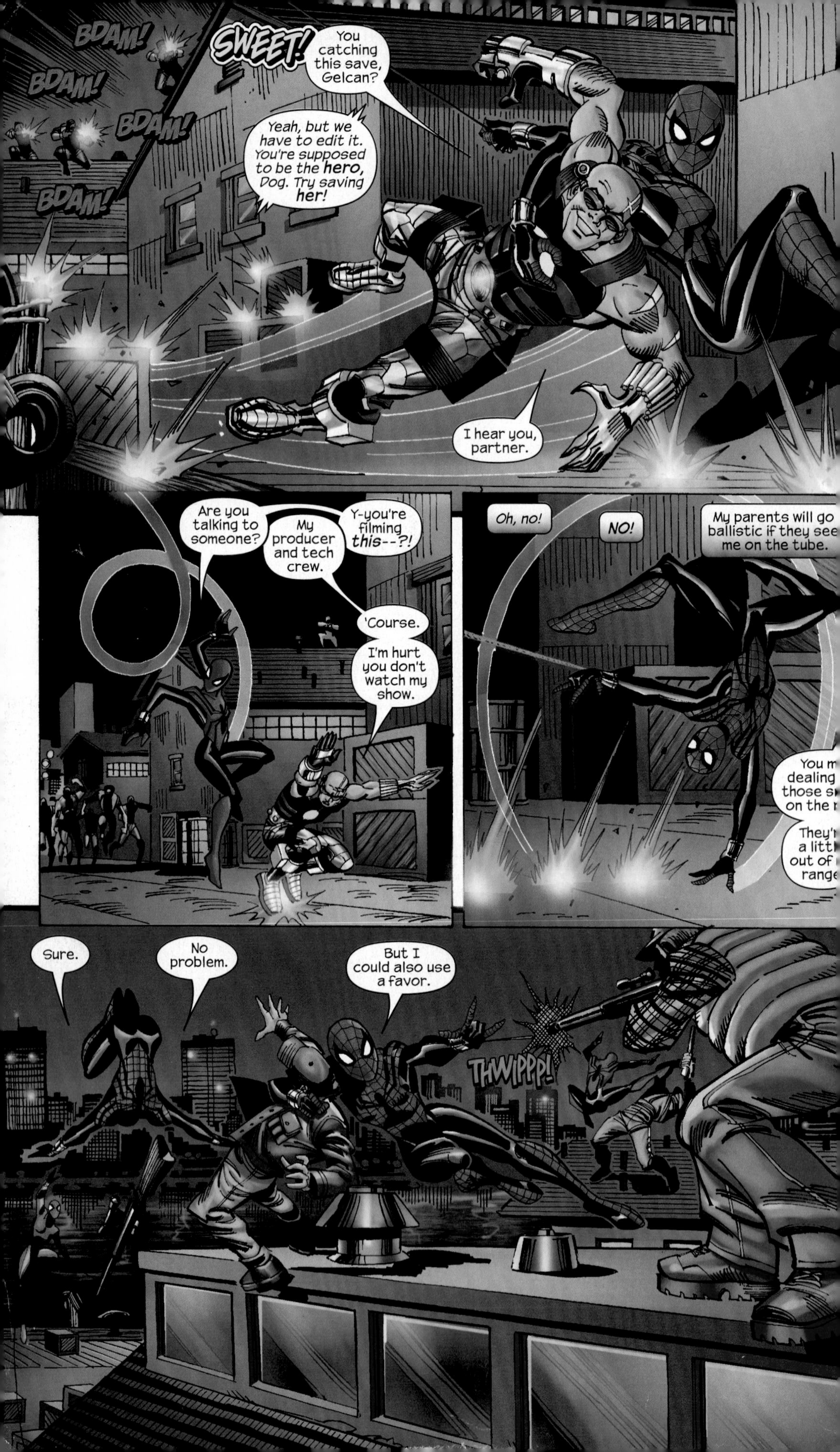
BDAM!
BDAM!
BDAM!
BDAM!
SWEET!
You catching this save, Gelcan?
Yeah, but we have to edit it. You're supposed to be the **hero,** Dog. Try saving **her!**
I hear you, partner.
Are you talking to someone?
My producer and tech crew.
Y-you're filming *this*--?!
'Course.
I'm hurt you don't watch my show.
Oh, no!
NO!
My parents will go ballistic if they see me on the tube.
Sure.
No problem.
But I could also use a favor.
THWIPPP!

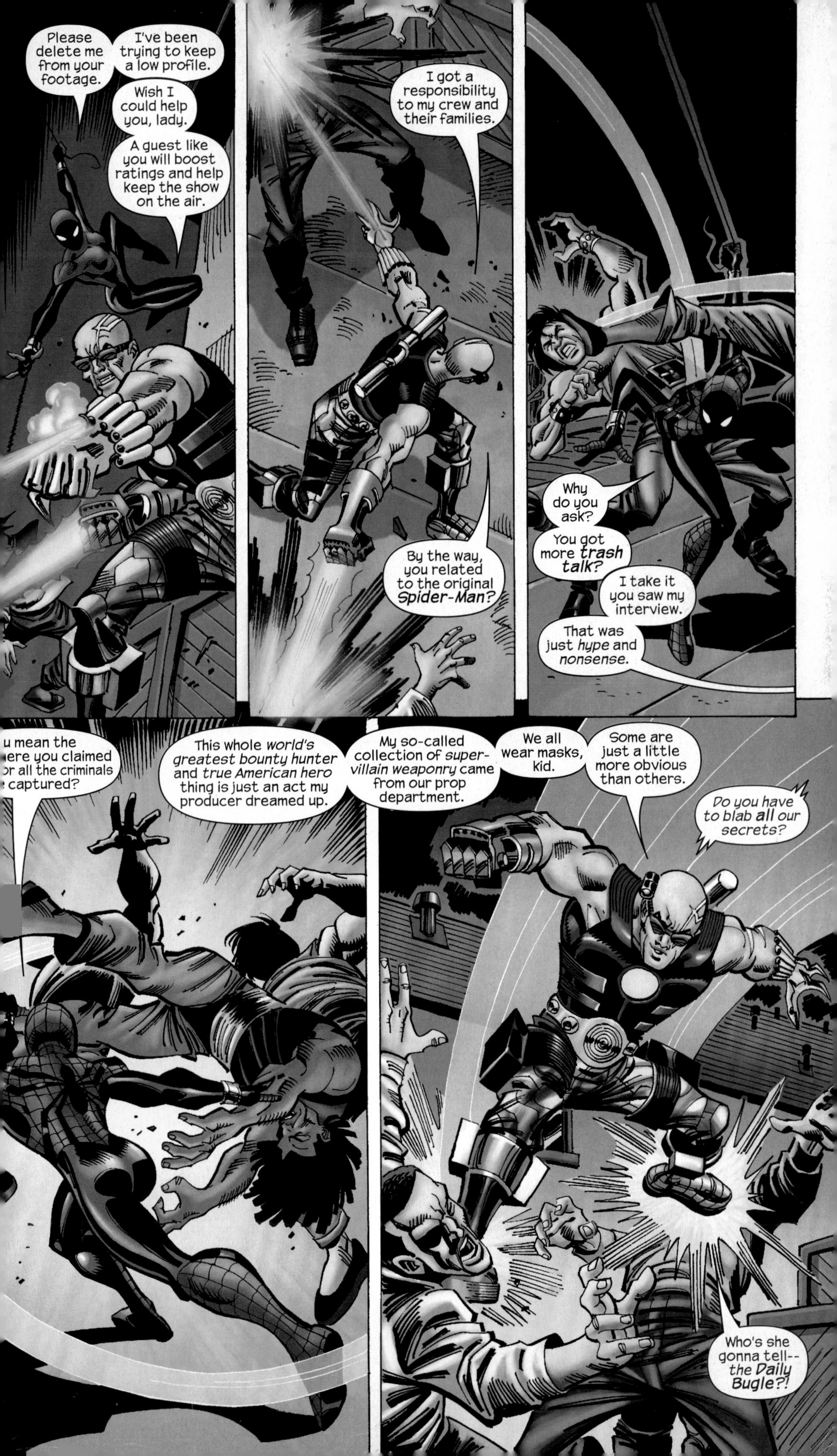
Please delete me from your footage.
I've been trying to keep a low profile.
Wish I could help you, lady.
A guest like you will boost ratings and help keep the show on the air.
I got a responsibility to my crew and their families.
By the way, you related to the original Spider-Man?
Why do you ask?
You got more trash talk?
I take it you saw my interview.
That was just hype and nonsense.
u mean the ere you claimed or all the criminals captured?
This whole world's greatest bounty hunter and true American hero thing is just an act my producer dreamed up.
My so-called collection of super-villain weaponry came from our prop department.
We all wear masks, kid.
Some are just a little more obvious than others.
Do you have to blab all our secrets?
Who's she gonna tell-- the Daily Bugle?!

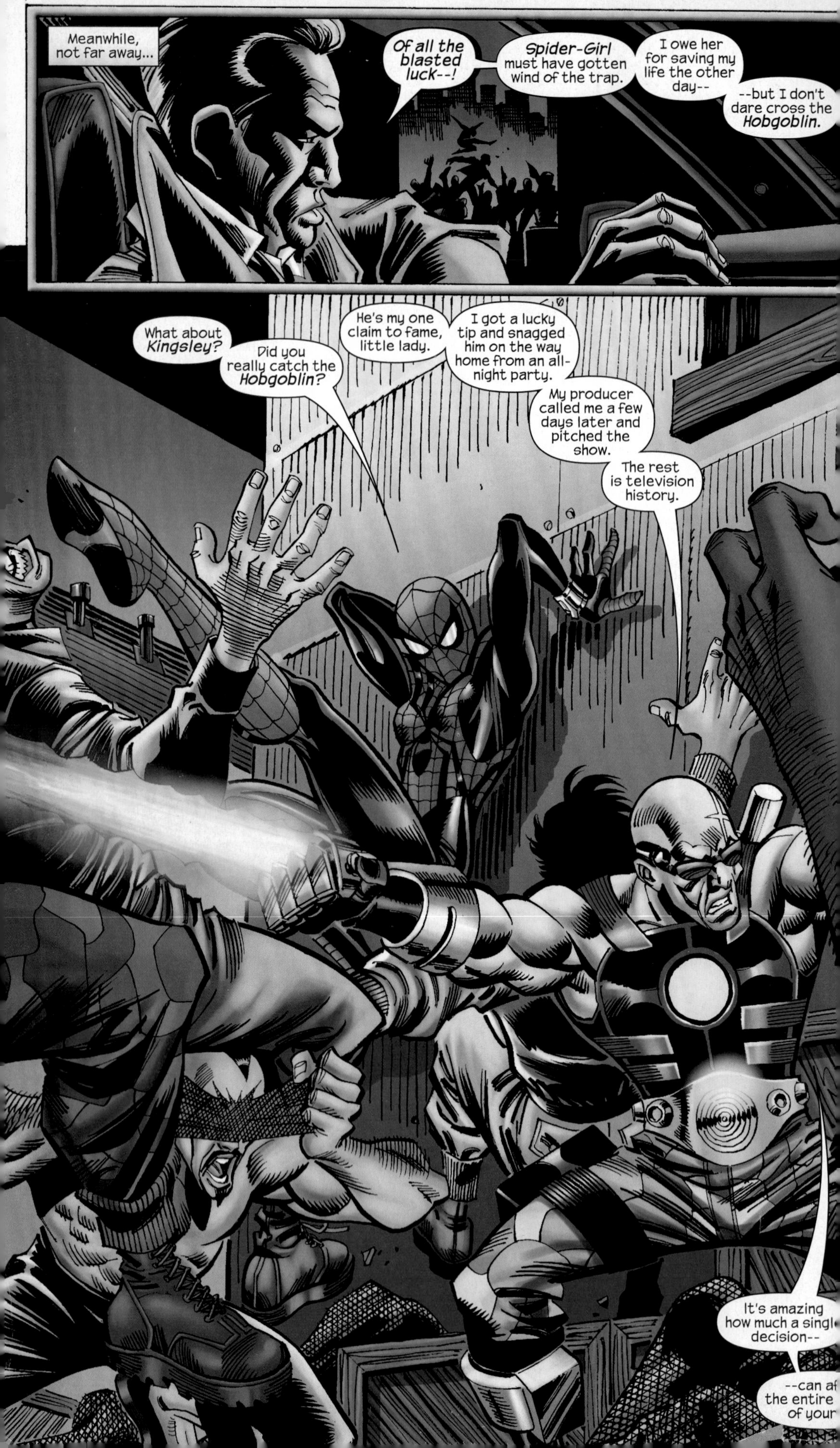
Meanwhile, not far away...
Of all the blasted luck--!
Spider-Girl must have gotten wind of the trap.
I owe her for saving my life the other day--
--but I don't dare cross the Hobgoblin.
What about Kingsley?
Did you really catch the Hobgoblin?
He's my one claim to fame, little lady.
I got a lucky tip and snagged him on the way home from an all-night party.
My producer called me a few days later and pitched the show.
The rest is television history.
It's amazing how much a singl decision--
--can af the entire of your

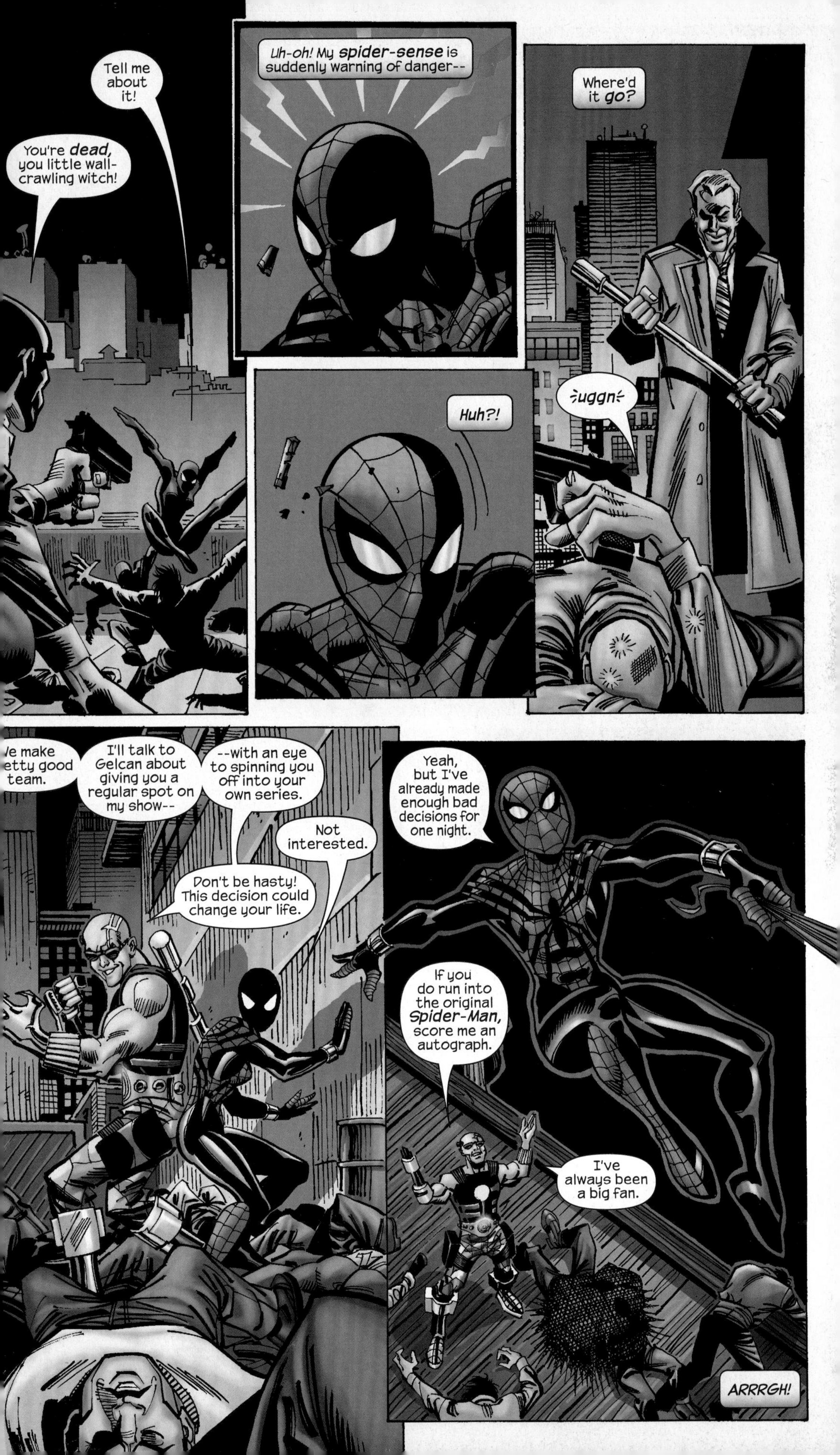

Tell me about it!
You're dead, you little wall-crawling witch!
Uh-oh! My spider-sense is suddenly warning of danger--
Huh?!
Where'd it go?
uggn
/e make
etty good
team.
I'll talk to Gelcan about giving you a regular spot on my show--
--with an eye to spinning you off into your own series.
Not interested.
Don't be hasty! This decision could change your life.
Yeah, but I've already made enough bad decisions for one night.
If you do run into the original Spider-Man, score me an autograph.
I've always been a big fan.
ARRRGH!

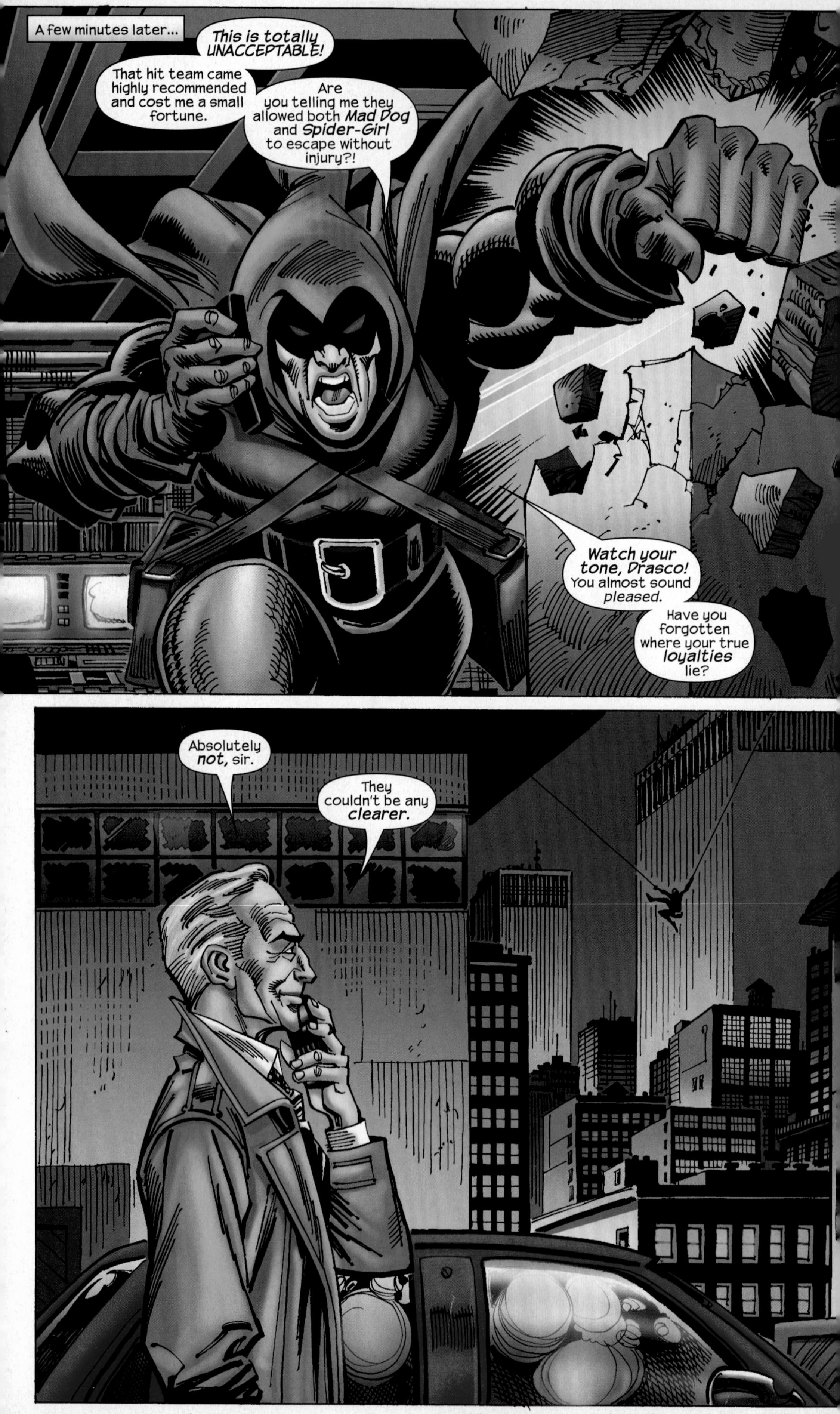
A few minutes later...
This is totally UNACCEPTABLE!
That hit team came highly recommended and cost me a small fortune.
Are you telling me they allowed both Mad Dog and Spider-Girl to escape without injury?!
Watch your tone, Drasco! You almost sound pleased.
Have you forgotten where your true loyalties lie?
Absolutely not, sir.
They couldn't be any clearer.

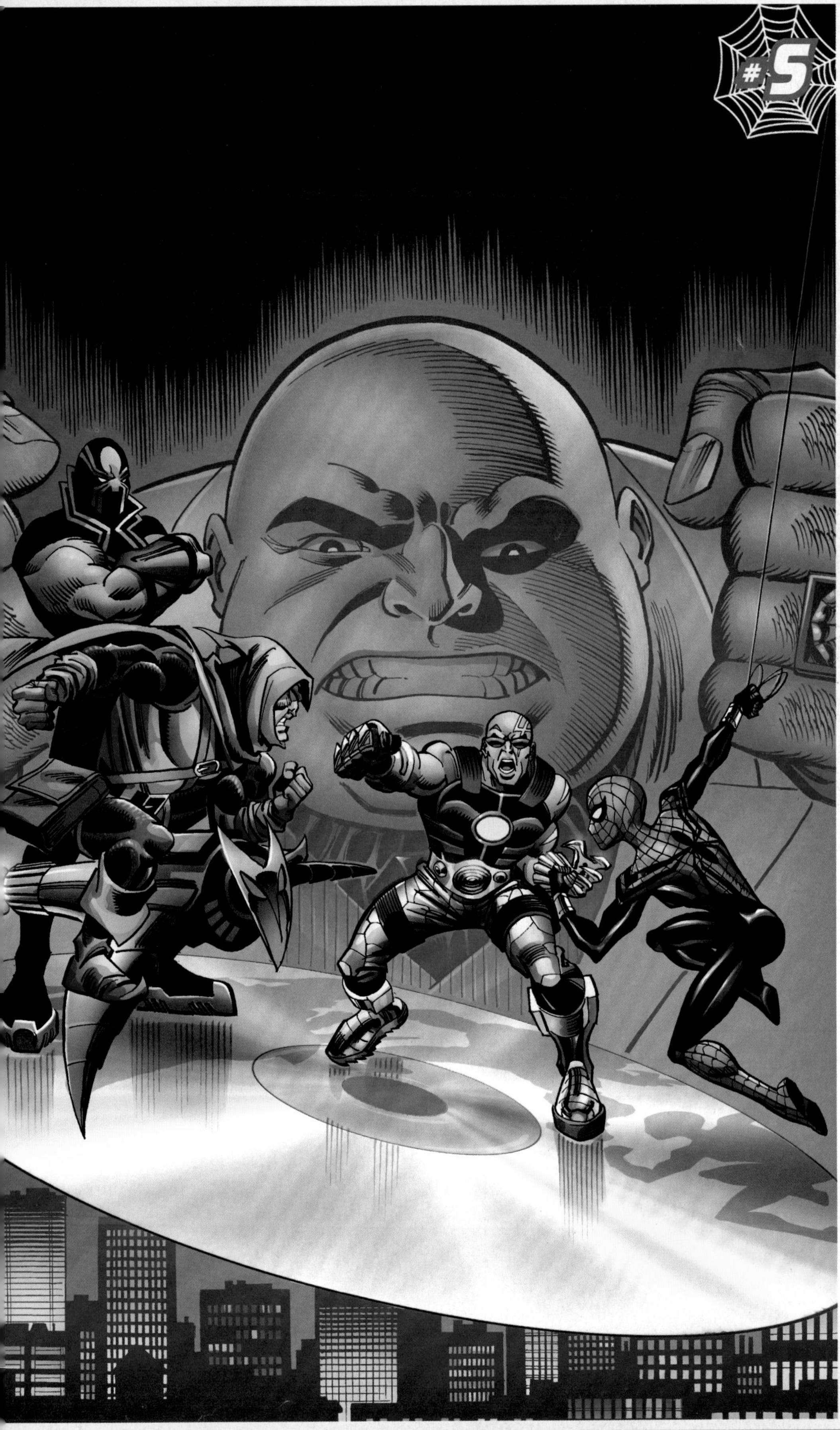
#5

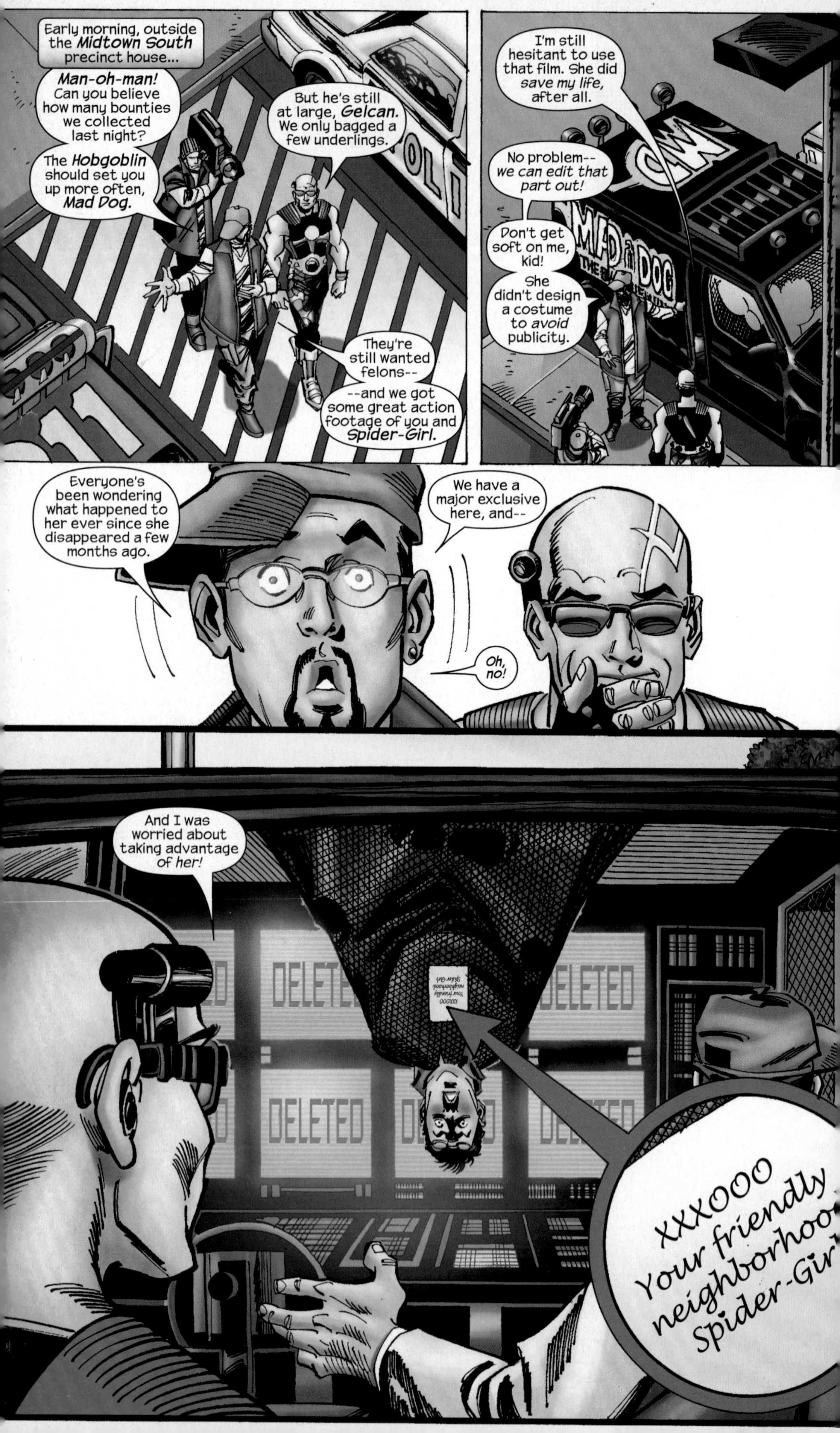

Early morning, outside the *Midtown South* precinct house...
Man-oh-man! Can you believe how many bounties we collected last night?
The *Hobgoblin* should set you up more often, *Mad Dog.*
But he's still at large, *Gelcan.* We only bagged a few underlings.
They're still wanted felons--
--and we got some great action footage of you and *Spider-Girl.*
I'm still hesitant to use that film. She did *save my life,* after all.
No problem-- *we can edit that part out!*
Don't get soft on me, kid!
She didn't design a costume to *avoid* publicity.
MAD DOG
Everyone's been wondering what happened to her ever since she disappeared a few months ago.
We have a major exclusive here, and--
Oh, no!
And I was worried about taking advantage of *her!*
DELETED
DELETED
DELETED
DELETED
DELETED
XXXOOO Your friendly neighborhoo Spider-Gir

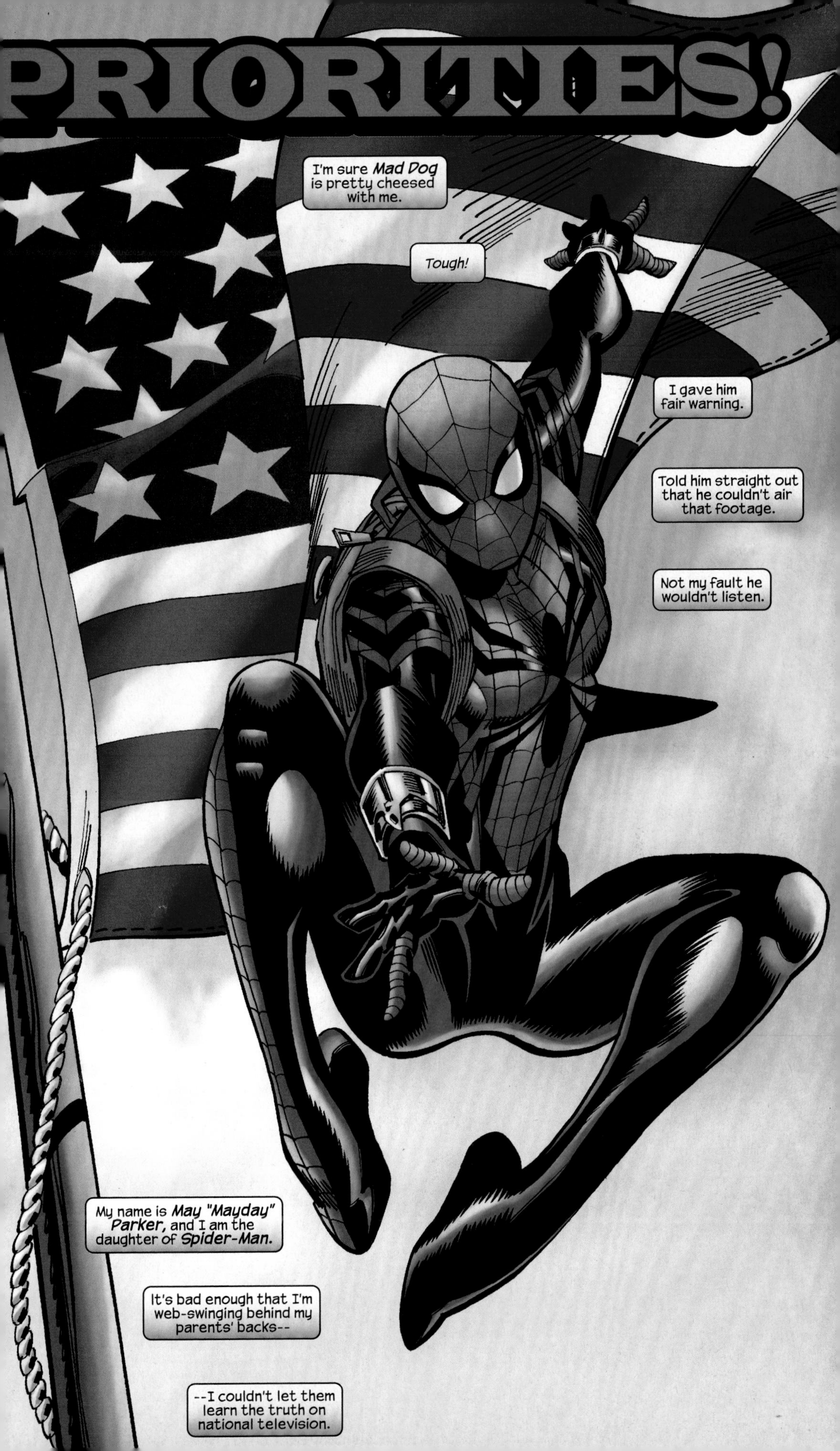
PRIORITIES!
I'm sure Mad Dog is pretty cheesed with me.
Tough!
I gave him fair warning.
Told him straight out that he couldn't air that footage.
Not my fault he wouldn't listen.
My name is May "Mayday" Parker, and I am the daughter of Spider-Man.
It's bad enough that I'm web-swinging behind my parents' backs--
--I couldn't let them learn the truth on national television.

I'm just lucky I found the van so quickly.

I figured Mad Dog would be at the station house all night.

Of course, there's always a chance he mentioned me in his formal statements to the police--

--but there's nothing I can do about that.

MIDTOWN HIGH SCHOOL

Looks like I actually made it to school early for a change.

My *spider-s* isn't tingli

--which means there's no danger of being spotted while I slip into my civvies.

I have at least an hour or so before my first class.

Cool!

Getting up early certainly has its advantages.

I can use the time to prepare for this afternoon's student council debate.

That'll leave me free to run an errand at lunchtime.

I need to hav another littl chat with *Dan Kingsley,* the Hobgoblin brother.

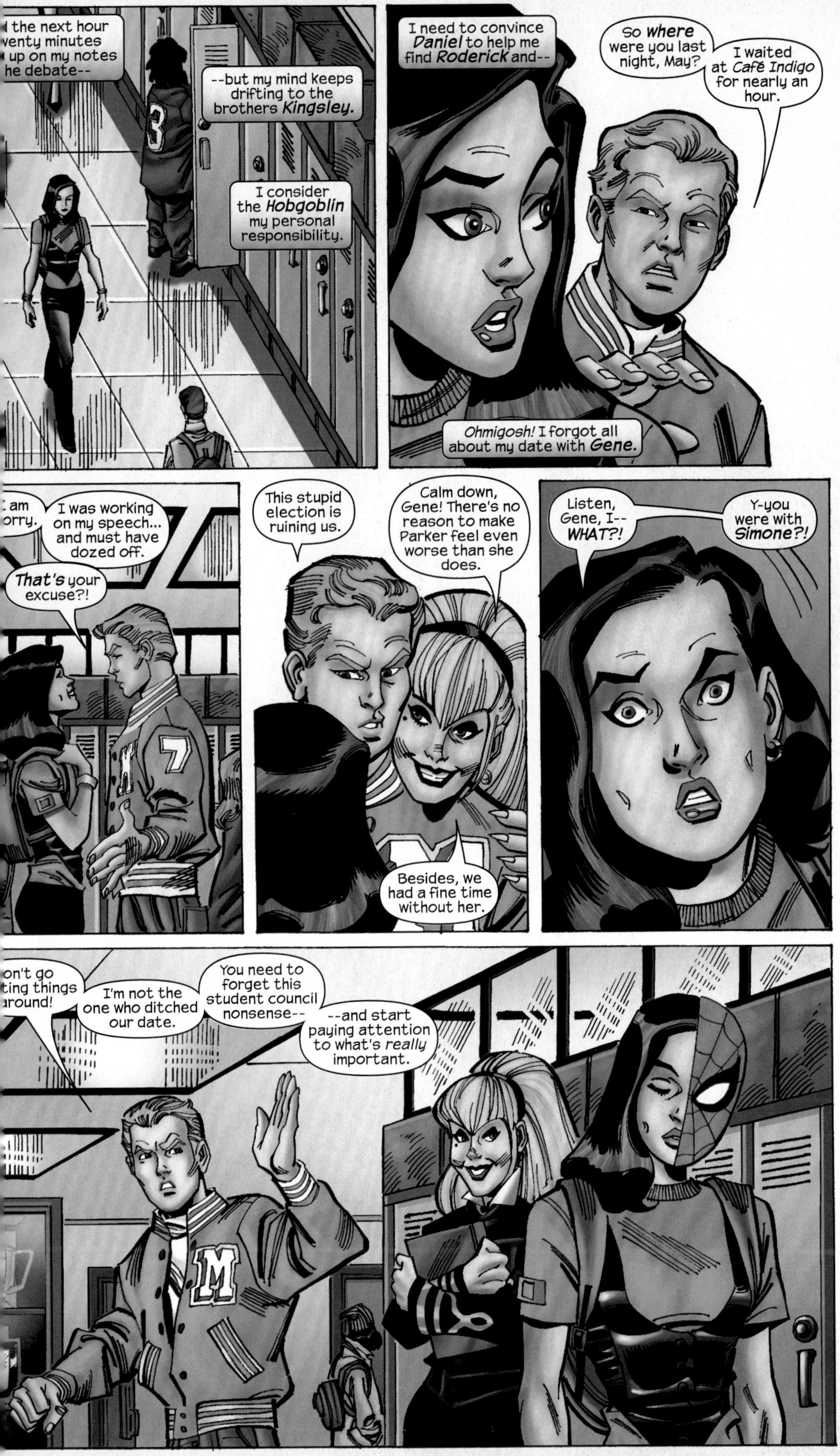

the next hour
venty minutes
up on my notes
he debate--
--but my mind keeps drifting to the brothers *Kingsley.*
I consider the *Hobgoblin* my personal responsibility.
I need to convince *Daniel* to help me find *Roderick* and--
So *where* were you last night, May?
I waited at *Café Indigo* for nearly an hour.
Ohmigosh! I forgot all about my date with *Gene.*
am
orry.
I was working on my speech... and must have dozed off.
That's your excuse?!
This stupid election is ruining us.
Calm down, Gene! There's no reason to make Parker feel even worse than she does.
Besides, we had a fine time without her.
Listen, Gene, I-- *WHAT?!*
Y-you were with *Simone?!*
on't go
ting things
around!
I'm not the one who ditched our date.
You need to forget this student council nonsense--
--and start paying attention to what's *really* important.

Poor little Parker! Looks like she's about to lose the election--

--and her boyfriend.

I can't speak to the boyfriend issue, Simone--

--but Mayday's looking pretty good election-wise.

And you're so objective, Kirby.

I'll admit to a vested interest. That's why I asked a few underclassmen to take an informal poll for me.

Seems yo locked up th vote while M nearly eve else

She's go to troub you, gi

The cream always rises.

Yeah, but you're way past your expiration date.

Did you really conduct a poll, Davida?

Nah, but I made her sweat.

Simone is no dummy.

She keeps busting on you because she knows she's cooked.

No one is going to put a mean girl on student council.

The students deserve better.

We want someone who is going to give us total commitment.

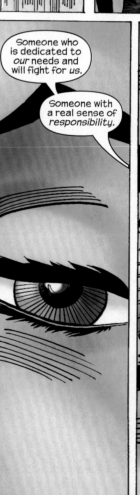

Someone who is dedicated to our needs and will fight for us.

Someone with a real sense of responsibility.

Someone who has her prioritie straight and wil always put us first.

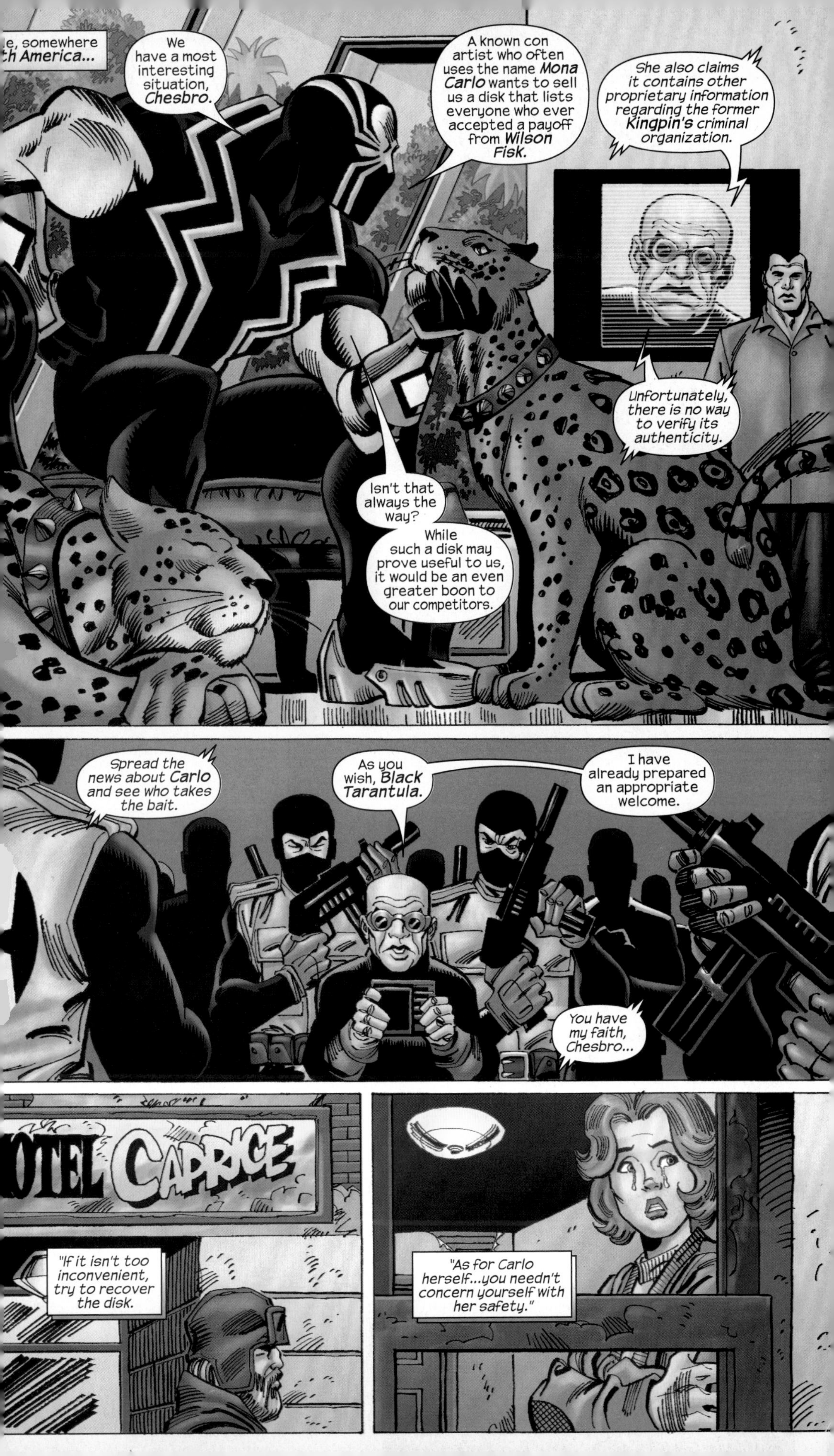

e, somewhere
th America...
We have a most interesting situation, Chesbro.
A known con artist who often uses the name Mona Carlo wants to sell us a disk that lists everyone who ever accepted a payoff from Wilson Fisk.
She also claims it contains other proprietary information regarding the former Kingpin's criminal organization.
Unfortunately, there is no way to verify its authenticity.
Isn't that always the way?
While such a disk may prove useful to us, it would be an even greater boon to our competitors.
Spread the news about Carlo and see who takes the bait.
As you wish, Black Tarantula.
I have already prepared an appropriate welcome.
You have my faith, Chesbro...
OTEL CAPRICE
"If it isn't too inconvenient, try to recover the disk.
"As for Carlo herself...you needn't concern yourself with her safety."

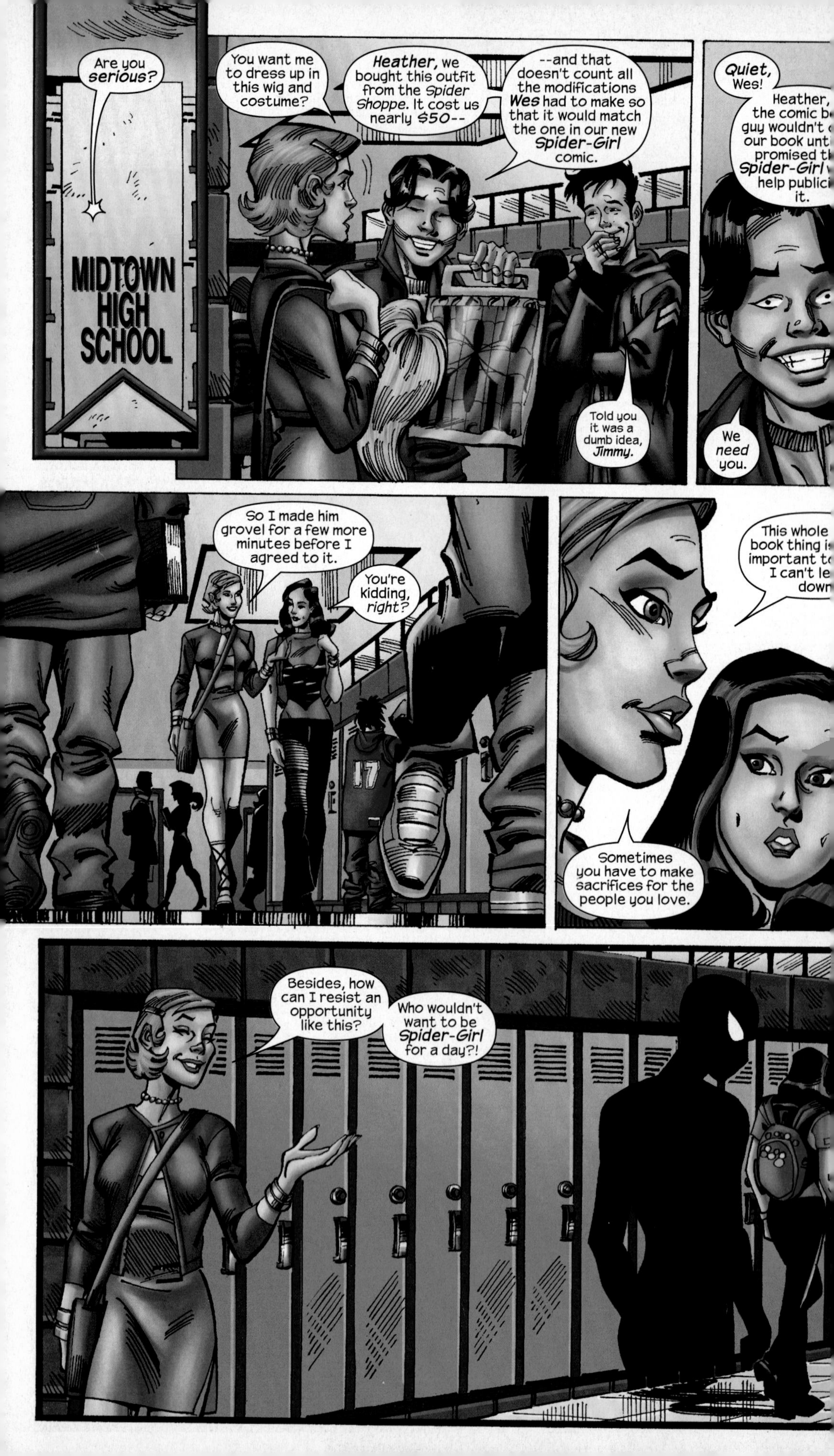

Are you serious?
MIDTOWN HIGH SCHOOL
You want me to dress up in this wig and costume?
Heather, we bought this outfit from the Spider Shoppe. It cost us nearly $50--
--and that doesn't count all the modifications Wes had to make so that it would match the one in our new Spider-Girl comic.
Told you it was a dumb idea, Jimmy.
Quiet, Wes!
Heather, the comic b guy wouldn't our book unt promised t Spider-Girl help public it.
We need you.
So I made him grovel for a few more minutes before I agreed to it.
You're kidding, right?
This whole book thing i important t I can't le down
Sometimes you have to make sacrifices for the people you love.
Besides, how can I resist an opportunity like this?
Who wouldn't want to be Spider-Girl for a day?!

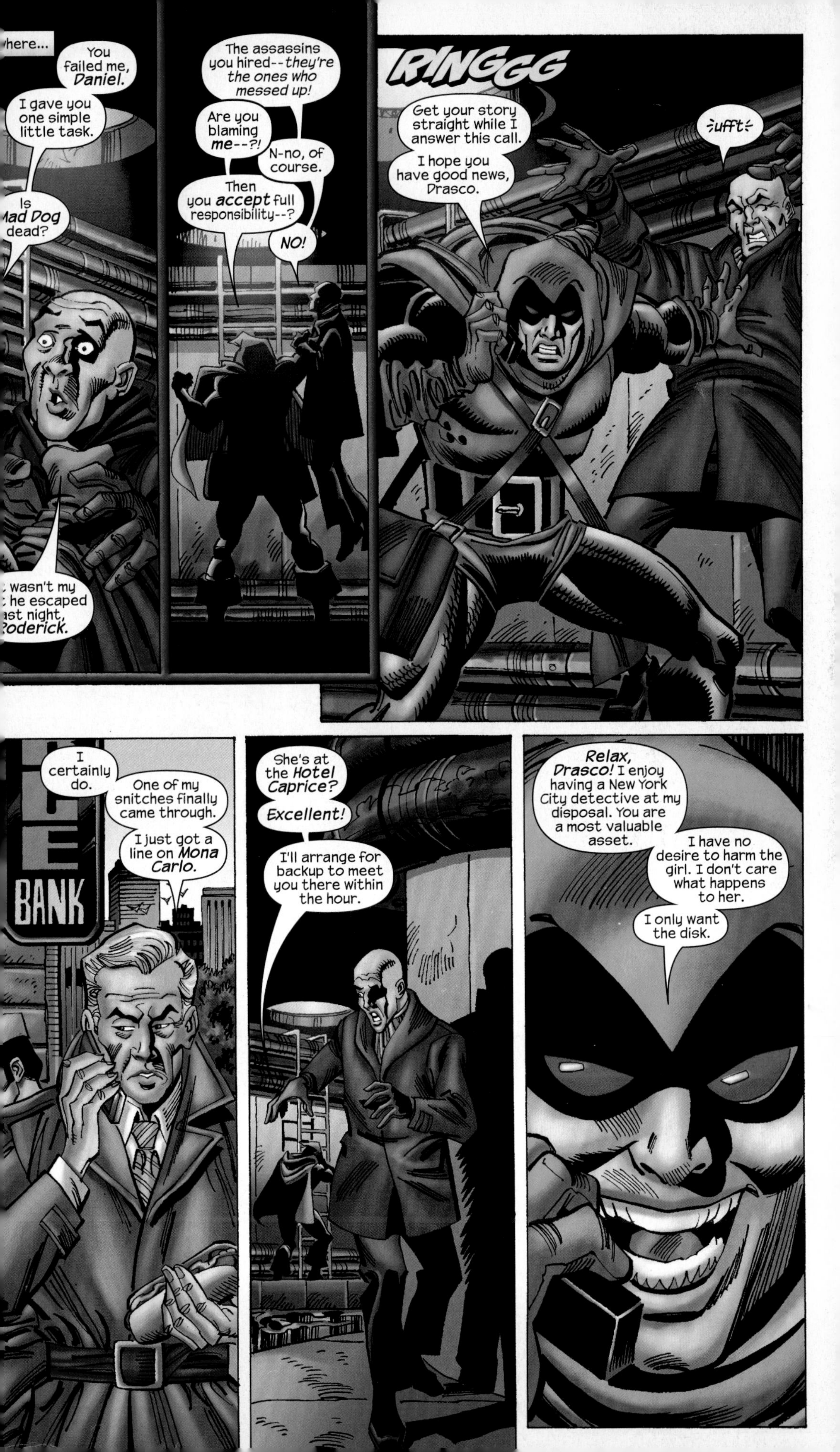

here...
You failed me, Daniel.
I gave you one simple little task.
Is Mad Dog dead?
wasn't my he escaped ast night, Roderick.
The assassins you hired--they're the ones who messed up!
Are you blaming me--?!
N-no, of course.
Then you accept full responsibility--?
NO!
RINGGG
Get your story straight while I answer this call.
I hope you have good news, Drasco.
ufft
I certainly do.
One of my snitches finally came through.
I just got a line on Mona Carlo.
BANK
She's at the Hotel Caprice?
Excellent!
I'll arrange for backup to meet you there within the hour.
Relax, Drasco! I enjoy having a New York City detective at my disposal. You are a most valuable asset.
I have no desire to harm the girl. I don't care what happens to her.
I only want the disk.

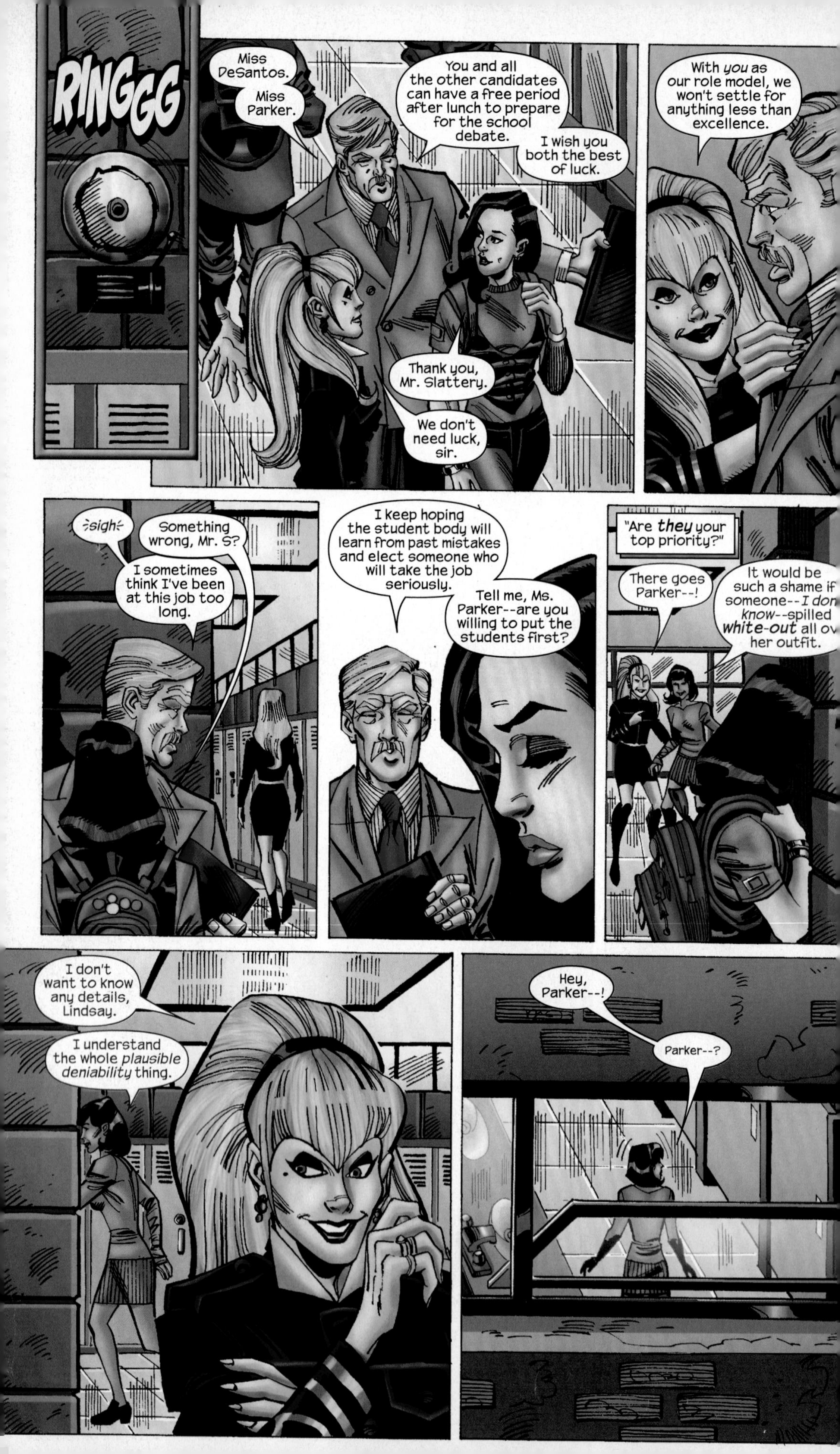
RINGGG
Miss DeSantos.
Miss Parker.
You and all the other candidates can have a free period after lunch to prepare for the school debate.
I wish you both the best of luck.
Thank you, Mr. Slattery.
We don't need luck, sir.
With *you* as our role model, we won't settle for anything less than excellence.
sigh
Something wrong, Mr. S?
I sometimes think I've been at this job too long.
I keep hoping the student body will learn from past mistakes and elect someone who will take the job seriously.
Tell me, Ms. Parker--are you willing to put the students first?
"Are *they* your top priority?"
There goes Parker--!
It would be such a shame if someone--*I don't know*--spilled ***white-out*** all over her outfit.
I don't want to know any details, Lindsay.
I understand the whole *plausible deniability* thing.
Hey, Parker--!
Parker--?

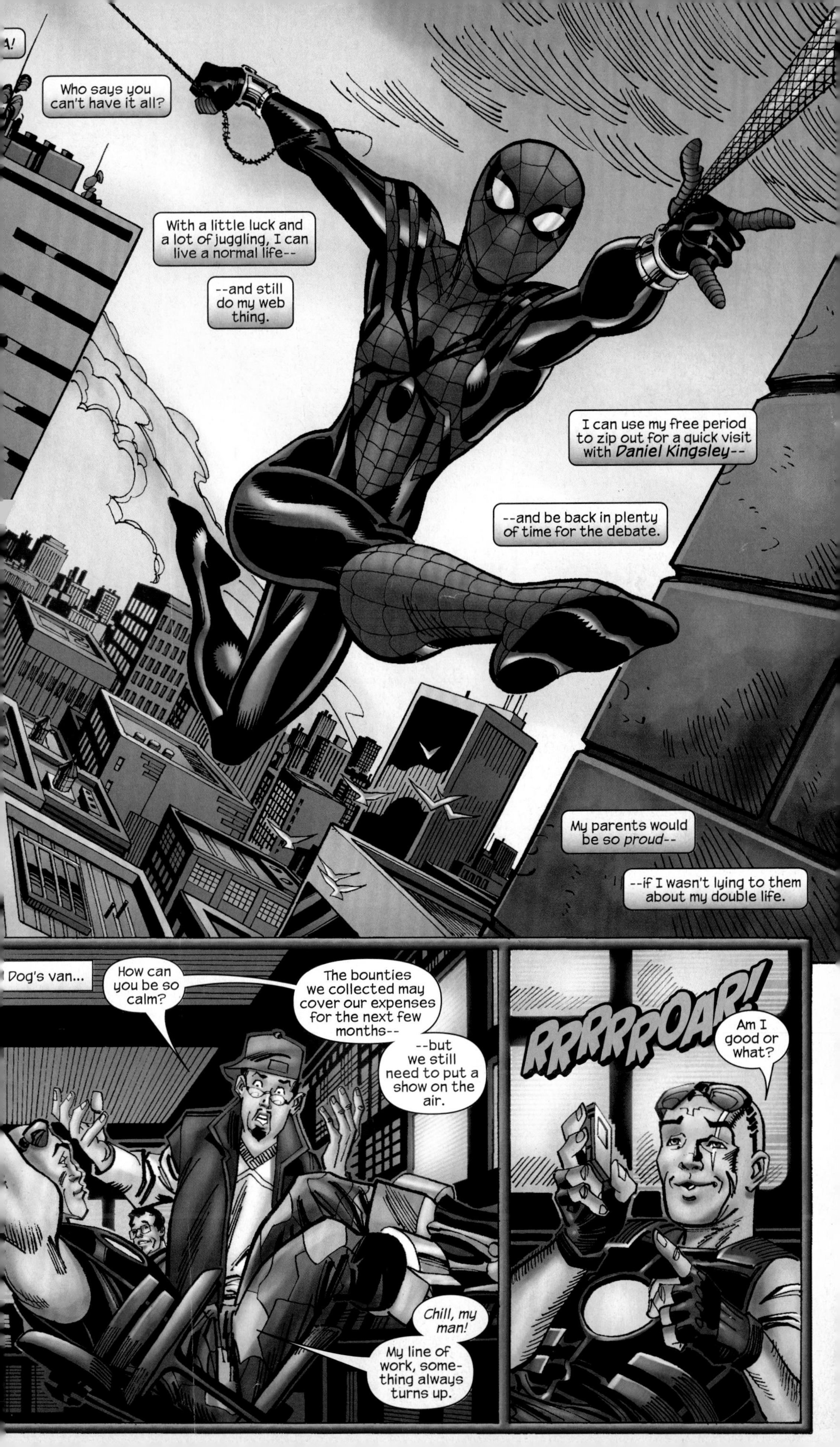
A!
Who says you can't have it all?
With a little luck and a lot of juggling, I can live a normal life--
--and still do my web thing.
I can use my free period to zip out for a quick visit with *Daniel Kingsley*--
--and be back in plenty of time for the debate.
My parents would be so *proud*--
--if I wasn't lying to them about my double life.
Dog's van...
How can you be so calm?
The bounties we collected may cover our expenses for the next few months--
--but we still need to put a show on the air.
Chill, my man!
My line of work, some- thing always turns up.
RRRRROAR!
Am I good or what?

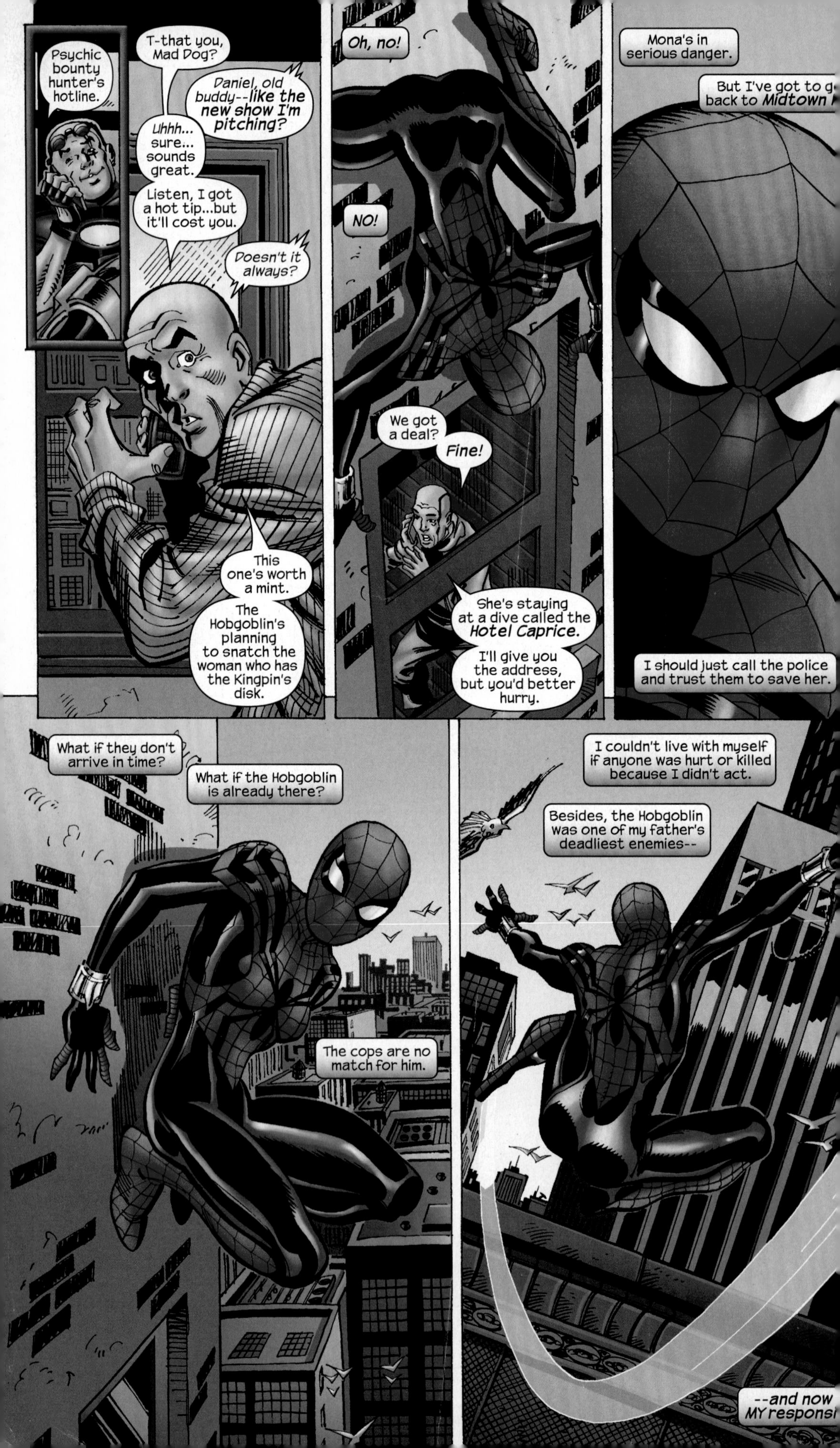
Psychic bounty hunter's hotline.
T-that you, Mad Dog?
Daniel, old buddy--like the new show I'm pitching?
Uhhh... sure... sounds great.
Listen, I got a hot tip...but it'll cost you.
Doesn't it always?
This one's worth a mint.
The Hobgoblin's planning to snatch the woman who has the Kingpin's disk.
Oh, no!
NO!
We got a deal?
Fine!
She's staying at a dive called the Hotel Caprice.
I'll give you the address, but you'd better hurry.
Mona's in serious danger.
I should just call the police and trust them to save her.
What if they don't arrive in time?
What if the Hobgoblin is already there?
The cops are no match for him.
I couldn't live with myself if anyone was hurt or killed because I didn't act.
Besides, the Hobgoblin was one of my father's deadliest enemies--

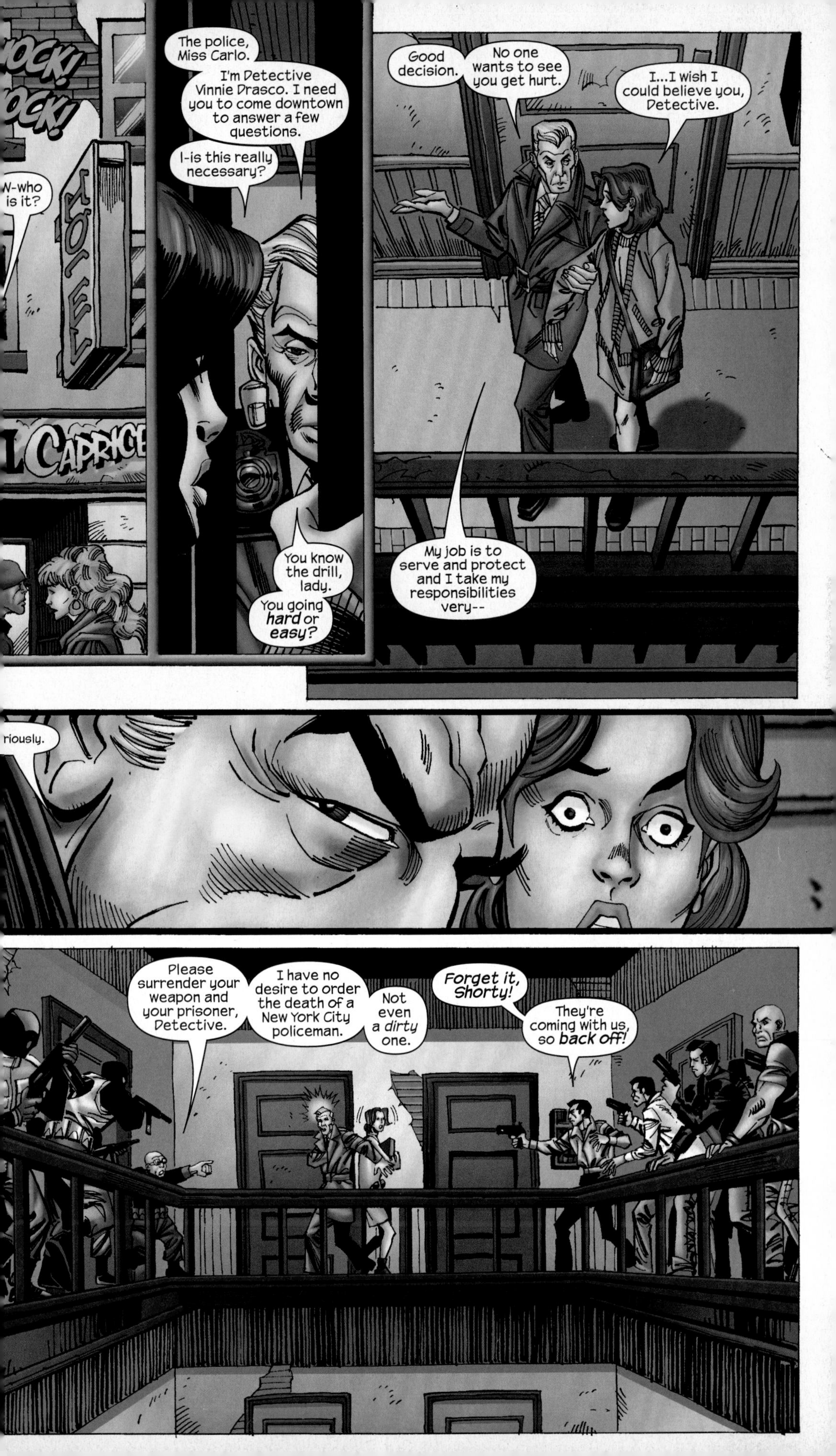

KNOCK! KNOCK!
W-who is it?
The police, Miss Carlo.
I'm Detective Vinnie Drasco. I need you to come downtown to answer a few questions.
I-is this really necessary?
You know the drill, lady.
You going *hard* or *easy?*
HOTEL
CAPRICE
Good decision.
No one wants to see you get hurt.
I...I wish I could believe you, Detective.
My job is to serve and protect and I take my responsibilities very--
riously.
Please surrender your weapon and your prisoner, Detective.
I have no desire to order the death of a New York City policeman.
Not even a *dirty* one.
Forget it, Shorty!
They're coming with us, so *back off!*

KRAKRAKRA CAKRASHH

STAIRS

Is it my imagination--

--or does life seem to be one endless *popularity* contest?!

Spider-Girl!

W-sh h

Looks like Hobgoblin sent goo

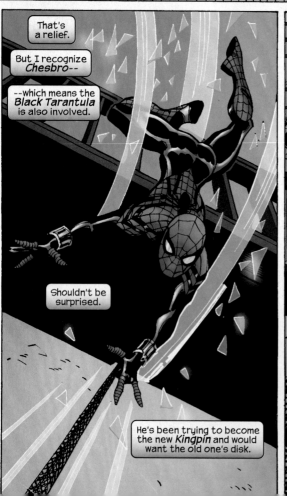

That's a relief.

But I recognize Chesbro--

--which means the *Black Tarantula* is also involved.

Shouldn't be surprised.

He's been trying to become the new *Kingpin* and would want the old one's disk.

Blast that stupid web-swinger!

We can't let her--ARRK

TWAKK

Don't knock yourselves *out* on my account, boys!

I'm happy to do it for you.

Where are the police?

I phoned in an anonymous They should be here by no

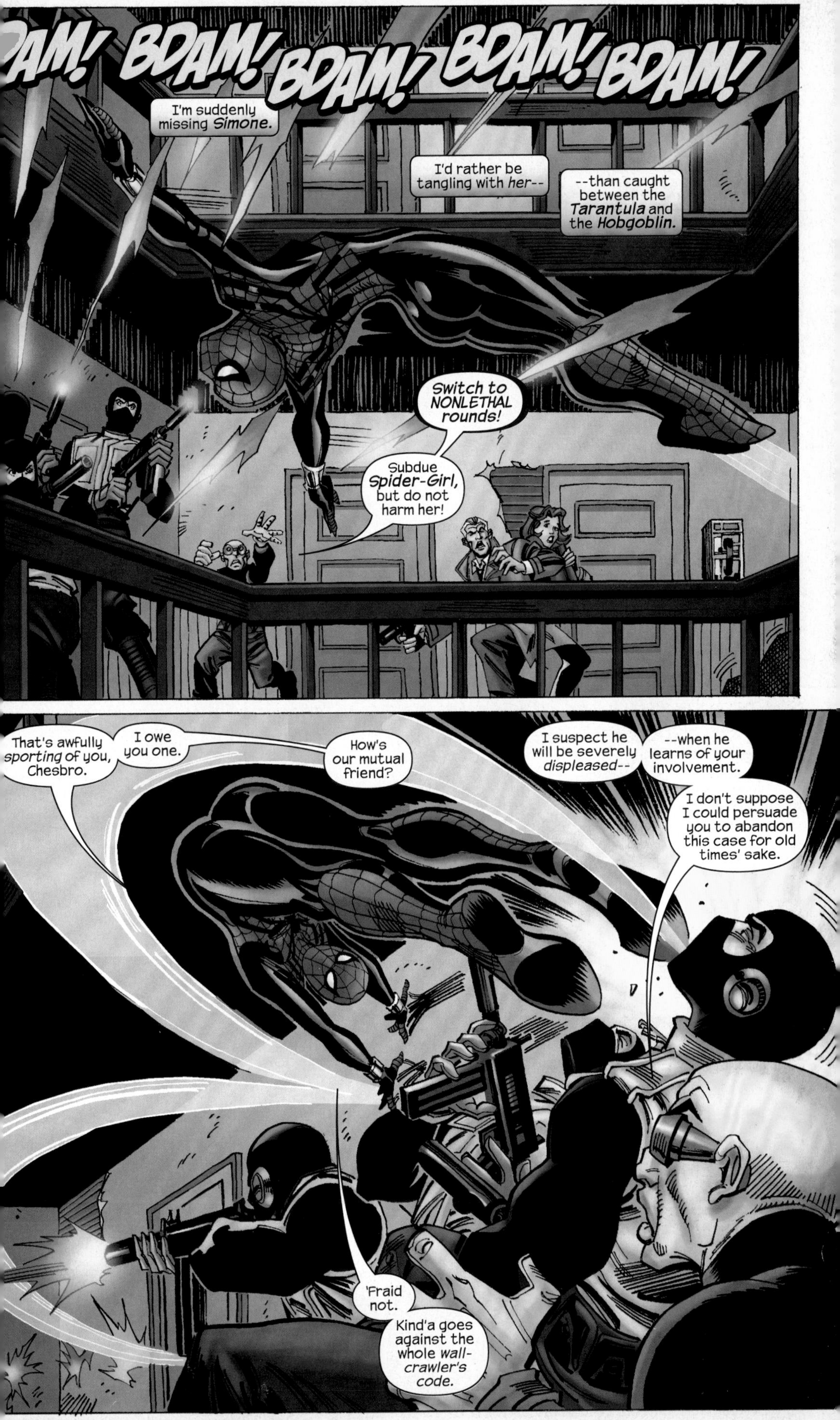

BDAM! BDAM! BDAM! BDAM! BDAM!
I'm suddenly missing Simone.
I'd rather be tangling with her--
--than caught between the Tarantula and the Hobgoblin.
Switch to NONLETHAL rounds!
Subdue Spider-Girl, but do not harm her!
That's awfully sporting of you, Chesbro.
I owe you one.
How's our mutual friend?
I suspect he will be severely displeased--
--when he learns of your involvement.
I don't suppose I could persuade you to abandon this case for old times' sake.
'Fraid not.
Kind'a goes against the whole wall-crawler's code.

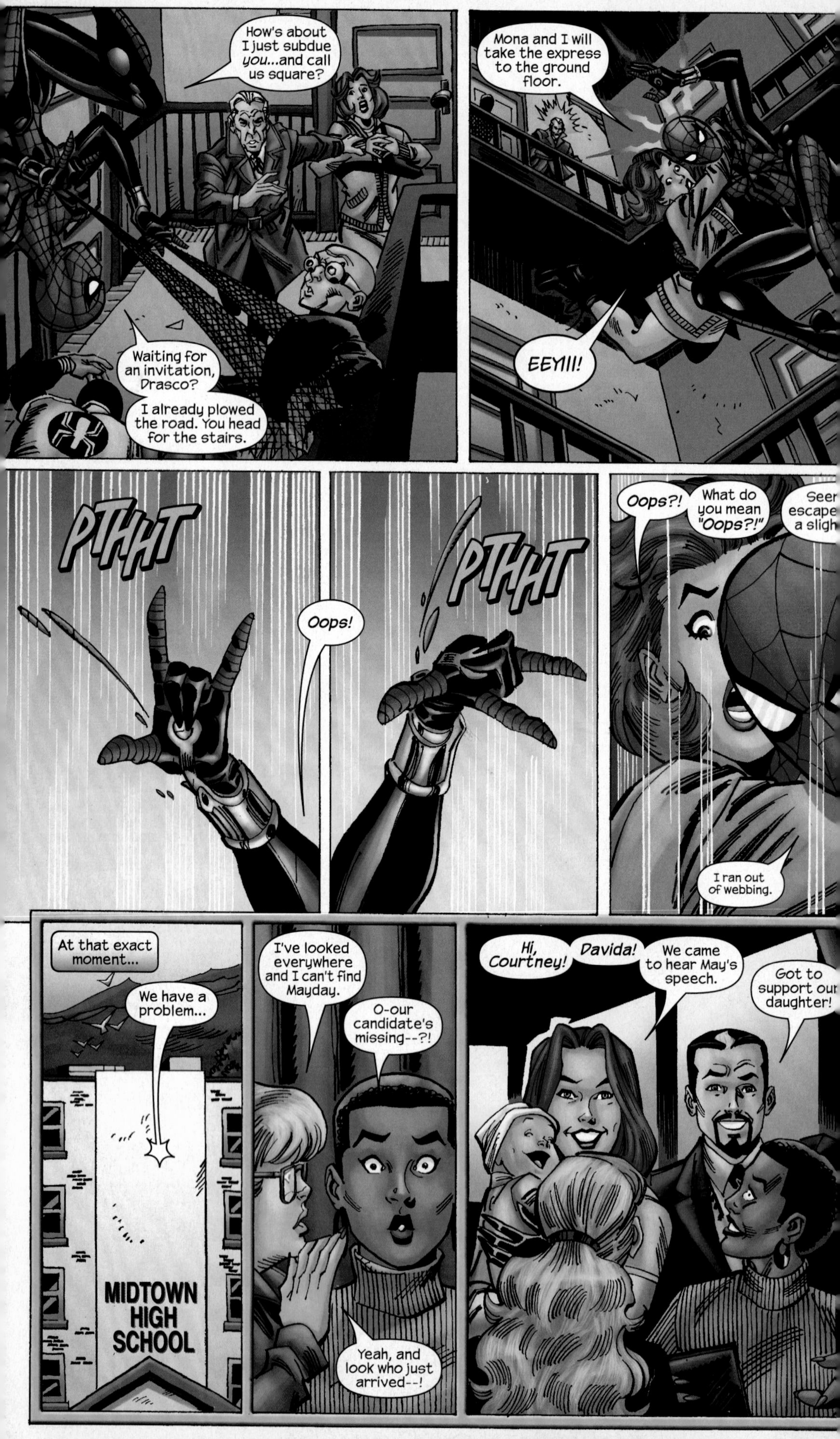
How's about I just subdue *you*...and call us square?
Waiting for an invitation, Drasco?
I already plowed the road. You head for the stairs.
Mona and I will take the express to the ground floor.
EEYIII!
PTHHT
Oops!
PTHHT
Oops?!
What do you mean "Oops?!"
I ran out of webbing.
At that exact moment...
We have a problem...
MIDTOWN HIGH SCHOOL
I've looked everywhere and I can't find Mayday.
O-our candidate's missing--?!
Yeah, and look who just arrived--!
Hi, Courtney!
Davida!
We came to hear May's speech.
Got to support our daughter!

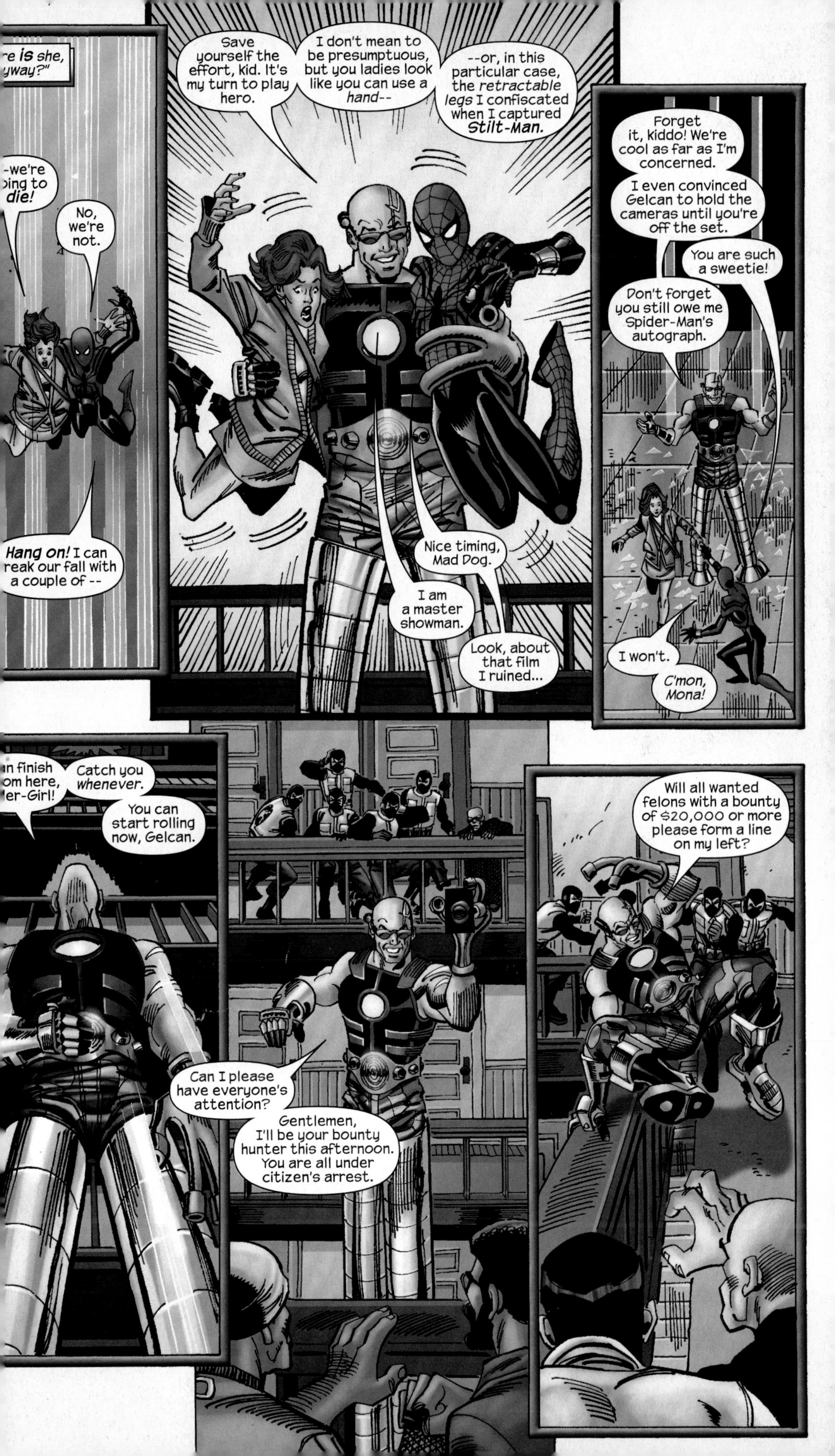
re is she, yway?"
-we're oing to die!
No, we're not.
Hang on! I can reak our fall with a couple of --
Save yourself the effort, kid. It's my turn to play hero.
I don't mean to be presumptuous, but you ladies look like you can use a hand--
--or, in this particular case, the retractable legs I confiscated when I captured Stilt-Man.
Nice timing, Mad Dog.
I am a master showman.
Look, about that film I ruined...
Forget it, kiddo! We're cool as far as I'm concerned.
I even convinced Gelcan to hold the cameras until you're off the set.
You are such a sweetie!
Don't forget you still owe me Spider-Man's autograph.
I won't.
C'mon, Mona!
n finish om here, der-Girl!
Catch you whenever.
You can start rolling now, Gelcan.
Can I please have everyone's attention?
Gentlemen, I'll be your bounty hunter this afternoon. You are all under citizen's arrest.
Will all wanted felons with a bounty of $20,000 or more please form a line on my left?

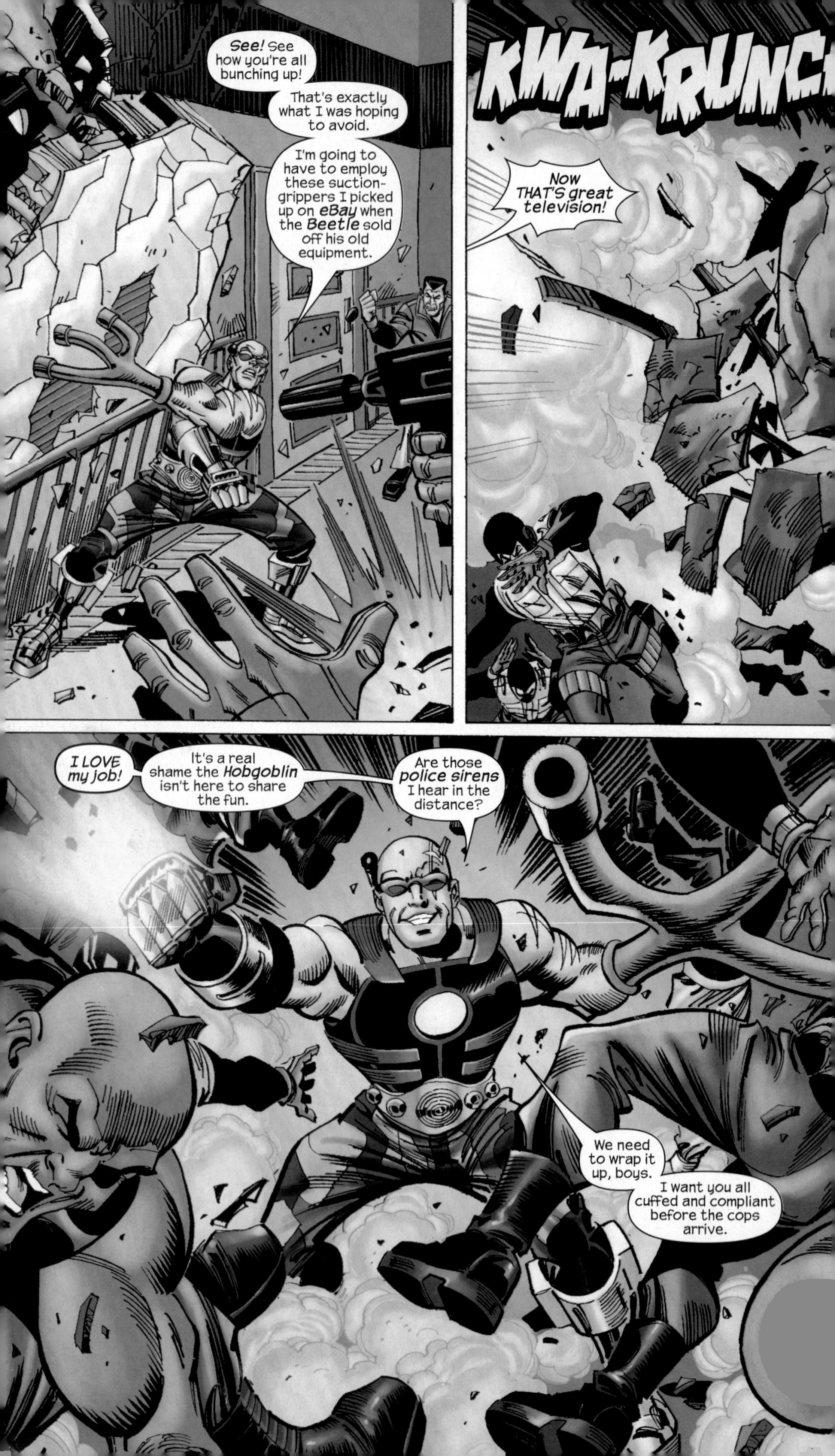
See! See how you're all bunching up!
That's exactly what I was hoping to avoid.
I'm going to have to employ these suction-grippers I picked up on eBay when the Beetle sold off his old equipment.
KWA-KRUNCH
Now THAT'S great television!
I LOVE my job!
It's a real shame the Hobgoblin isn't here to share the fun.
Are those police sirens I hear in the distance?
We need to wrap it up, boys.
I want you all cuffed and compliant before the cops arrive.

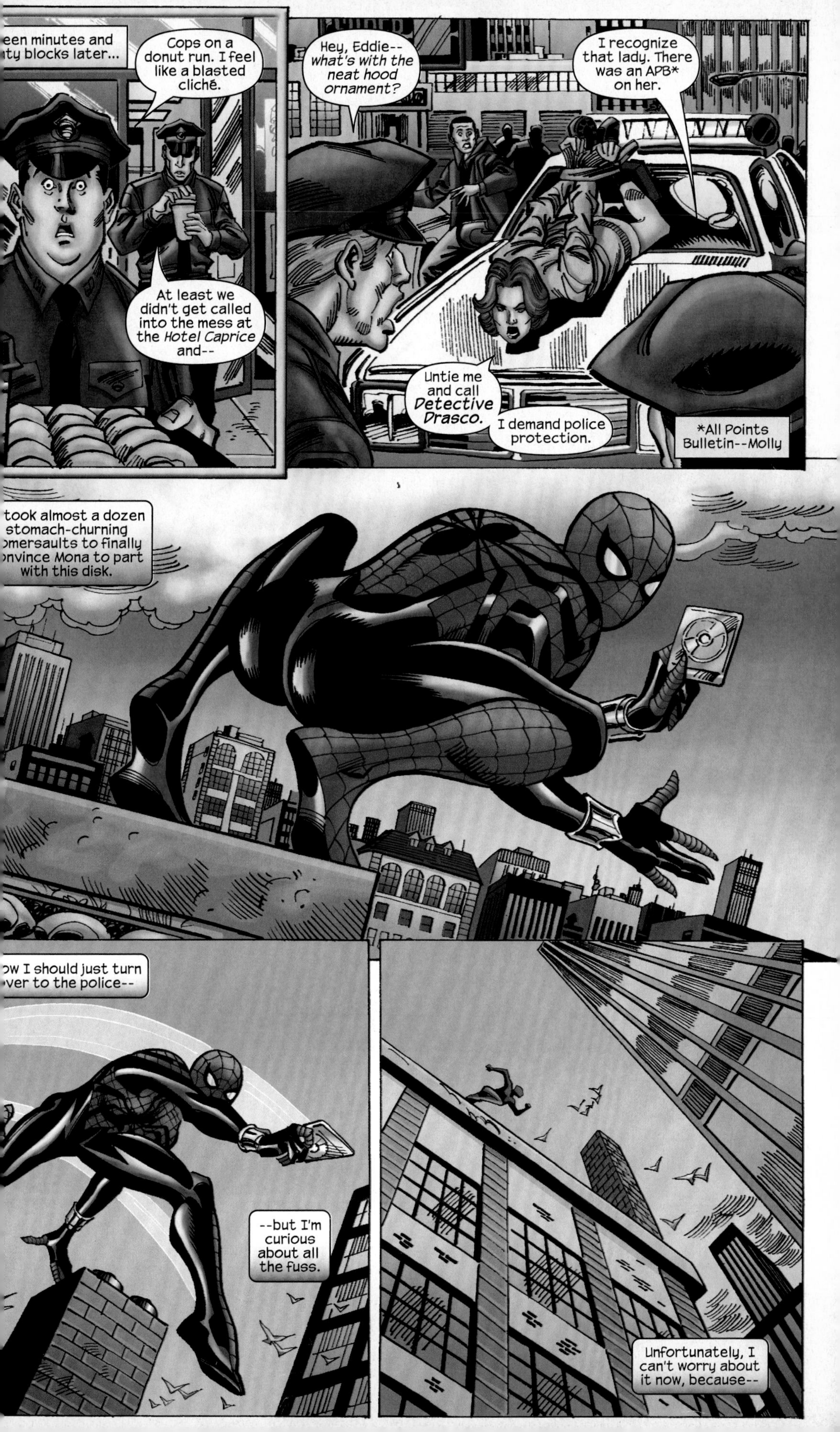

een minutes and
ty blocks later...
Cops on a donut run. I feel like a blasted cliché.
At least we didn't get called into the mess at the Hotel Caprice and--
Hey, Eddie-- what's with the neat hood ornament?
I recognize that lady. There was an APB* on her.
Untie me and call Detective Drasco.
I demand police protection.
*All Points Bulletin--Molly
took almost a dozen stomach-churning omersaults to finally onvince Mona to part with this disk.
ow I should just turn ver to the police--
--but I'm curious about all the fuss.
Unfortunately, I can't worry about it now, because--

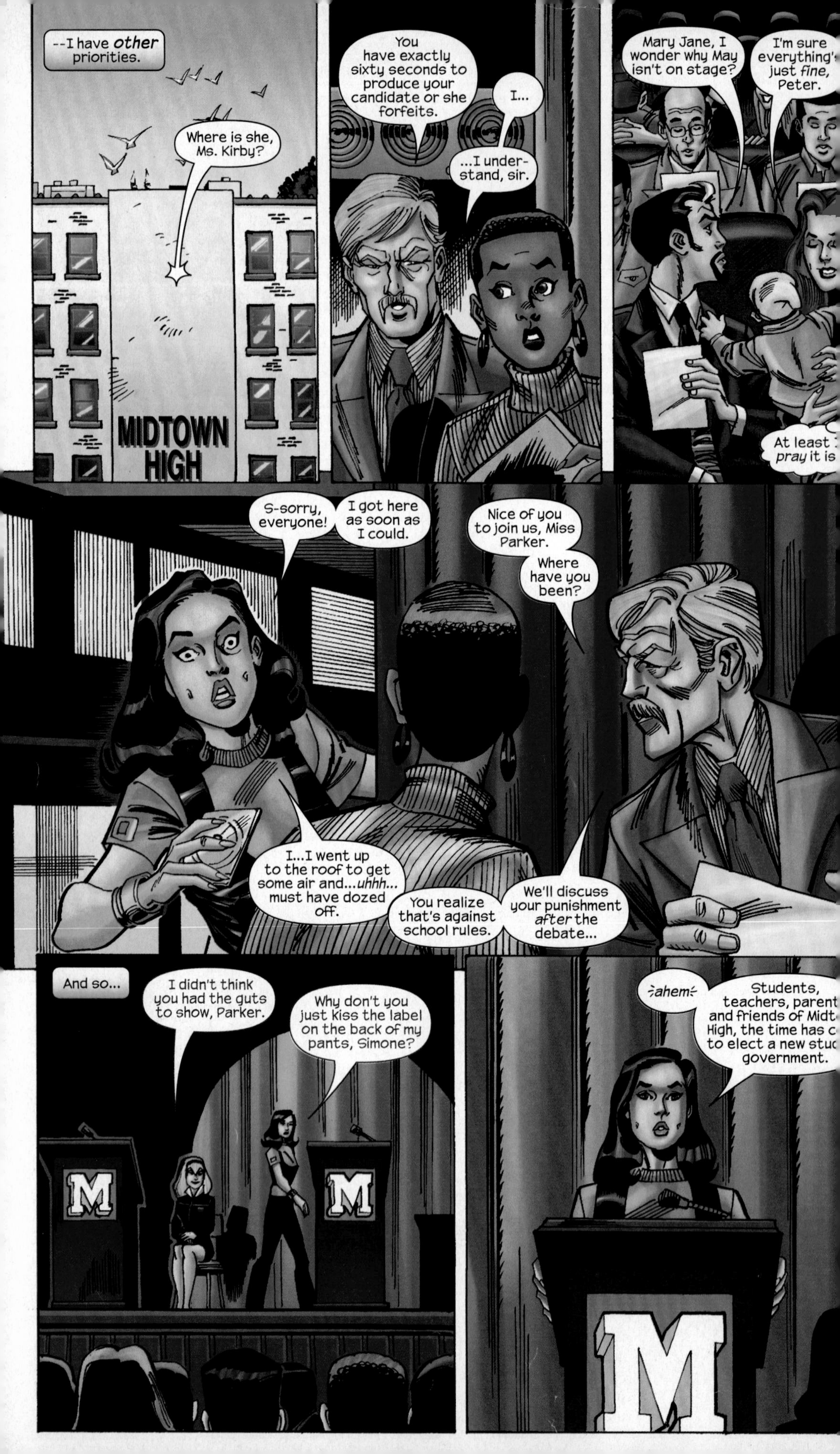
--I have *other* priorities.
Where is she, Ms. Kirby?
MIDTOWN HIGH
You have exactly sixty seconds to produce your candidate or she forfeits.
I...
...I understand, sir.
Mary Jane, I wonder why May isn't on stage?
I'm sure everything's just *fine*, Peter.
At least I *pray* it is
S-sorry, everyone!
I got here as soon as I could.
Nice of you to join us, Miss Parker.
Where have you been?
I...I went up to the roof to get some air and...*uhhh*... must have dozed off.
You realize that's against school rules.
We'll discuss your punishment *after* the debate...
And so...
I didn't think you had the guts to show, Parker.
Why don't you just kiss the label on the back of my pants, Simone?
ahem
Students, teachers, parent and friends of Midt High, the time has c to elect a new stu government.

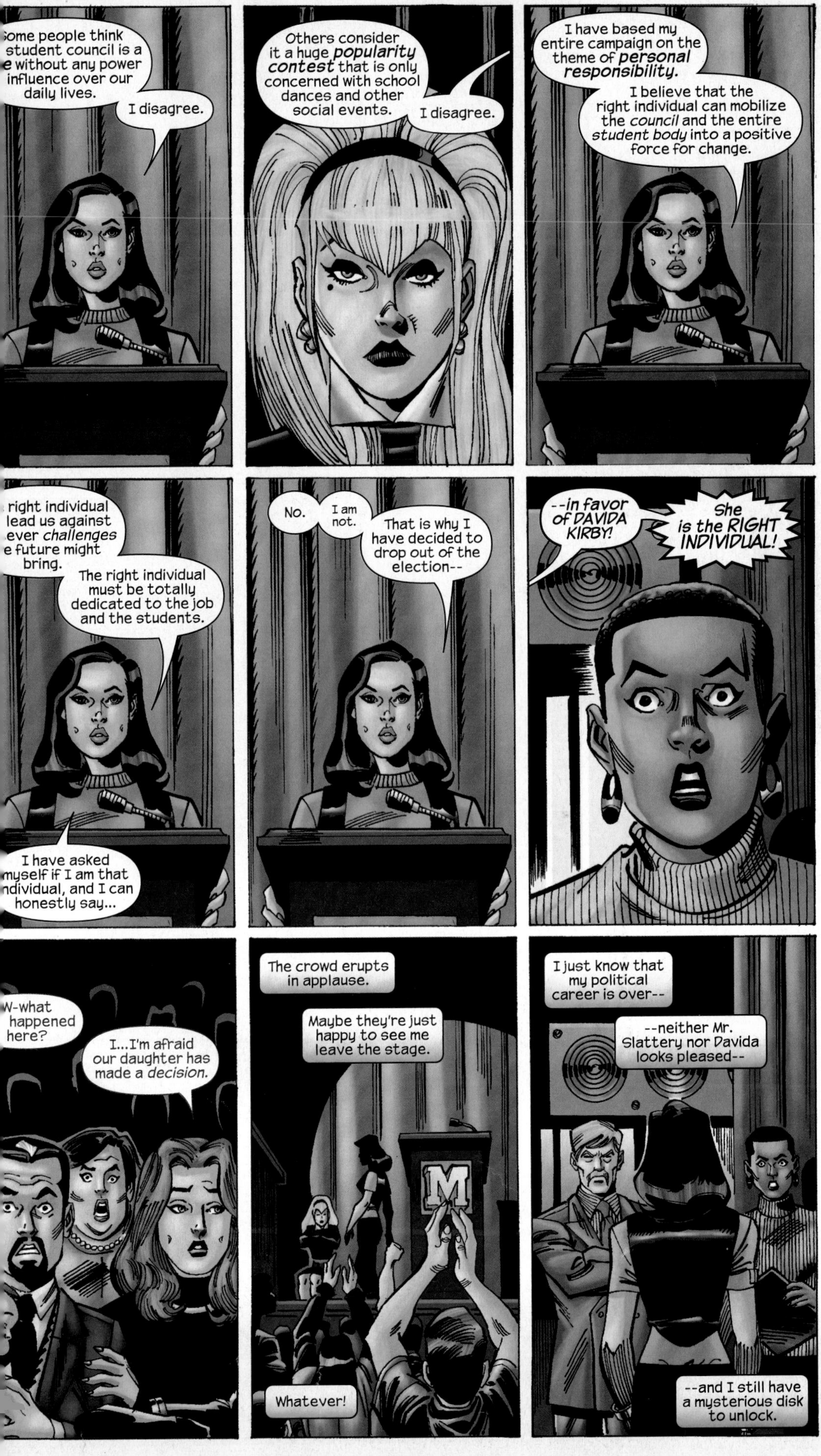

ome people think student council is a e without any power influence over our daily lives.
I disagree.
Others consider it a huge popularity contest that is only concerned with school dances and other social events.
I disagree.
I have based my entire campaign on the theme of personal responsibility.
I believe that the right individual can mobilize the council and the entire student body into a positive force for change.
right individual lead us against ever challenges e future might bring.
The right individual must be totally dedicated to the job and the students.
I have asked myself if I am that ndividual, and I can honestly say...
No.
I am not.
That is why I have decided to drop out of the election--
--in favor of DAVIDA KIRBY!
She is the RIGHT INDIVIDUAL!
W-what happened here?
I...I'm afraid our daughter has made a decision.
The crowd erupts in applause.
Maybe they're just happy to see me leave the stage.
Whatever!
I just know that my political career is over--
--neither Mr. Slattery nor Davida looks pleased--
--and I still have a mysterious disk to unlock.

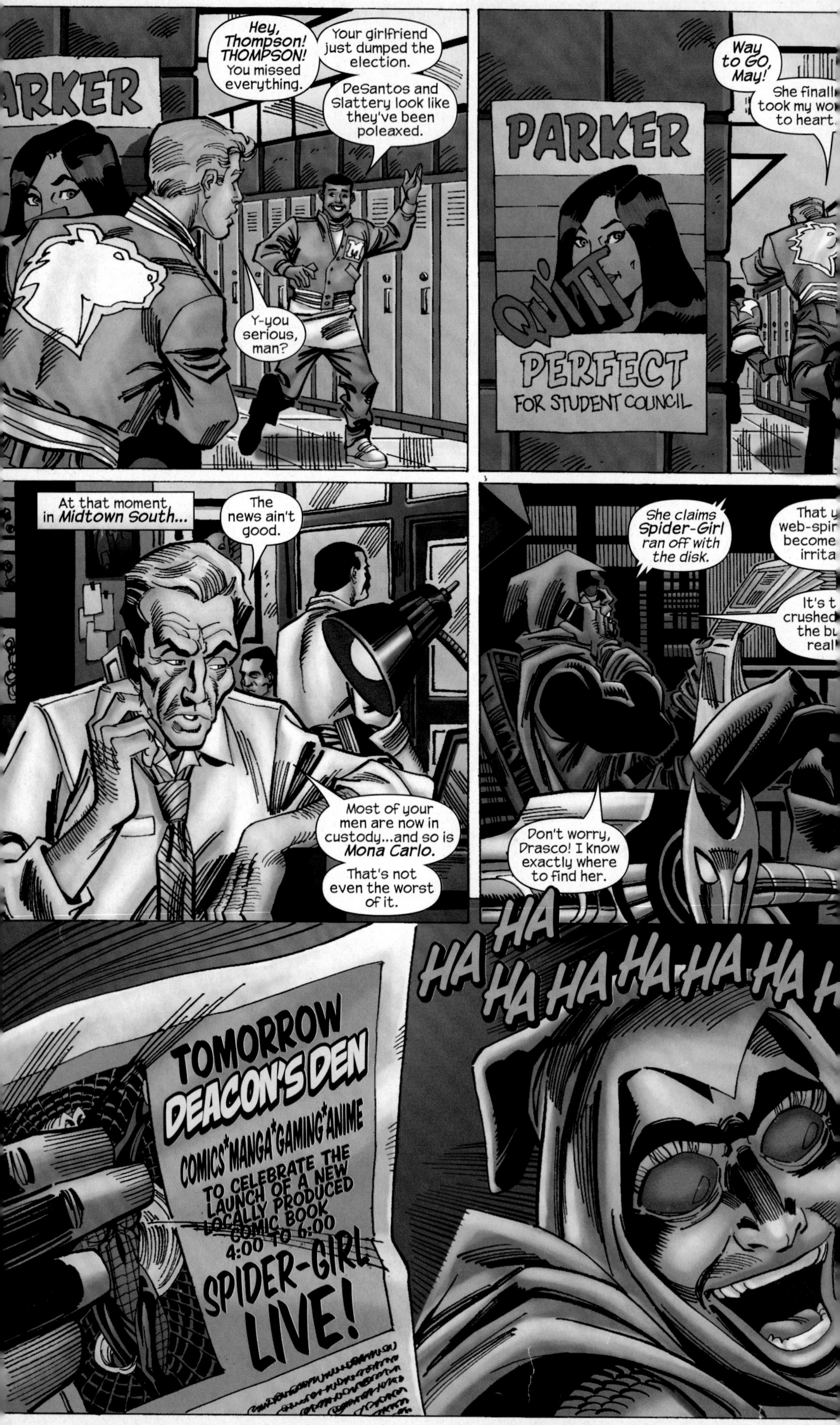

ARKER
Hey, Thompson! THOMPSON! You missed everything.
Your girlfriend just dumped the election.
DeSantos and Slattery look like they've been poleaxed.
Y-you serious, man?
PARKER
QUIT
PERFECT
FOR STUDENT COUNCIL
Way to GO, May!
She finall took my wo to heart
At that moment, in Midtown South...
The news ain't good.
Most of your men are now in custody...and so is Mona Carlo.
That's not even the worst of it.
She claims Spider-Girl ran off with the disk.
That y web-spir become irrita
It's t crushed the bu real
Don't worry, Drasco! I know exactly where to find her.
HA HA HA HA HA HA HA HA HA H
TOMORROW
DEACON'S DEN
COMICS*MANGA*GAMING*ANIME
TO CELEBRATE THE LAUNCH OF A NEW LOCALLY PRODUCED COMIC BOOK
4:00 TO 6:00
SPIDER-GIRL LIVE!

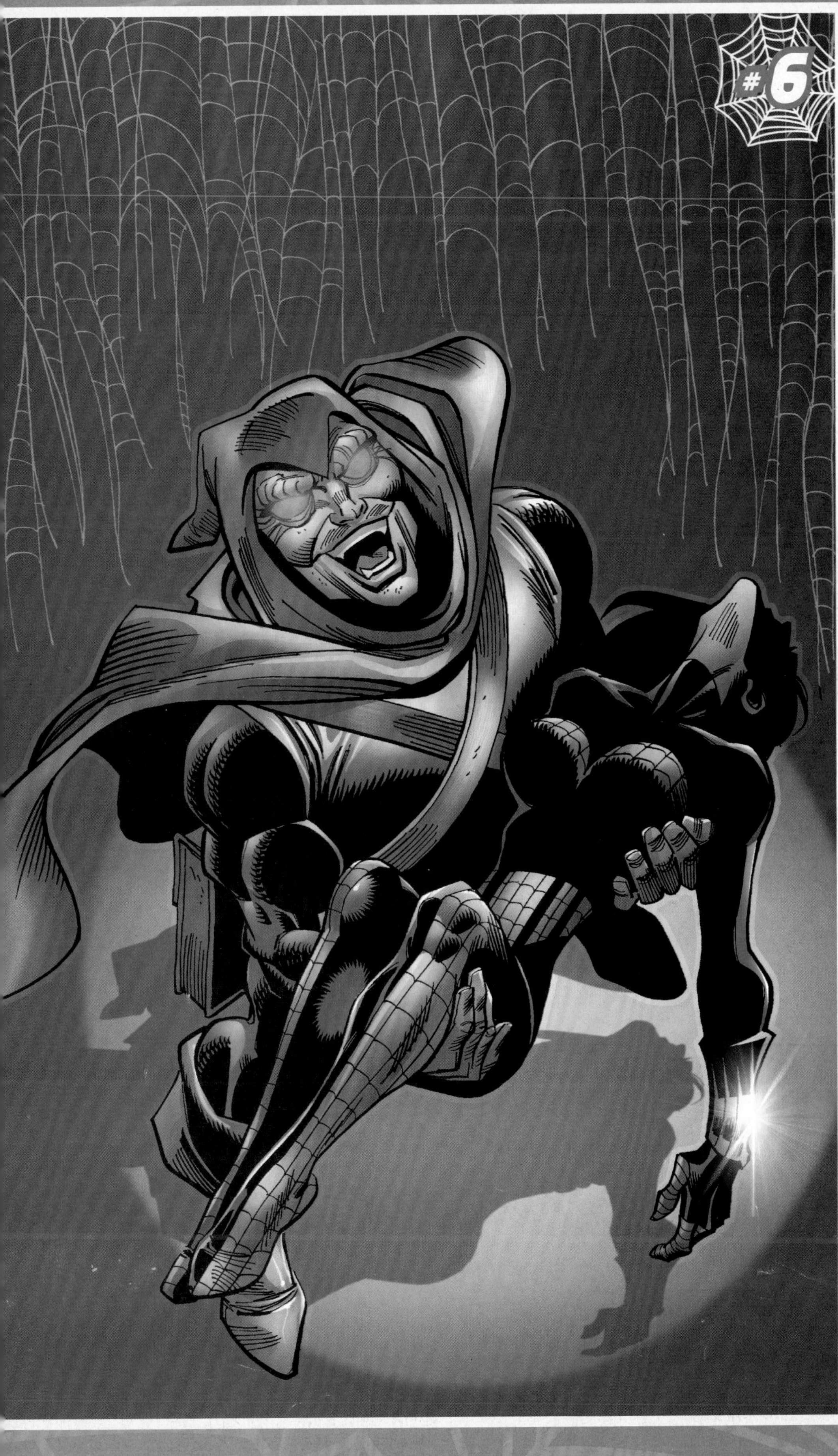
#6

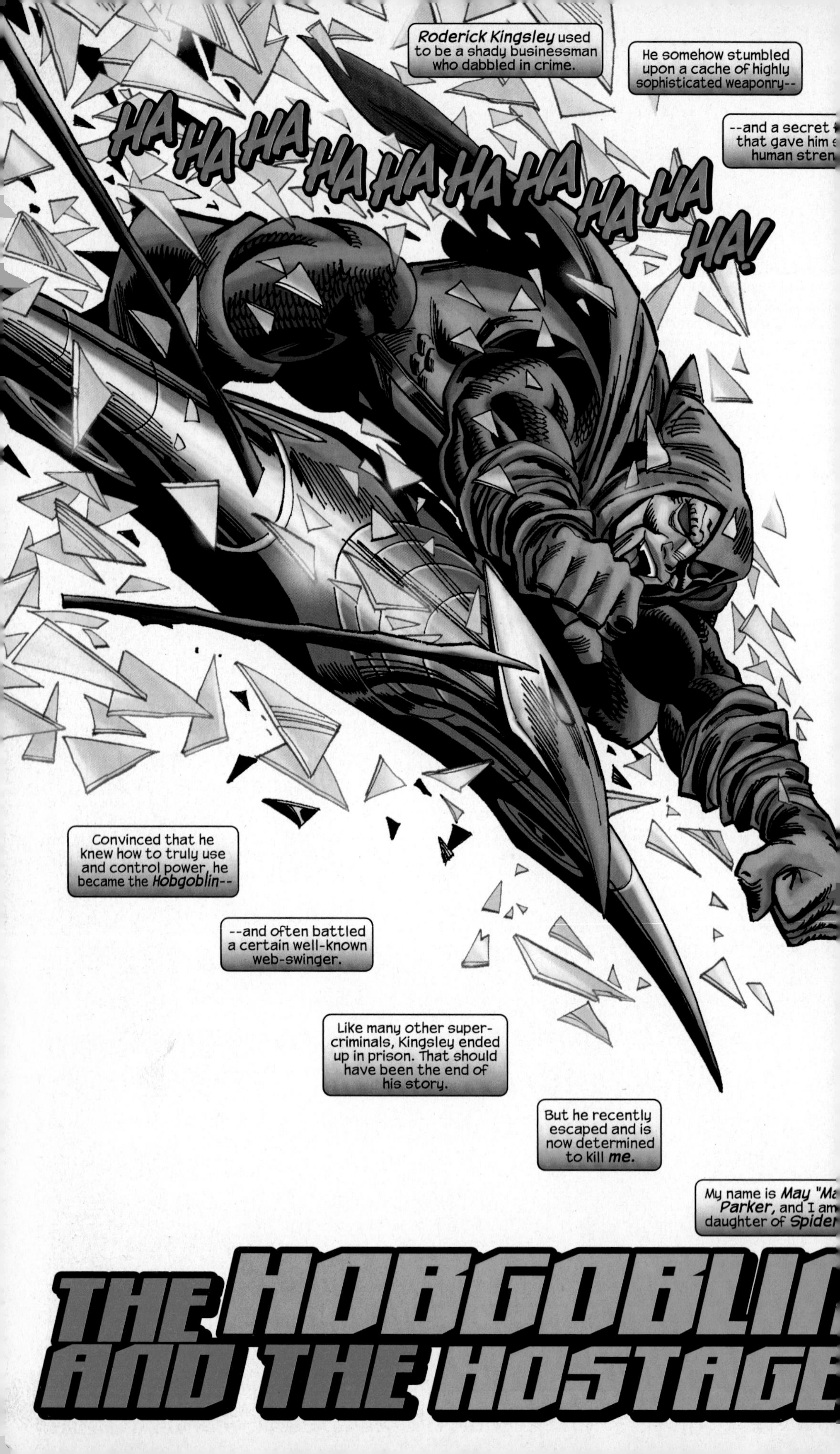
Roderick Kingsley used to be a shady businessman who dabbled in crime.
He somehow stumbled upon a cache of highly sophisticated weaponry--
--and a secret
that gave him
human stren
HA HA HA HA HA HA HA HA HA HA HA HA!
Convinced that he knew how to truly use and control power, he became the Hobgoblin--
--and often battled a certain well-known web-swinger.
Like many other super-criminals, Kingsley ended up in prison. That should have been the end of his story.
But he recently escaped and is now determined to kill me.
My name is May "Ma
Parker, and I am
daughter of Spider
THE HOBGOBLI
AND THE HOSTAGE

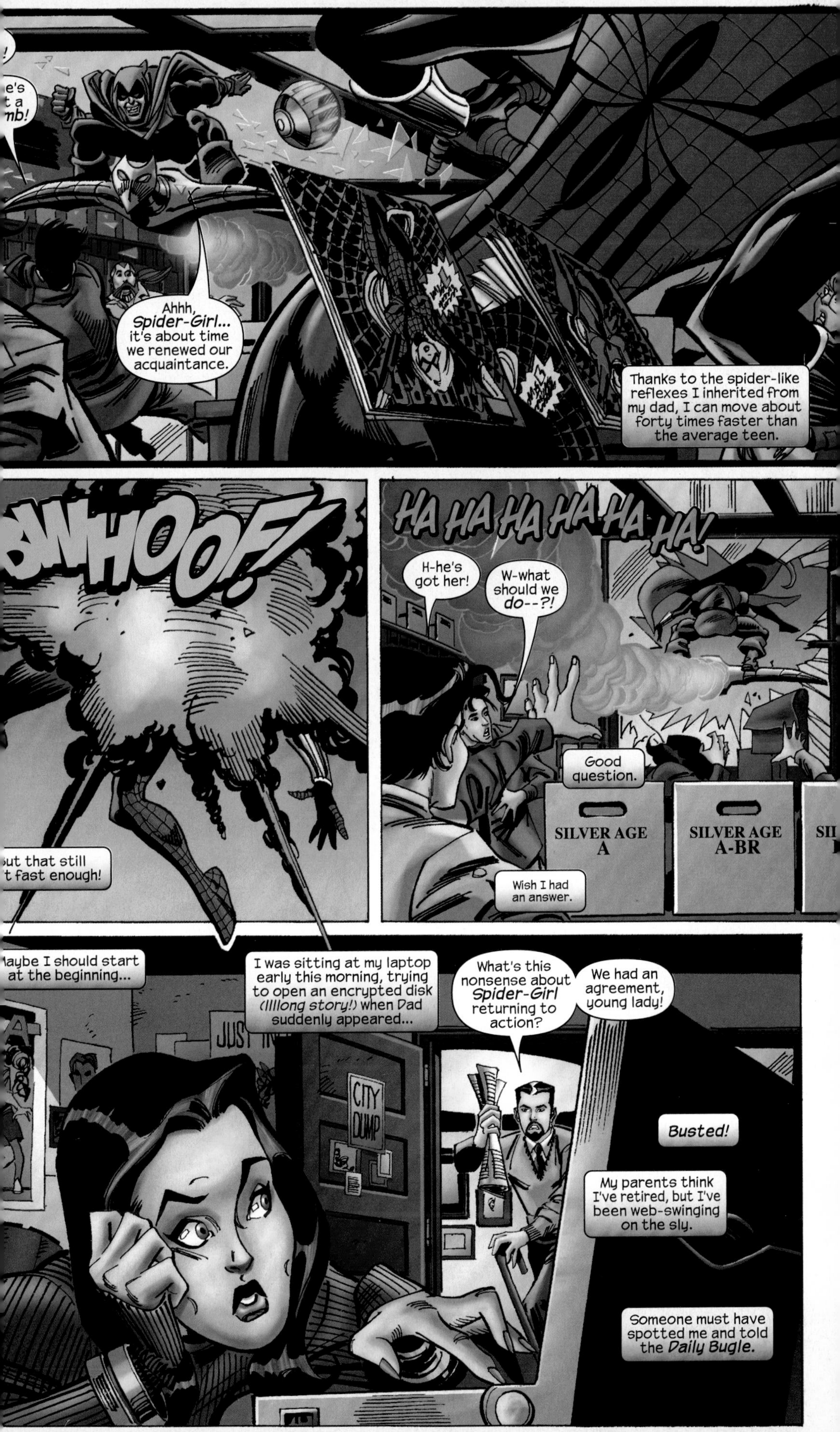

Ahhh, Spider-Girl... it's about time we renewed our acquaintance.
Thanks to the spider-like reflexes I inherited from my dad, I can move about forty times faster than the average teen.
WHOOF!
HA HA HA HA HA HA HA!
H-he's got her!
W-what should we do--?!
Good question.
Wish I had an answer.
SILVER AGE A
SILVER AGE A-BR
I was sitting at my laptop early this morning, trying to open an encrypted disk (llllong story!) when Dad suddenly appeared...
What's this nonsense about Spider-Girl returning to action?
We had an agreement, young lady!
CITY DUMP
Busted!
My parents think I've retired, but I've been web-swinging on the sly.
Someone must have spotted me and told the Daily Bugle.

I'm just about to come clean and beg for Dad's mercy when...

I can't believe you agreed to appear at a comic book store. *A comic book store?!* Who goes to comic book stores?!

A lot more people than you think.

But that ad has nothing to do with me.

SPIDER-GIRL LIVE

As I get ready for school--

--I quickly tell Dad all about *Jimmy Yama, Wes Westin* and their version of *Spider-Girl*.

So this is just a publicity stunt to sell comics?

I owe you an apology, May.

I shou have tru you

Uhhh...

Ye

I could hear that outburst from down here. I don't know how you wiggled out of it, but we should talk.

I don't feel right about lying to your father. I have to tell him that I helped you go out as *Spider-Girl.*

I...I know, Mom.

I guess we should have a family meeting to discuss everything.

Will that include your reasons for suddenly dropping out of the student council race?

Yeah... *everything.*

Even though I'll probably be grounded for life.

My parents ar going to freak they learn I rece got hold of a di

--that the *police,* the *Hobgoblin* and the *Black Tarantula* want--

--because it's supposed to contain the secret files of *Wilson Fisk,* the former Kingpin of crime.

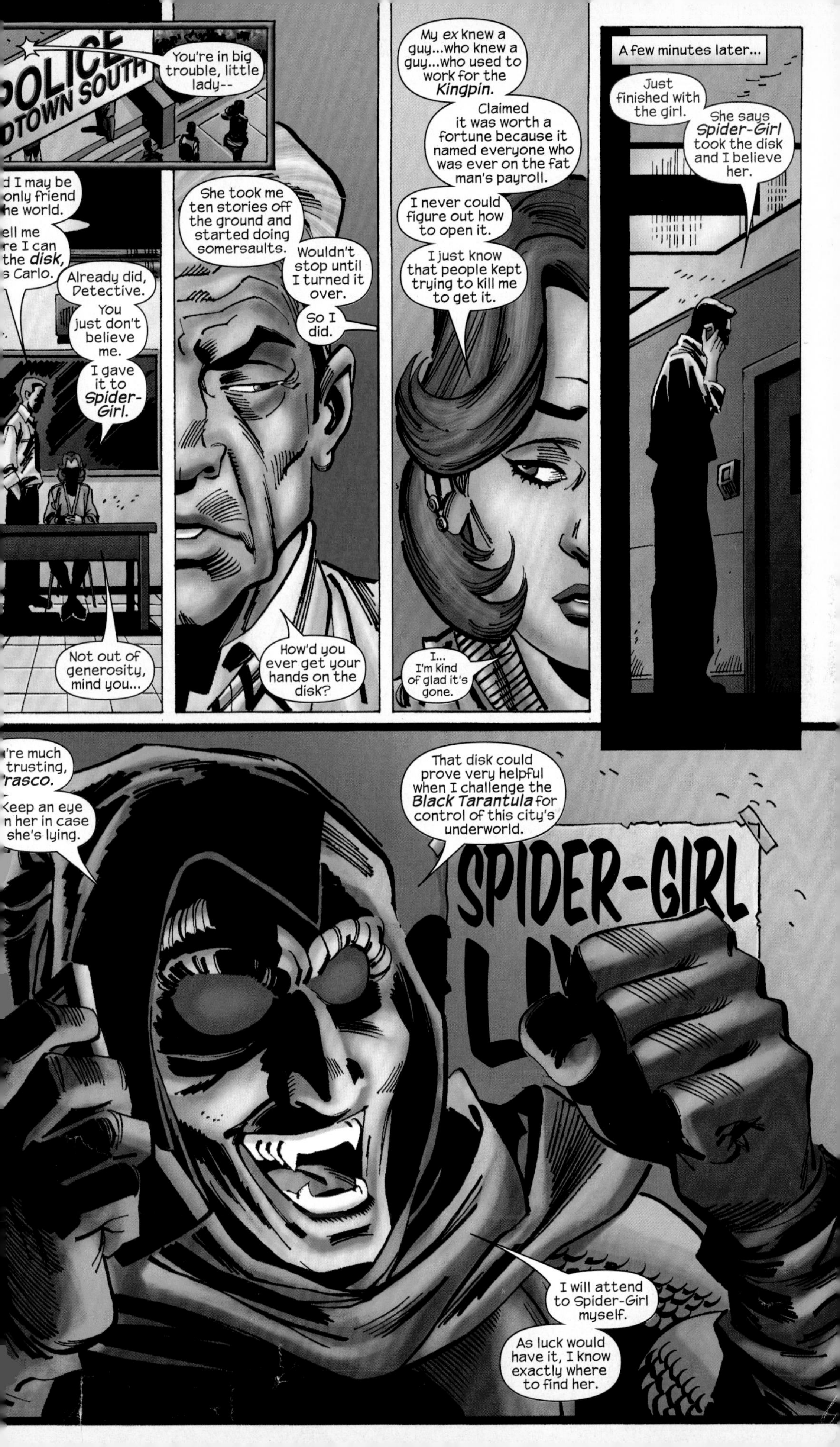

POLICE
DTOWN SOUTH
You're in big trouble, little lady--
d I may be only friend he world.
ell me re I can the disk, s Carlo.
Already did, Detective.
You just don't believe me.
I gave it to Spider-Girl.
Not out of generosity, mind you...
She took me ten stories off the ground and started doing somersaults.
Wouldn't stop until I turned it over.
So I did.
How'd you ever get your hands on the disk?
My ex knew a guy...who knew a guy...who used to work for the Kingpin.
Claimed it was worth a fortune because it named everyone who was ever on the fat man's payroll.
I never could figure out how to open it.
I just know that people kept trying to kill me to get it.
I... I'm kind of glad it's gone.
A few minutes later...
Just finished with the girl.
She says Spider-Girl took the disk and I believe her.
're much trusting, rasco.
Keep an eye n her in case she's lying.
That disk could prove very helpful when I challenge the Black Tarantula for control of this city's underworld.
SPIDER-GIRL
I will attend to Spider-Girl myself.
As luck would have it, I know exactly where to find her.

MIDTOWN HIGH SCHOOL

You're *kidding*, right?

Jimmy wants you to dress up as *Spider-Girl?!* Heather, I mean-- *come on!*

Yeah, I know it sounds kind of hinky on so many levels.

But this comic book is important to Jimmy and he asks so little.

Sometimes you've got to make sacrifices for the people you love.

Ain't that the truth.

Be I've wonde I'd loo cos

No, not really.

I-is that your locker?

Who would *do* such a thing?

I wish I knew. I assumed this harassment would stop when I stopped running for student council.

QUITTE

Mayday, it's just a frustrated voter.

I know I was disappointed when you dropped out of the election.

I can't believe some jerk is still hassling you, May.

It's no big deal, Gene.

No big deal?! Nobody messes with Gene Thompson's girlfriend.

I'm going to hunt this creep down and teach him a lesson he'll never forget.

Just forg Gene! Viol never so anythir

Maybe not, but it may put an end to *Mr. Graffiti.*

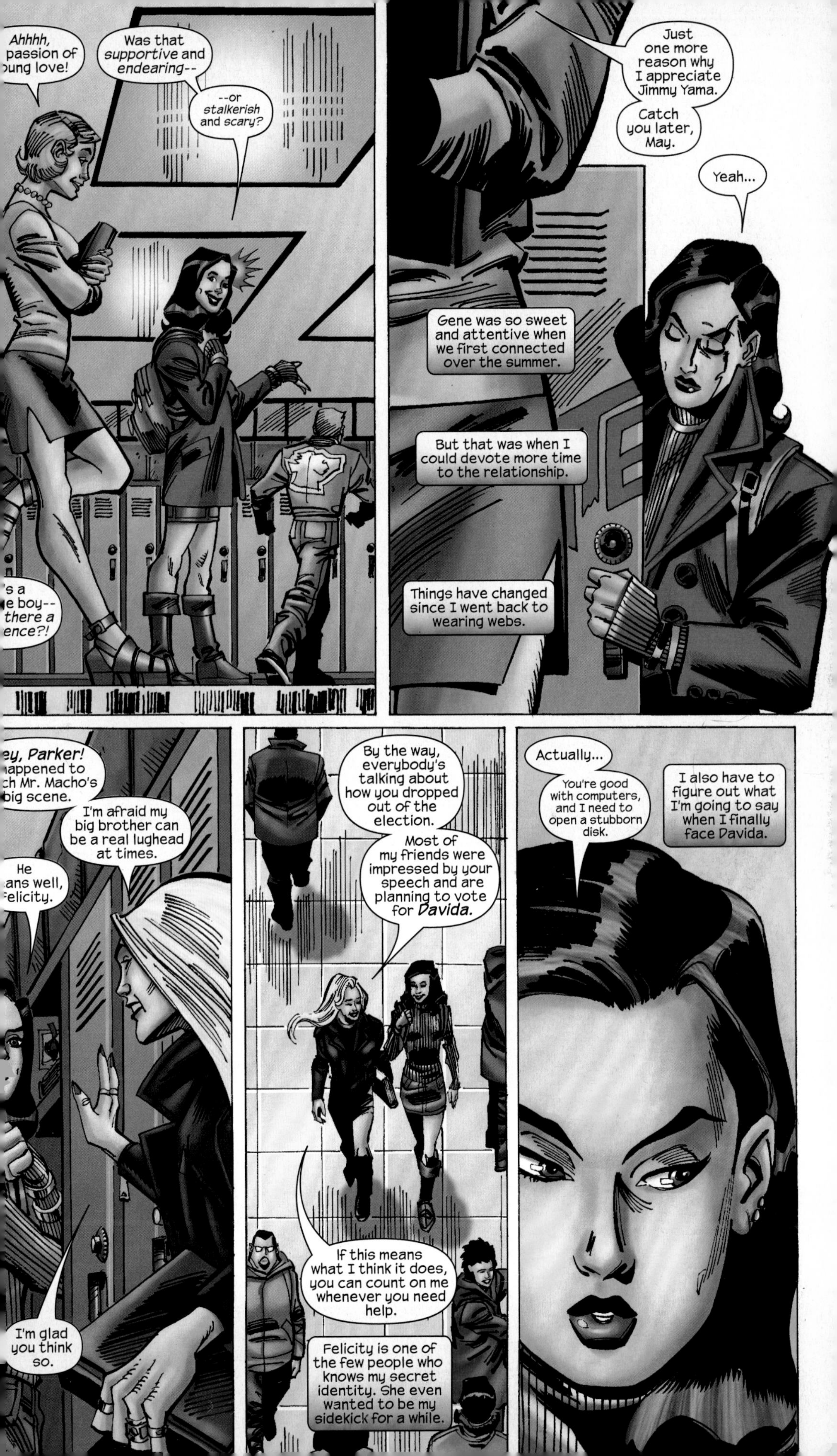
Ahhhh, passion of ung love!
Was that supportive and endearing--
--or stalkerish and scary?
's a e boy-- there a ence?!
Just one more reason why I appreciate Jimmy Yama.
Catch you later, May.
Yeah...
Gene was so sweet and attentive when we first connected over the summer.
But that was when I could devote more time to the relationship.
Things have changed since I went back to wearing webs.
ey, Parker! appened to ch Mr. Macho's big scene.
I'm afraid my big brother can be a real lughead at times.
He ans well, elicity.
I'm glad you think so.
By the way, everybody's talking about how you dropped out of the election.
Most of my friends were impressed by your speech and are planning to vote for Davida.
If this means what I think it does, you can count on me whenever you need help.
Felicity is one of the few people who knows my secret identity. She even wanted to be my sidekick for a while.
Actually...
You're good with computers, and I need to open a stubborn disk.
I also have to figure out what I'm going to say when I finally face Davida.

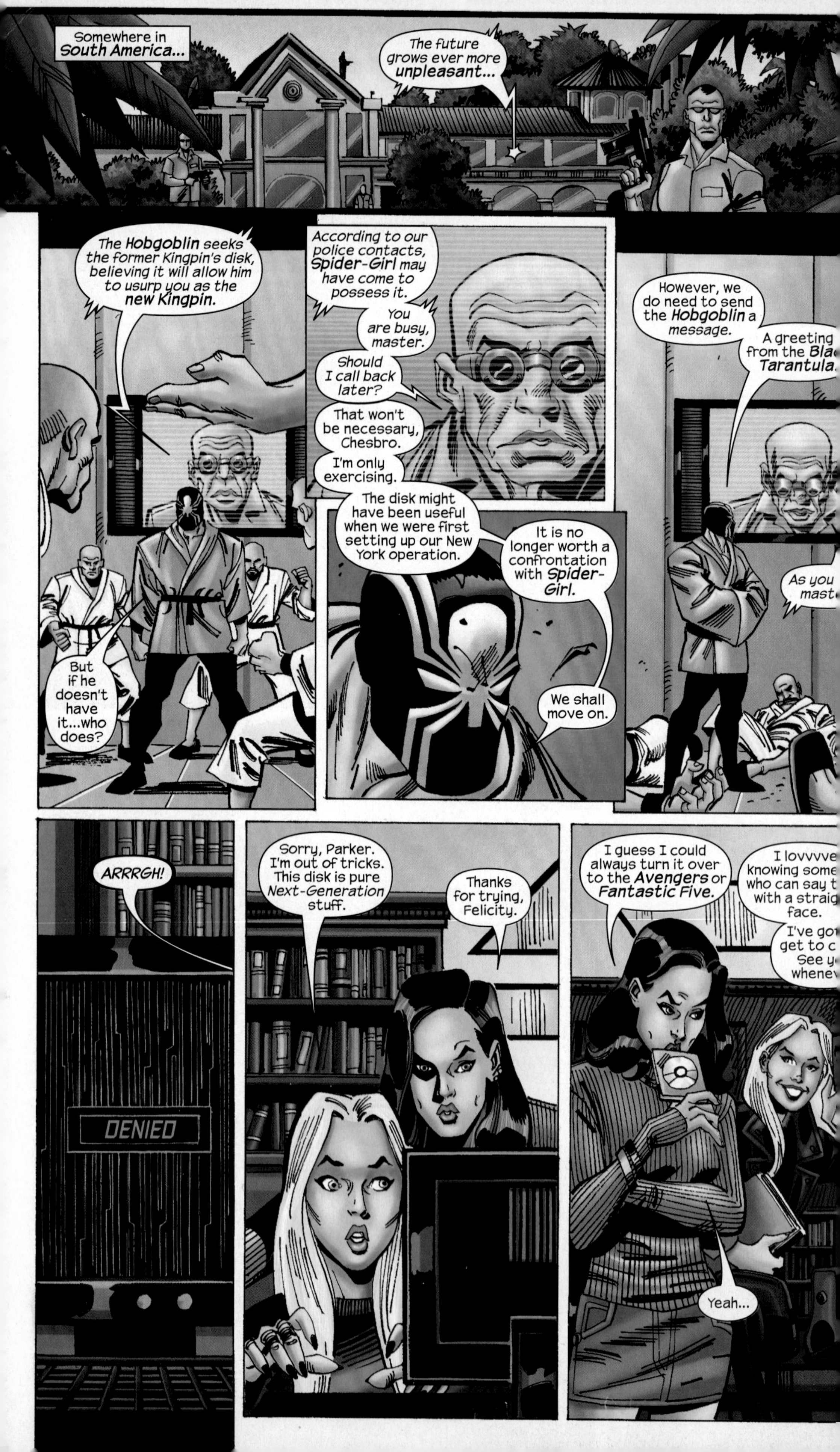
Somewhere in South America...
The future grows ever more unpleasant...
The Hobgoblin seeks the former Kingpin's disk, believing it will allow him to usurp you as the new Kingpin.
According to our police contacts, Spider-Girl may have come to possess it.
You are busy, master.
Should I call back later?
That won't be necessary, Chesbro.
I'm only exercising.
But if he doesn't have it...who does?
The disk might have been useful when we were first setting up our New York operation.
It is no longer worth a confrontation with Spider-Girl.
We shall move on.
However, we do need to send the Hobgoblin a message.
A greeting from the Bla
Tarantula.
As you mast
ARRRGH!
DENIED
Sorry, Parker. I'm out of tricks. This disk is pure Next-Generation stuff.
Thanks for trying, Felicity.
I guess I could always turn it over to the Avengers or Fantastic Five.
Yeah...
I lovvvve knowing some who can say t with a straig face.
I've go get to c See y whene

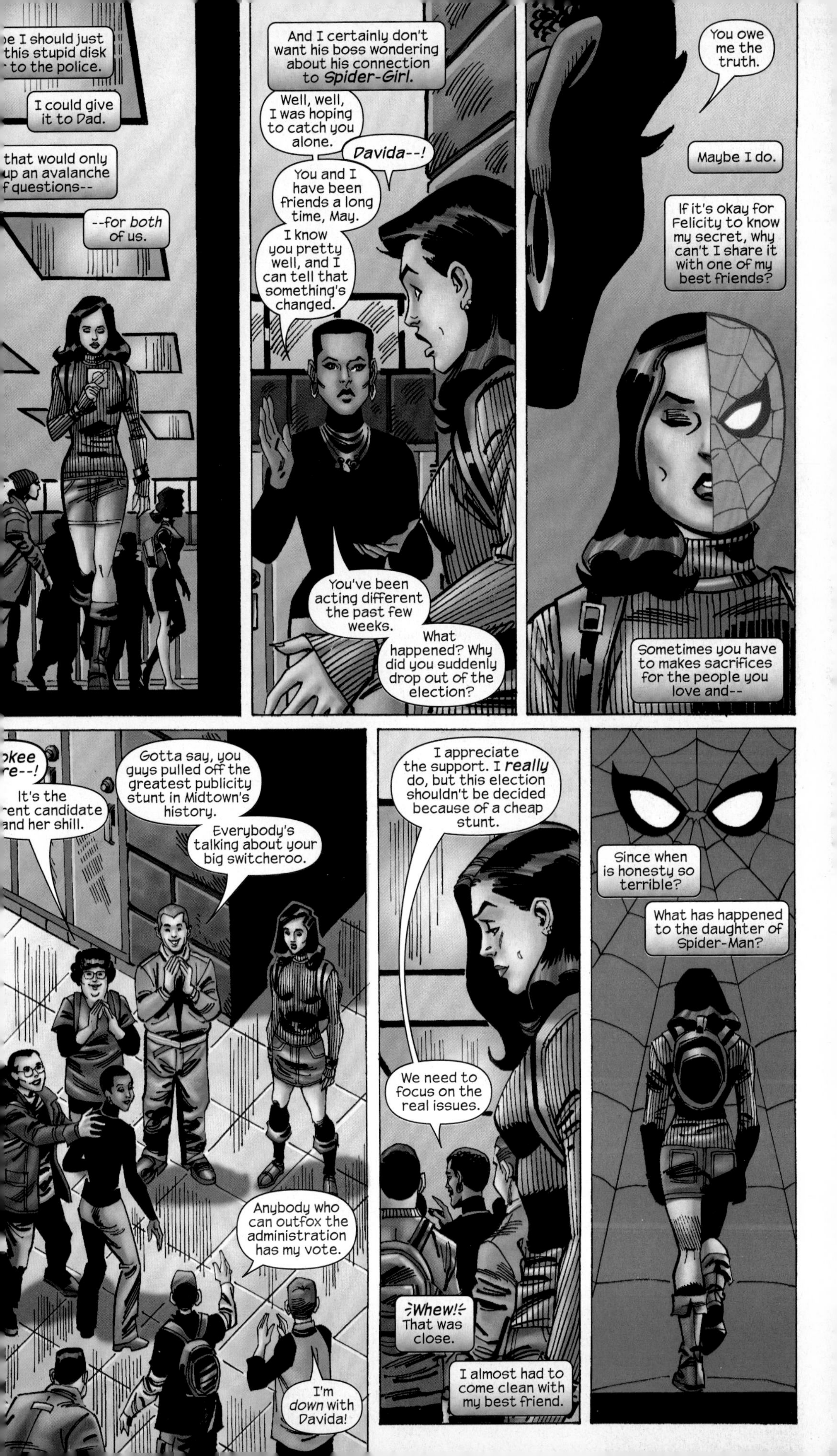

e I should just this stupid disk to the police.
I could give it to Dad.
that would only up an avalanche f questions--
--for both of us.
And I certainly don't want his boss wondering about his connection to Spider-Girl.
Well, well, I was hoping to catch you alone.
Davida--!
You and I have been friends a long time, May.
I know you pretty well, and I can tell that something's changed.
You've been acting different the past few weeks.
What happened? Why did you suddenly drop out of the election?
You owe me the truth.
Maybe I do.
If it's okay for Felicity to know my secret, why can't I share it with one of my best friends?
Sometimes you have to makes sacrifices for the people you love and--
kee re--!
It's the rent candidate and her shill.
Gotta say, you guys pulled off the greatest publicity stunt in Midtown's history.
Everybody's talking about your big switcheroo.
Anybody who can outfox the administration has my vote.
I'm down with Davida!
I appreciate the support. I really do, but this election shouldn't be decided because of a cheap stunt.
We need to focus on the real issues.
Whew! That was close.
I almost had to come clean with my best friend.
Since when is honesty so terrible?
What has happened to the daughter of Spider-Man?

NEW DEACON'S DEN *★ COMICS ★ MANGA*

Shortly after the last class at Midtown High...

How does my butt look, Wes?

Uhhh... J-just great!

The real Spider-Girl must be even more courageous than I realized to go out in a costume like this.

You look amazing, spectacular and sensational, Heather.

The fans will love you.

Ready to greet the crowd?

SPIDER-GIRL #1 ON SALE NOW

MARVEL SOLD HERE!

Davida seemed pretty cheesed.

Car you bla her

Yo owe a hea u

No argument here.

Should I also tell *Courtney* about *Spider-Girl*?

It wouldn't be fair to exclude her if *Davida* knows.

Does that mean I also need to inform Jimmy, Heather, Gene, Moose, JJ, Chris and the rest of the gang?!

♪ HELLO, BOYS! ♪

SPIDER-GIRL LIVE

Face front, true believers! This is the greatest, most exciting comic of all time!

Or on this particular table.

Just look at this crowd! I'm so happy for Jimmy and Wes.

They worked so hard on their book.

You're right, Court. We should just enjoy their big moment and--

Oh, noooo!

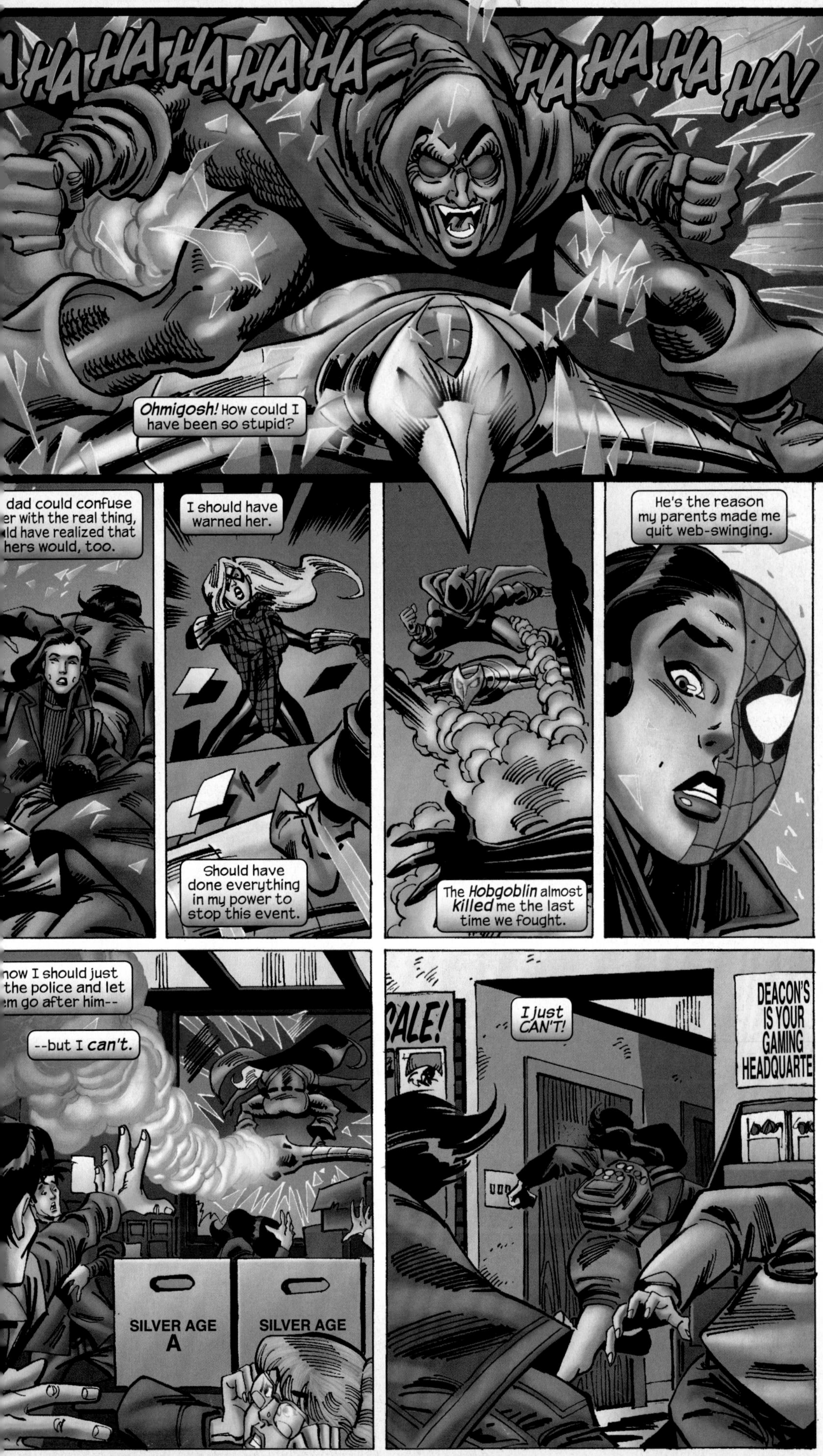
HA HA HA HA HA HA HA HA HA HA HA HA!
Ohmigosh! How could I have been so stupid?
dad could confuse er with the real thing, ld have realized that hers would, too.
I should have warned her.
Should have done everything in my power to stop this event.
The Hobgoblin almost killed me the last time we fought.
He's the reason my parents made me quit web-swinging.
now I should just the police and let em go after him--
--but I can't.
SILVER AGE A
SILVER AGE
SALE!
I just CAN'T!
DEACON'S IS YOUR GAMING HEADQUARTE

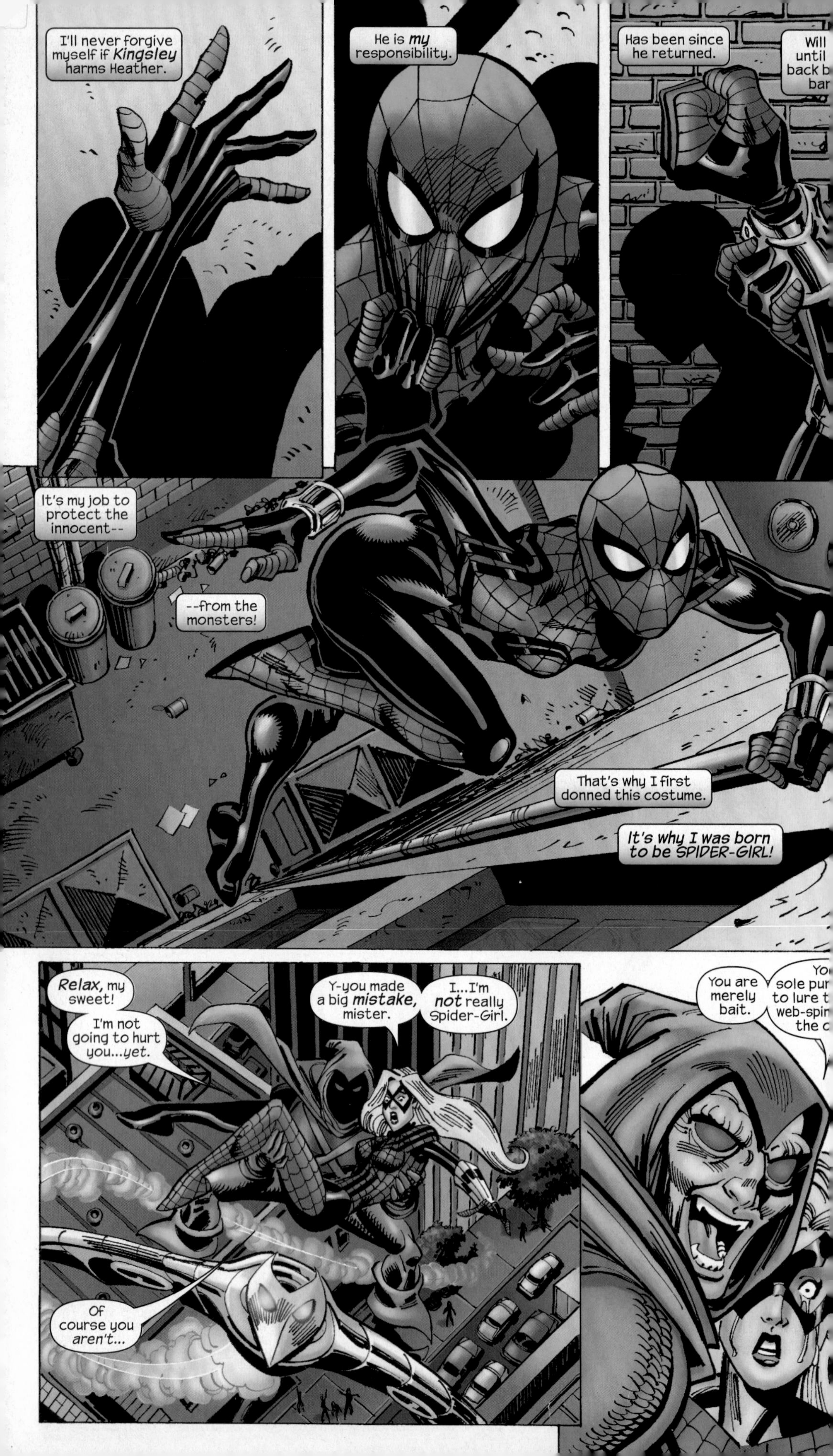
I'll never forgive myself if Kingsley harms Heather.
He is my responsibility.
Has been since he returned.
It's my job to protect the innocent--
--from the monsters!
That's why I first donned this costume.
It's why I was born to be SPIDER-GIRL!
Relax, my sweet!
I'm not going to hurt you...yet.
Y-you made a big mistake, mister.
I...I'm not really Spider-Girl.
Of course you aren't...
You are merely bait.

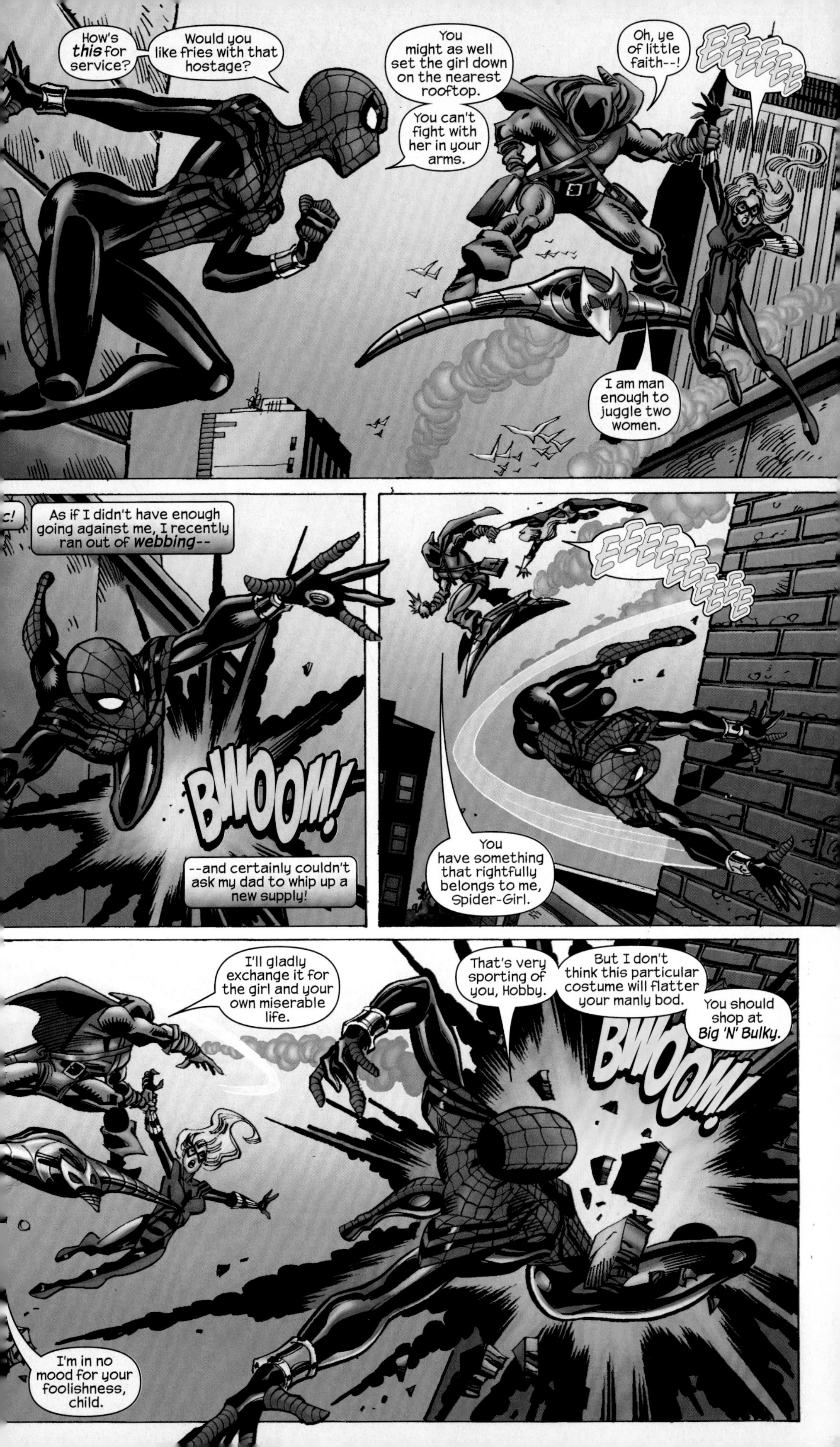
How's *this* for service?
Would you like fries with that hostage?
You might as well set the girl down on the nearest rooftop.
You can't fight with her in your arms.
Oh, ye of little faith--!
EEEEEE
I am man enough to juggle two women.
As if I didn't have enough going against me, I recently ran out of *webbing*--
BWOOM!
--and certainly couldn't ask my dad to whip up a new supply!
EEEEEEEEEEE
You have something that rightfully belongs to me, Spider-Girl.
I'll gladly exchange it for the girl and your own miserable life.
That's very sporting of you, Hobby.
But I don't think this particular costume will flatter your manly bod.
You should shop at *Big 'N' Bulky*.
BWOOM!
I'm in no mood for your foolishness, child.

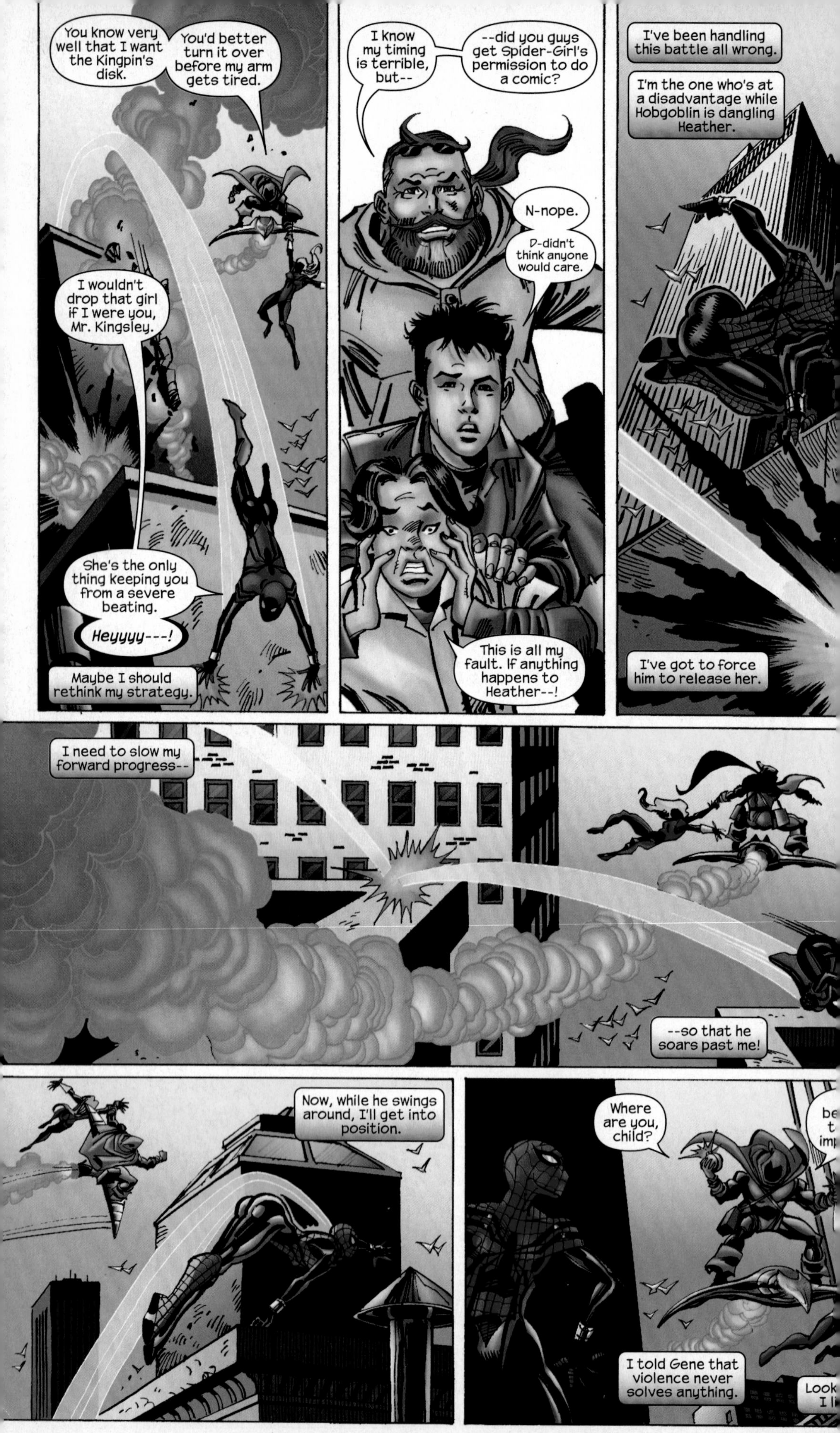
You know very well that I want the Kingpin's disk.
You'd better turn it over before my arm gets tired.
I wouldn't drop that girl if I were you, Mr. Kingsley.
She's the only thing keeping you from a severe beating.
Heyyyy---!
Maybe I should rethink my strategy.
I know my timing is terrible, but--
--did you guys get Spider-Girl's permission to do a comic?
N-nope.
D-didn't think anyone would care.
This is all my fault. If anything happens to Heather--!
I've been handling this battle all wrong.
I'm the one who's at a disadvantage while Hobgoblin is dangling Heather.
I've got to force him to release her.
I need to slow my forward progress--
--so that he soars past me!
Now, while he swings around, I'll get into position.
Where are you, child?
I told Gene that violence never solves anything.

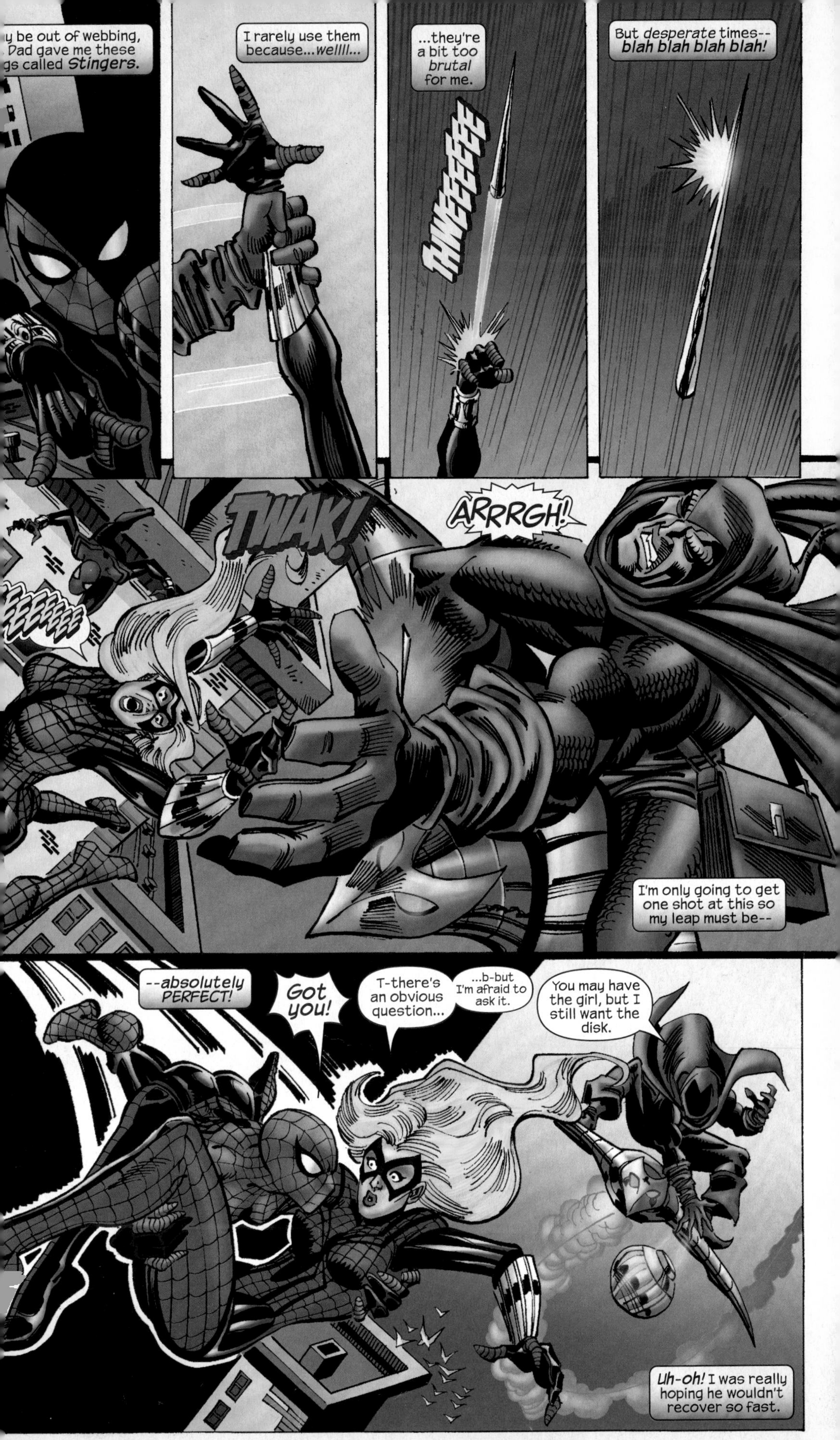

y be out of webbing, Dad gave me these gs called Stingers.
I rarely use them because...wellll...
...they're a bit too brutal for me.
THWEEEEEE
But desperate times-- blah blah blah blah!
TWAK!
ARRRGH!
EEEEEEE
I'm only going to get one shot at this so my leap must be--
--absolutely PERFECT!
Got you!
T-there's an obvious question...
...b-but I'm afraid to ask it.
You may have the girl, but I still want the disk.
Uh-oh! I was really hoping he wouldn't recover so fast.

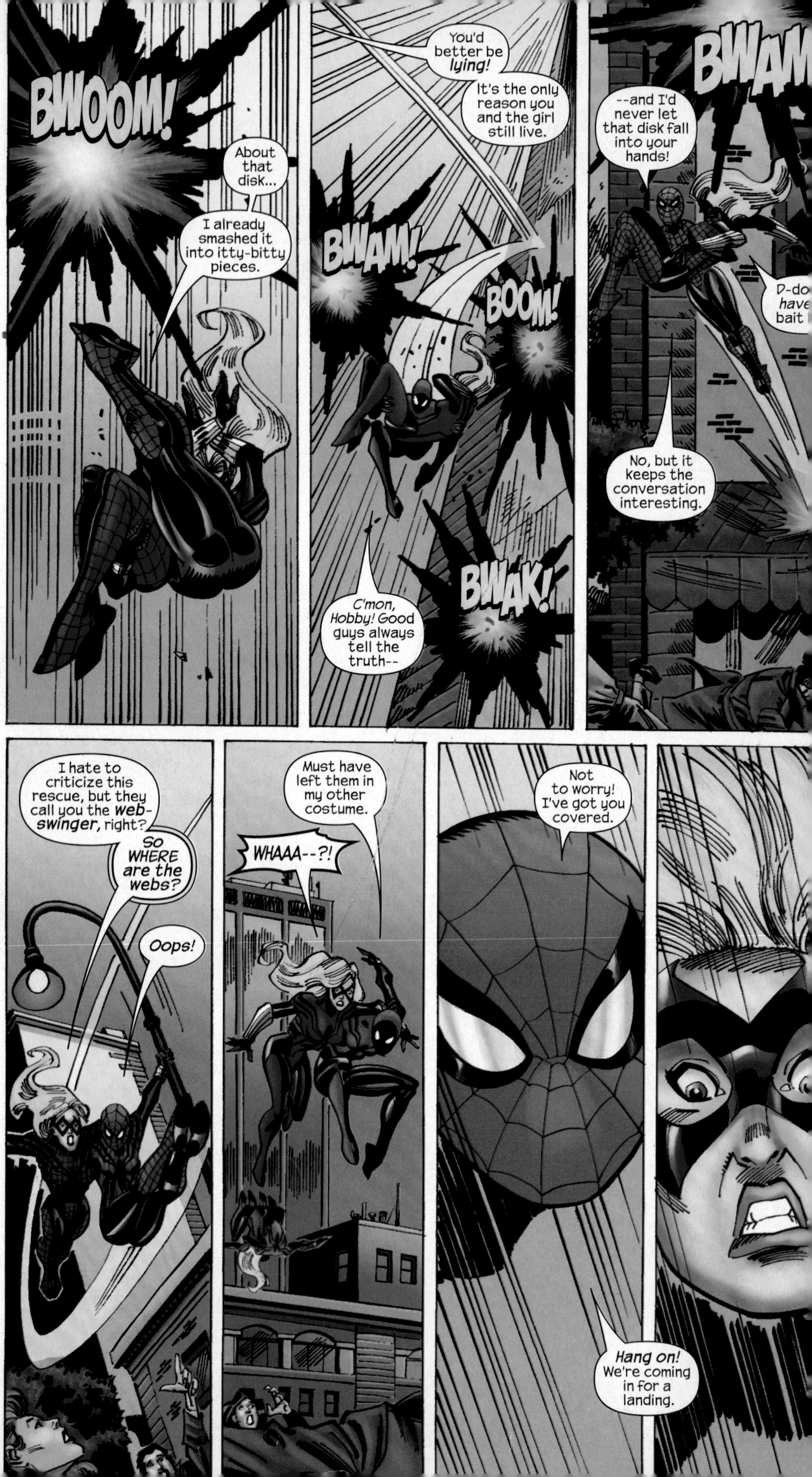

BWOOM!
About that disk...
I already smashed it into itty-bitty pieces.
You'd better be lying!
It's the only reason you and the girl still live.
BWAM!
BOOM!
BWAK!
C'mon, Hobby! Good guys always tell the truth--
BWAM
--and I'd never let that disk fall into your hands!
No, but it keeps the conversation interesting.
I hate to criticize this rescue, but they call you the web-swinger, right?
SO WHERE are the webs?
Oops!
Must have left them in my other costume.
WHAAA--?!
Not to worry! I've got you covered.
Hang on! We're coming in for a landing.

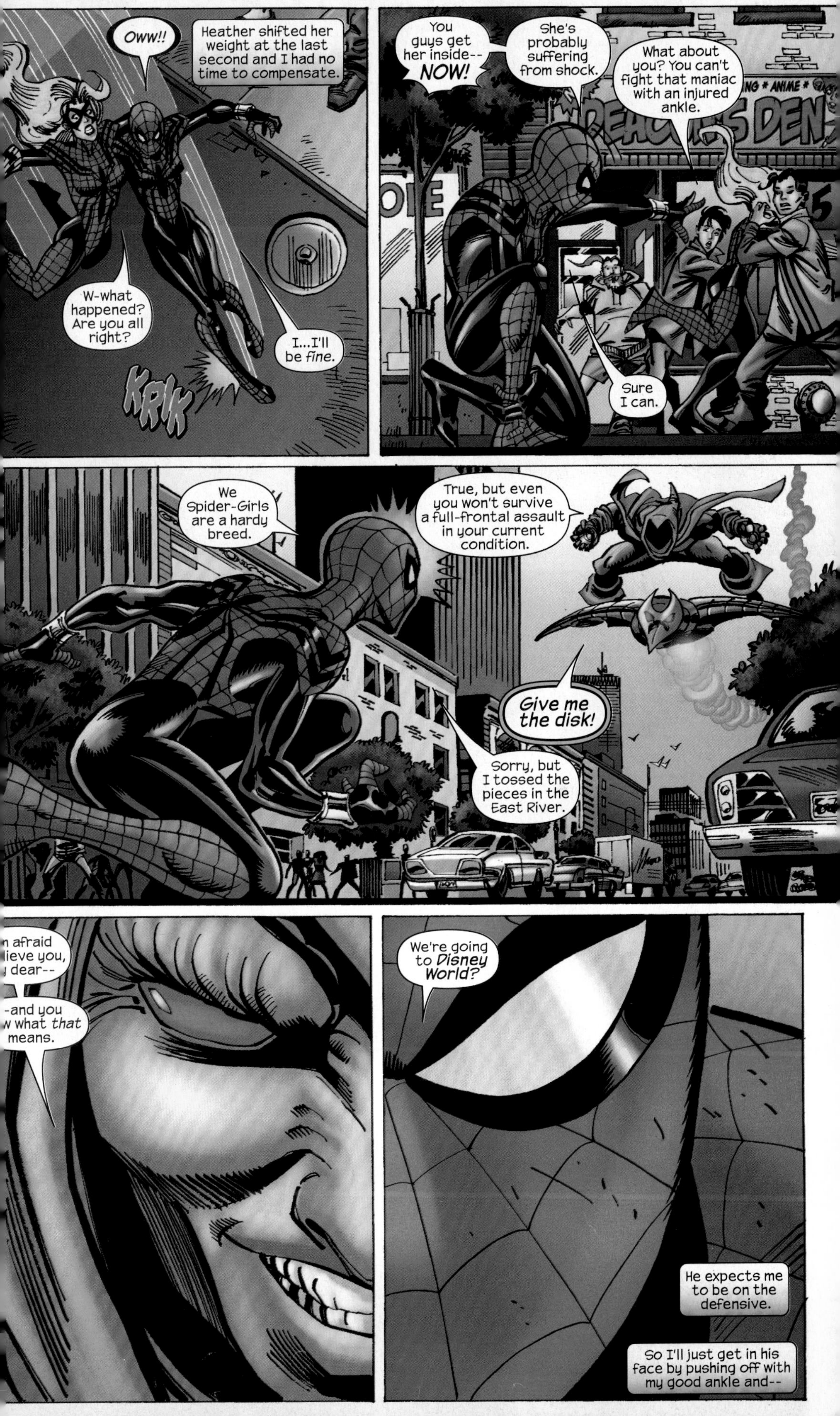
Oww!!
Heather shifted her weight at the last second and I had no time to compensate.
W-what happened? Are you all right?
I...I'll be fine.
KRIK
You guys get her inside-- NOW!
She's probably suffering from shock.
What about you? You can't fight that maniac with an injured ankle.
Sure I can.
We Spider-Girls are a hardy breed.
True, but even you won't survive a full-frontal assault in your current condition.
Give me the disk!
Sorry, but I tossed the pieces in the East River.
n afraid
ieve you,
dear--
-and you
v what that
means.
We're going to Disney World?
He expects me to be on the defensive.
So I'll just get in his face by pushing off with my good ankle and--

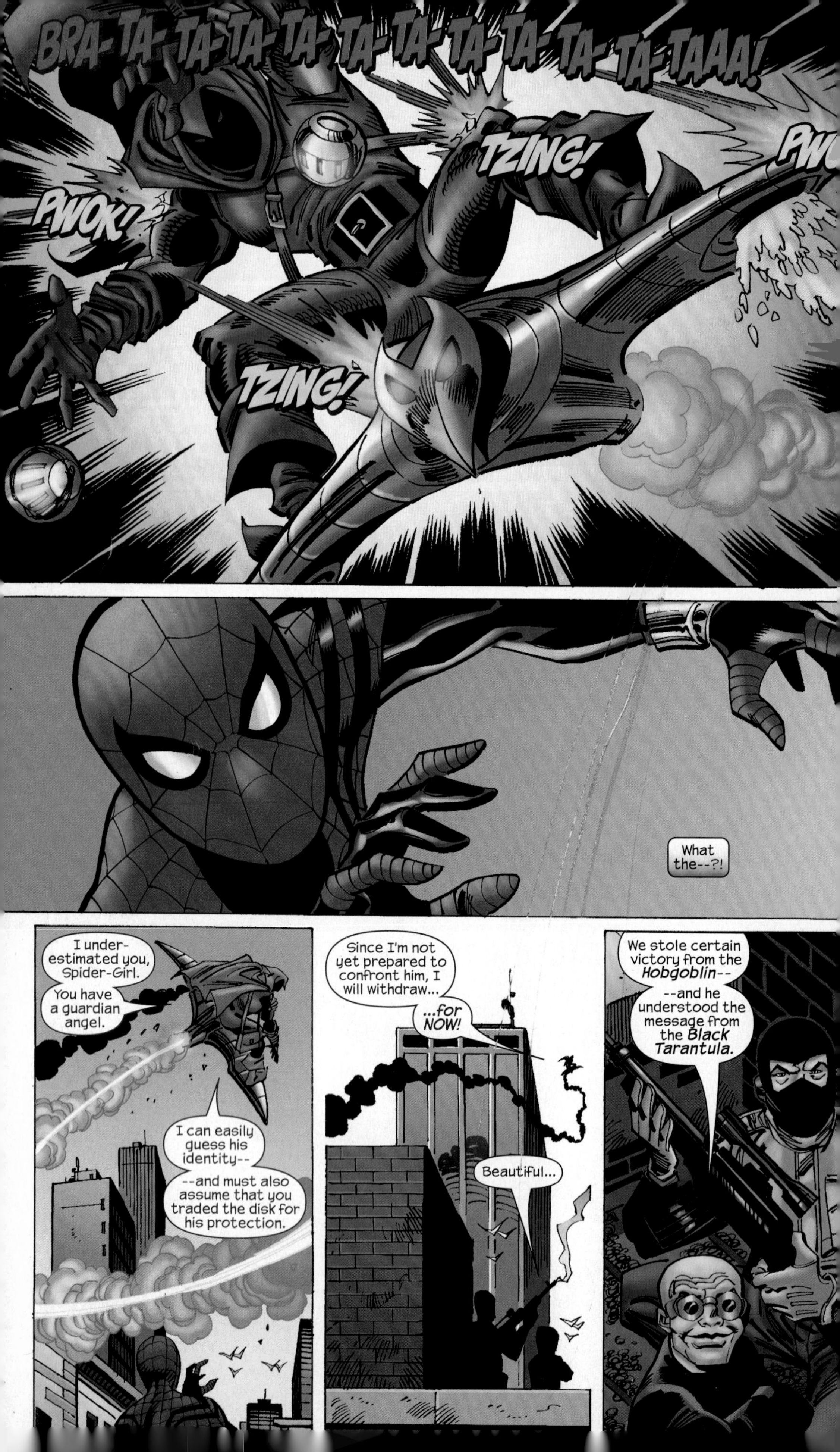
BRA-TA-TA-TA-TA-TA-TA-TA-TA-TA-TA-TAAA!
PWOK!
TZING!
TZING!
What the--?!
I under-estimated you, Spider-Girl.
You have a guardian angel.
I can easily guess his identity--
--and must also assume that you traded the disk for his protection.
Since I'm not yet prepared to confront him, I will withdraw...
...for NOW!
Beautiful...
We stole certain victory from the Hobgoblin--
--and he understood the message from the Black Tarantula.

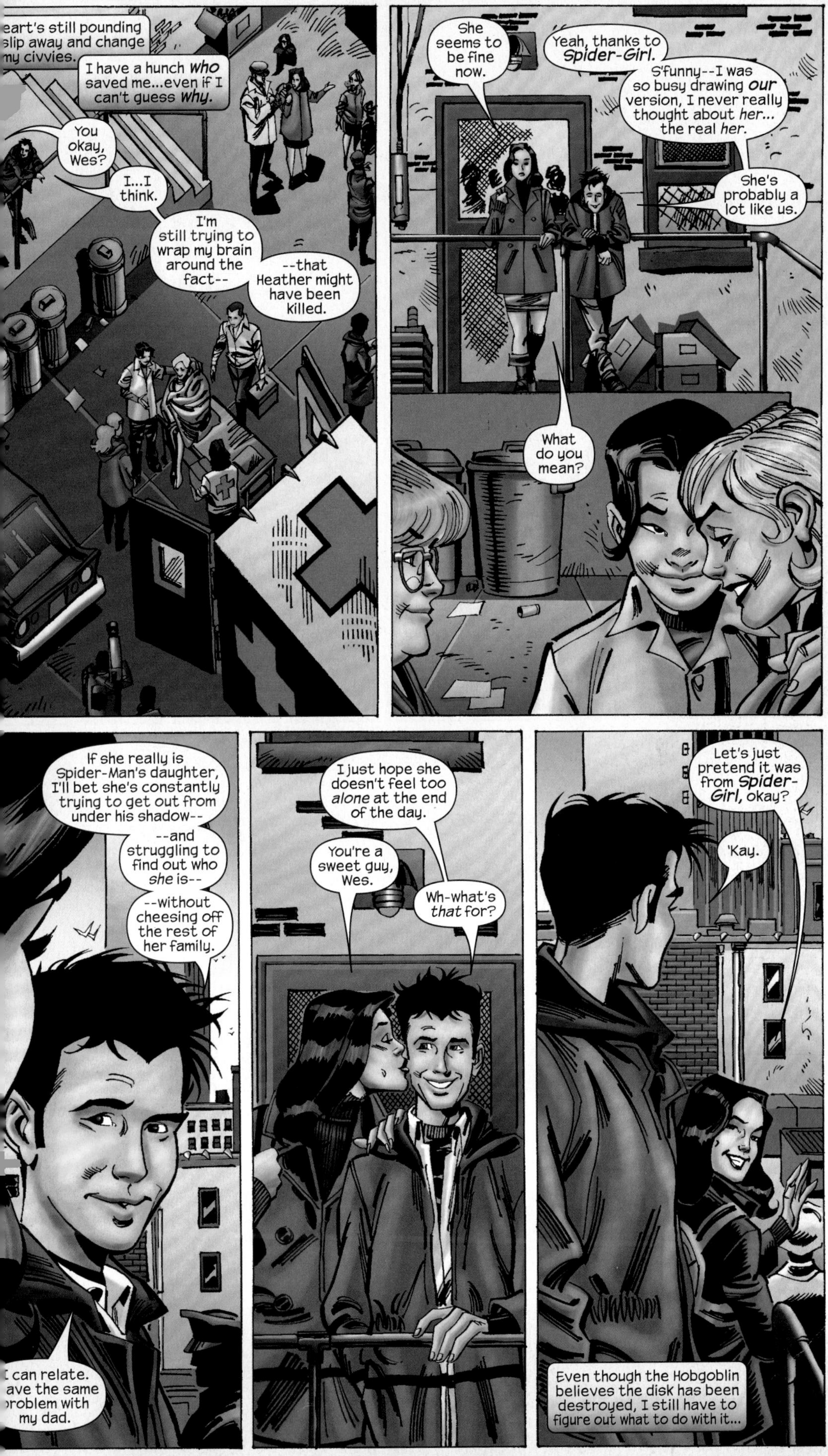

eart's still pounding
slip away and change
my civvies.
I have a hunch *who* saved me...even if I can't guess *why*.
You okay, Wes?
I...I think.
I'm still trying to wrap my brain around the fact--
--that Heather might have been killed.
She seems to be fine now.
Yeah, thanks to *Spider-Girl.*
S'funny--I was so busy drawing *our* version, I never really thought about *her*... the real *her*.
She's probably a lot like us.
What do you mean?
If she really is Spider-Man's daughter, I'll bet she's constantly trying to get out from under his shadow--
--and struggling to find out who *she* is--
--without cheesing off the rest of her family.
I can relate.
ave the same
roblem with
my dad.
I just hope she doesn't feel too *alone* at the end of the day.
You're a sweet guy, Wes.
Wh-what's *that* for?
Let's just pretend it was from *Spider-Girl,* okay?
'Kay.
Even though the Hobgoblin believes the disk has been destroyed, I still have to figure out what to do with it...

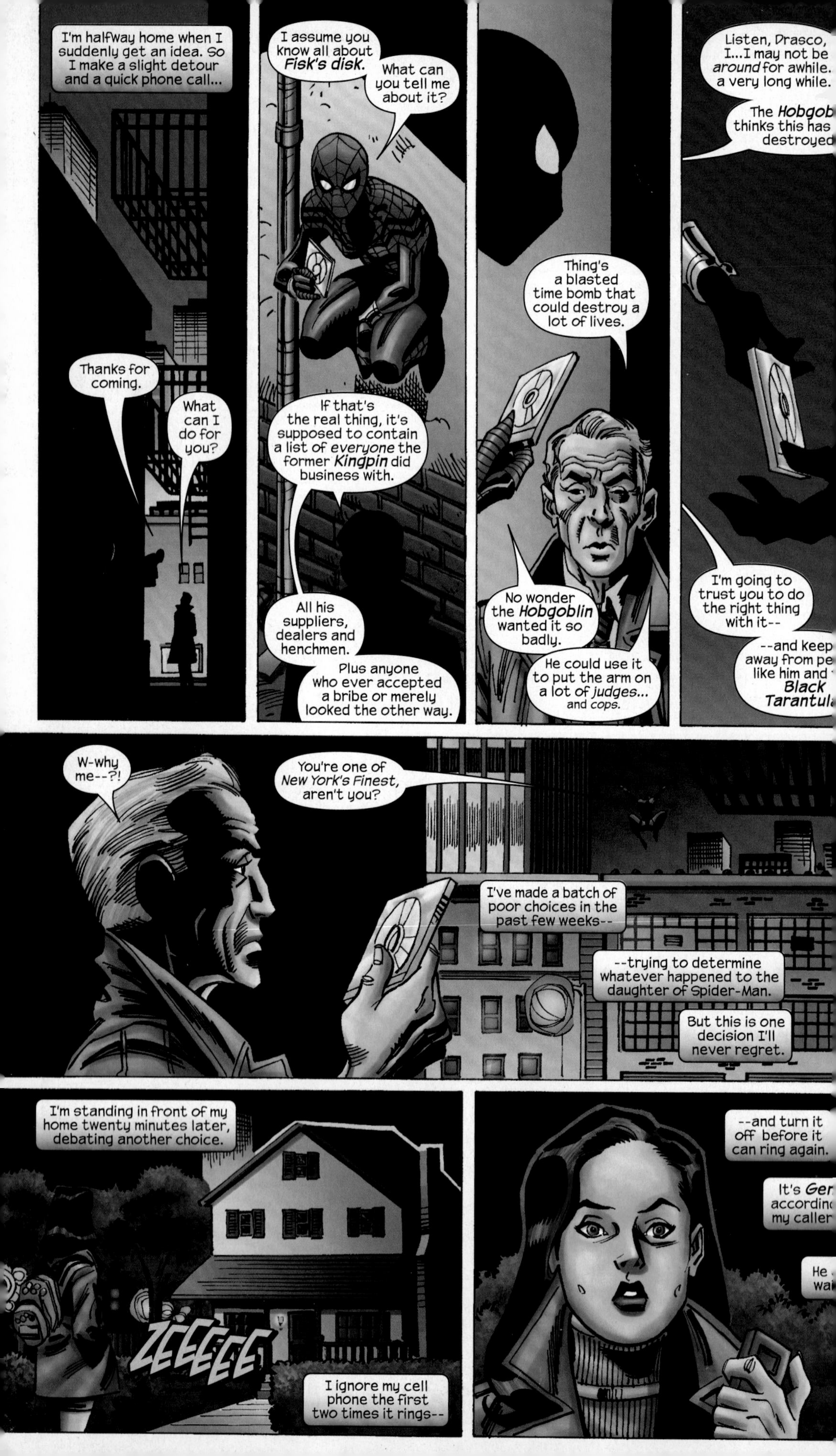
I'm halfway home when I suddenly get an idea. So I make a slight detour and a quick phone call...
Thanks for coming.
What can I do for you?
I assume you know all about Fisk's disk.
What can you tell me about it?
If that's the real thing, it's supposed to contain a list of everyone the former Kingpin did business with.
All his suppliers, dealers and henchmen.
Plus anyone who ever accepted a bribe or merely looked the other way.
Thing's a blasted time bomb that could destroy a lot of lives.
No wonder the Hobgoblin wanted it so badly.
He could use it to put the arm on a lot of judges... and cops.
Listen, Drasco, I...I may not be around for awhile. a very long while.
I'm going to trust you to do the right thing with it--
W-why me--?!
You're one of New York's Finest, aren't you?
I've made a batch of poor choices in the past few weeks--
--trying to determine whatever happened to the daughter of Spider-Man.
But this is one decision I'll never regret.
I'm standing in front of my home twenty minutes later, debating another choice.
ZEEEEEE
I ignore my cell phone the first two times it rings--
--and turn it off before it can ring again.

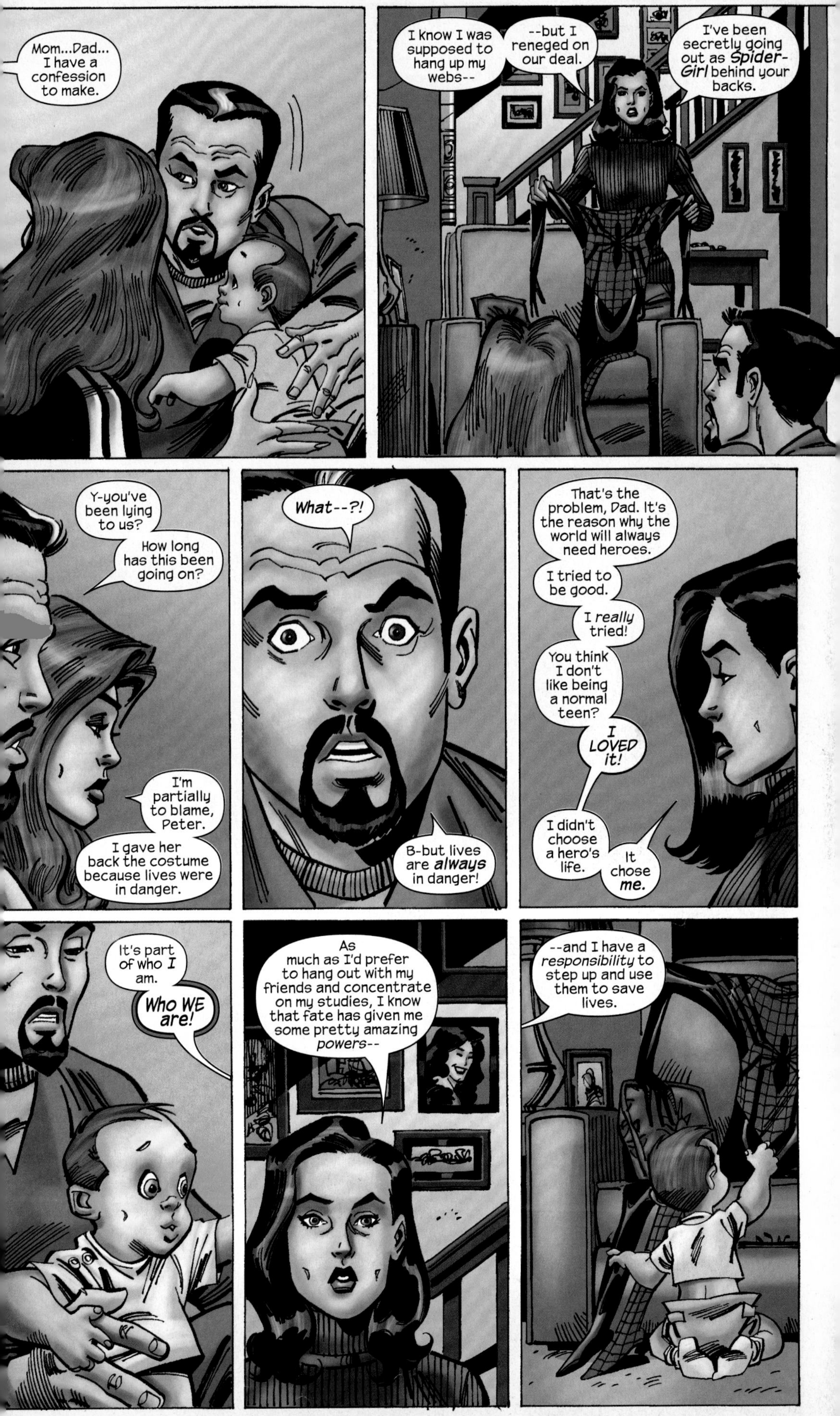
Mom...Dad... I have a confession to make.
I know I was supposed to hang up my webs--
--but I reneged on our deal.
I've been secretly going out as Spider-Girl behind your backs.
Y-you've been lying to us?
How long has this been going on?
I'm partially to blame, Peter.
I gave her back the costume because lives were in danger.
What--?!
B-but lives are always in danger!
That's the problem, Dad. It's the reason why the world will always need heroes.
I tried to be good.
I really tried!
You think I don't like being a normal teen?
I LOVED it!
I didn't choose a hero's life.
It chose me.
It's part of who I am.
Who WE are!
As much as I'd prefer to hang out with my friends and concentrate on my studies, I know that fate has given me some pretty amazing powers--
--and I have a responsibility to step up and use them to save lives.

I know this is hard on you. I can't imagine how much you worry every time I pull on those webs.

You're my parents. I love you and I'll try to do whatever you decide.

If you really want me to stop, I'll do my best.

But you have to understand that you can only *delay* my destiny. You can't *stop* it.

Even if I have to wait until my eighteenth birthday, I will return to web-swinging.

I will be Spider-Girl.

I just wonder how many lives will be lost in the meantime.

Thanks for hearing me out.

It means a lot.

If you'll excuse me, I need to get some fresh air.

And maybe throw up!

Th[e] conve[rsation] isn't [over] youn[g]

I know, Dad.

It's just *beginning...*

Well, I did it.

Finally came clean and embraced my destiny.

There's a pretty good chance my parents will ground me for life.

And I wouldn't blame them if they *did*.

I'm not sure what the future holds.

I just know that my name is *May "Mayday" Parker*.

I am the daughter of *Spider-Man*--

--and today is the first day of the rest of my life!

THE EN[D] for no[w]

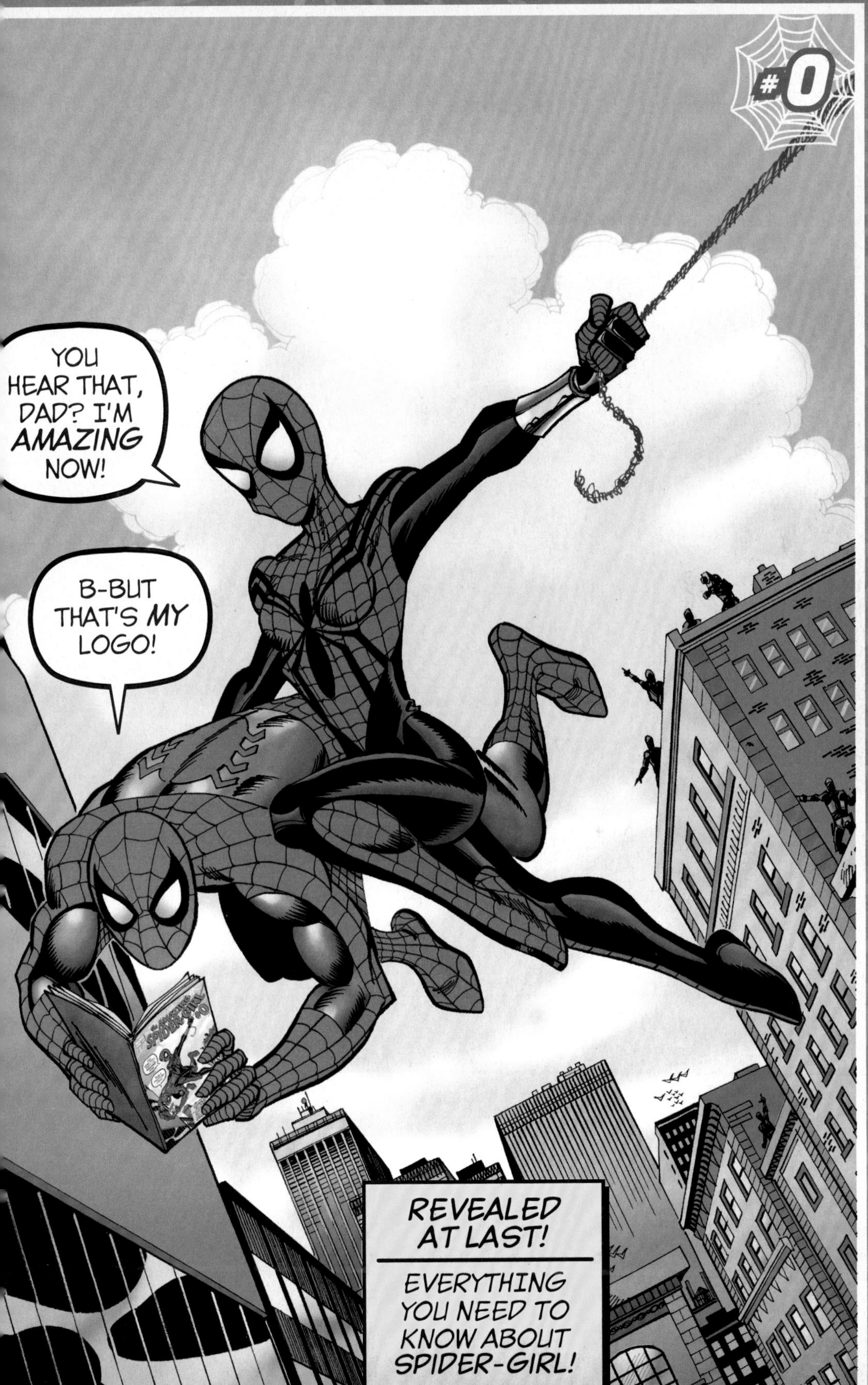
#0
YOU HEAR THAT, DAD? I'M AMAZING NOW!
B-BUT THAT'S MY LOGO!
REVEALED AT LAST!
EVERYTHING YOU NEED TO KNOW ABOUT SPIDER-GIRL!

the AMAZING SPIDER-GIRL

Dear Diary,

My name is **May Parker,** though most everybody calls me **Mayday** (a nickname I picked up from my basketball

have a secret (a bunch of them, actually) and decided to keep an "official" record of my life. I guess I should star

beginning, on the day my whole life changed and I discovered that I was the daughter of **Spider-Man.**

Writer: **Tom DeFalco**
Based on WHAT IF...? #105,
SPIDER-GIRL #0-100,
SPIDER-GIRL #1/2 and
SPIDER-GIRL 1999 ANNUAL

Featuring Artwork by: **Pat Olliffe,
Ron Frenz, John Romita Sr.,
J. Scott Campbell,
Al Williamson, Sal Buscema,
Bill Sienkiewicz, Scott Koblish**
and **Tim Townsend**
Cover Art: **Ron Frenz, Sal
Buscema** and **Gotham**

Editor: **Molly Lazer**
Senior Editor, Special Projects:
Jeff Younquist
Vice President of Sales:
David Gabriel
Special thanks to **Jennifer
Grünwald** & **Michael Short**

Production: **Jerron Quali**
Book Designer: **Dayle Che**
Vice President of Creative:
Tom Marvelli

Editor in Chief: **Joe Ques**
Publisher: **Dan Buckley**

case you just zapped in from another
nension and never heard of him, **Spider-**
n is one of the greatest costumed heroes of
modern age. His real name is **Peter Parker,**
d he possesses the proportionate strength,
ed, agility and equilibrium of a spider and
n cling to any surface. He even invented a
r of devices that produce artificial webbing.
also has an additional power that he calls his
der-sense, which is this weird, tingly feeling
t warns him of danger. *(And he makes the*
rld's greatest pancakes!)

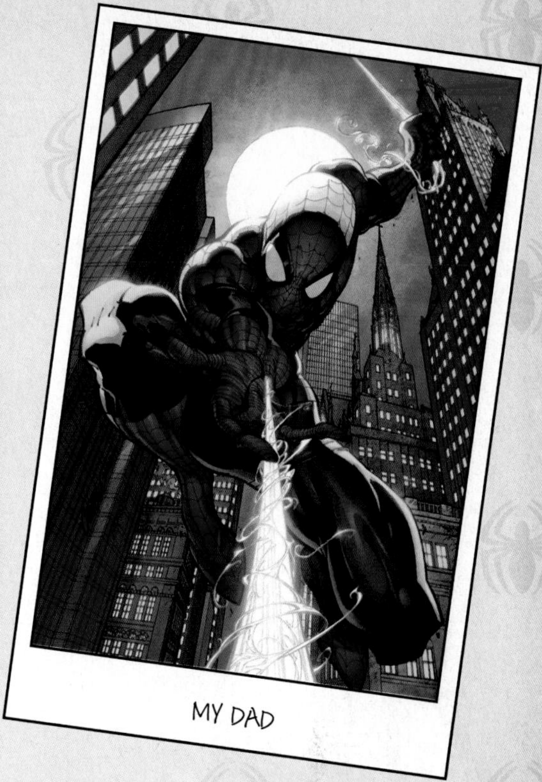

MY DAD

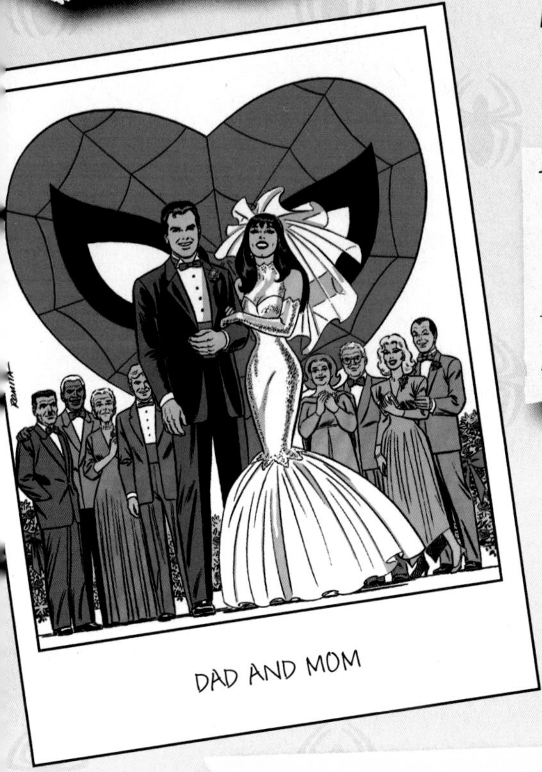

DAD AND MOM

Though I really don't know the details *(because I obviously wasn't around at the time)*, he fell in love with my mom, the former **Mary Jane Watson,** and they eventually got married. *(Yay for me!)*

After trying a variety of jobs, Dad became a forensic scientist for the police department and Mom worked as an executive in the fashion industry. I came along after a few years, and we had a pretty average life.

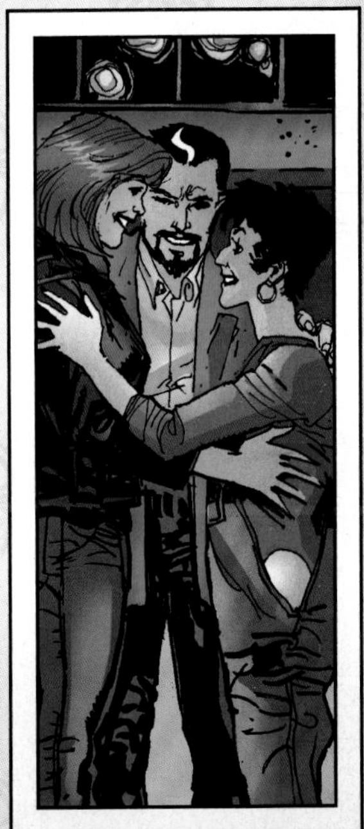

That changed during my sophomo[re]
year in high school. I was always in[to]
sports *(especially basketball)* and wa[s]
playing on my school team when m[y]
body suddenly kicked into overdriv[e]
and I realized that I wasn't exactly [the]
poster child for *"normal."*

Around the same time, **Normie Osborn** *(the grandson of the original **Green Goblin,** one of Spider-Man's greatest enemies)* decided to take up the family business and kill my dad.

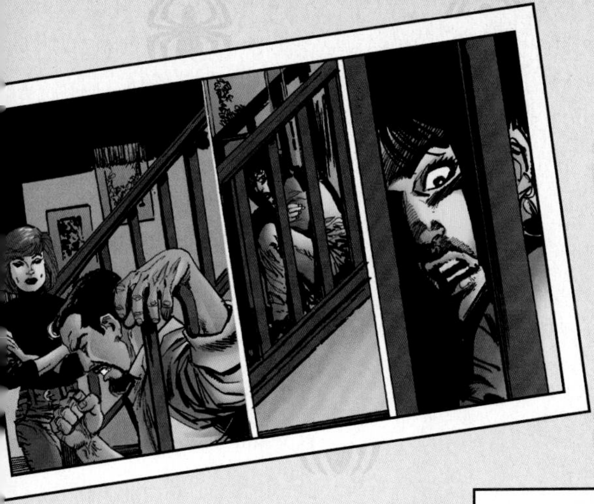

My parents were so freaked that they finally came clean. I learned the *truth* about my dad...and about myself.

I later found out that I was around
o years old when my dad confronted
rmie's grandfather for the last time.
ıring the battle, the **Goblin** died and
Dad lost his right leg. It took Dad a
e, but he had to accept the fact that
is wall-crawling days were over and
hang up his webs.

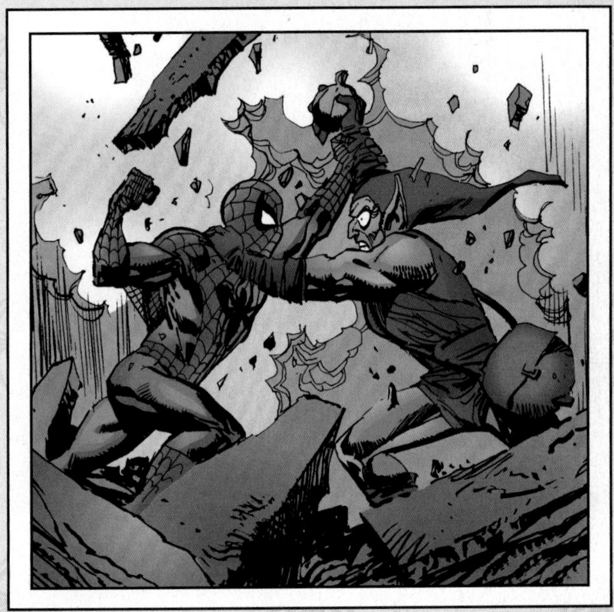

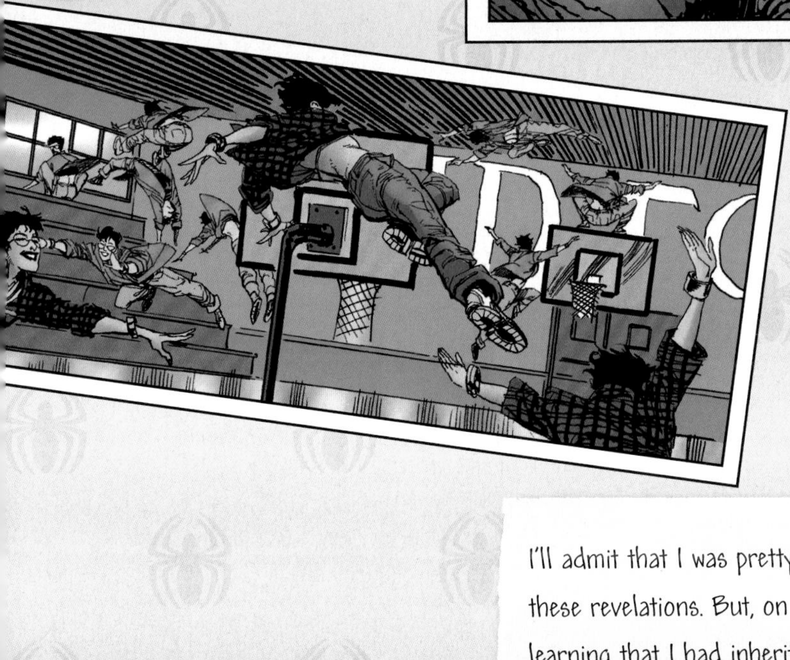

I'll admit that I was pretty weirded out by all these revelations. But, on the other hand, learning that I had inherited Dad's spider-powers--**HOO-HA!** ***That was mega-cool!***

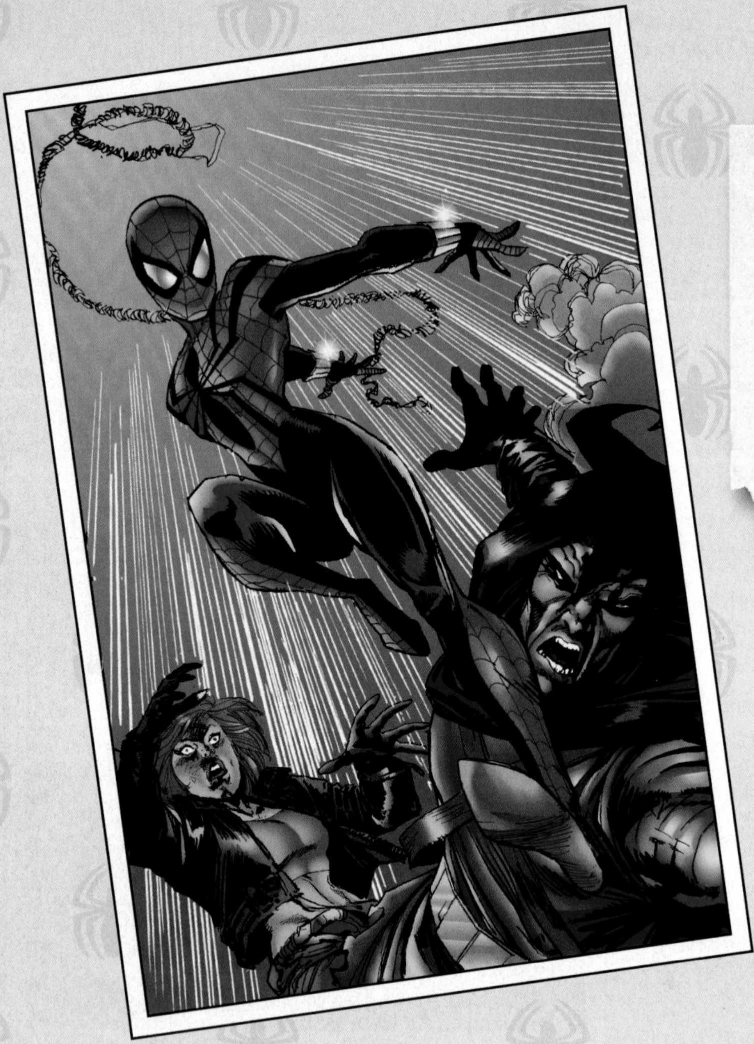

Anyway, I eventually modified one of the old spider-costume I found stored in the attic, fitt myself with a pair of web-shooters and quickly convince **Normie Osborn** that no one going to die on my watch.

I guess my parents and I assumed that this **Spider-Girl** thing was just a one-time event. We thought we could all go back to our normal lives once Normie was safely behind bars. No such luck!

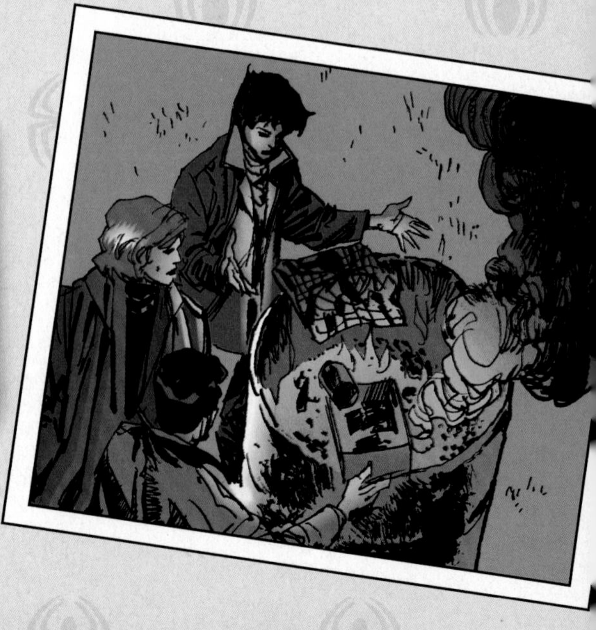

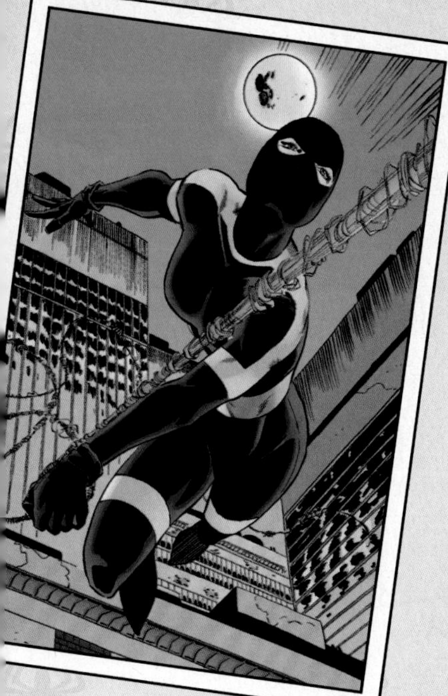

Seems my dad's sense of responsibility came with his powers. I soon found myself wearing a makeshift costume and sneaking out at night to play hero because I had learned a very important lesson--*when I succeed, people* ***live!***

Here's another secret--*being a* *uper hero* ***ain't*** *all it's cracked up to be!* I ran across some real winners ke **Mr. Nobody,** a psychopath who had a device that allowed him to eport wherever he wanted and was ventually modified to make him as intangible as a ghost.

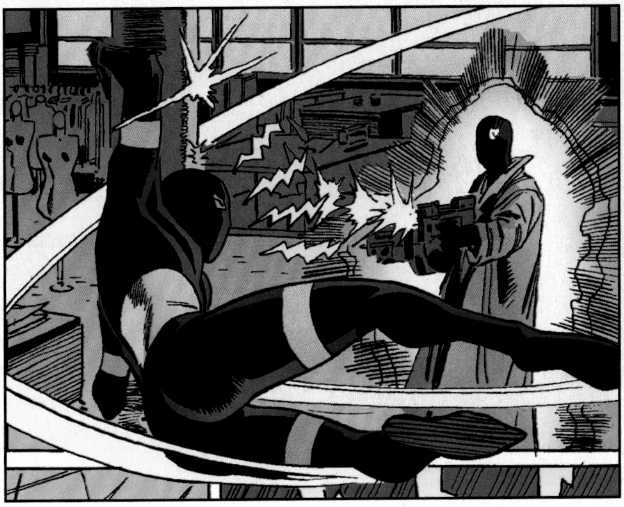

MR. NOBODY

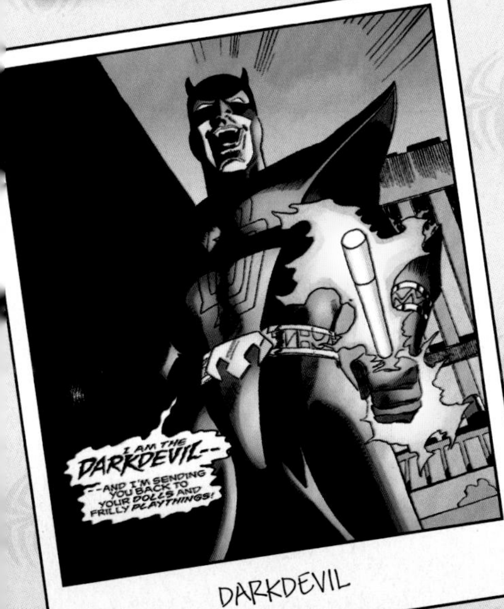
I AM THE DARKDEVIL--
--AND I'M SENDING YOU BACK TO YOUR DOLLS AND FRILLY PLAYTHINGS!

DARKDEVIL

Not only did I come to the attention of **Wilson Fisk,** the so-called **Kingpin of Crime,** but I also crossed paths with **Darkdevil,** a costumed vigilante with demon-like powers. When we first met, he kept trying to discourage me from being **Spider-Girl,** but I eventually won him over. *(Points for me!)*

THE FANTASTIC FIVE

I even became acquainted with the **Fantastic Five**, the current incarnation of the **Fantastic Four**. The new team consists of **Johnny Storm**, the **Human Torch**...his wife **Lyja Storm**, a shape-shifting Skrull who calls herself **Ms. Fantastic**...**Ben Grimm**, the ever-loving **Thing**...the always-dreamy **Franklin Richards**, a powerful telepath and telekinetic who goes by the name **Psi-Lord**...and **Big Brain**, a robot that used to house the brain of **Reed Richards**. (*Thanks to a little help on my part,* **Mr. Fantastic** *and his wife, the* **Invisible Woman**, *have recently rejoined the team.*)

I APOLOGIZE FOR INTRUDING UPON YOUR LEISURELY AFTERNOON...BUT I STRONGLY SUGGEST THAT YOU ALL *FIND*...AND CALMLY *WALK*...TO THE NEAREST *EXIT*...

SPYRAL

I also encountered **Spyral**, a freakoid who could travel through time and to alternate realities. The poor guy claimed that he was just trying to find his way back to his home world, but he sure created a lot of chaos on this one.

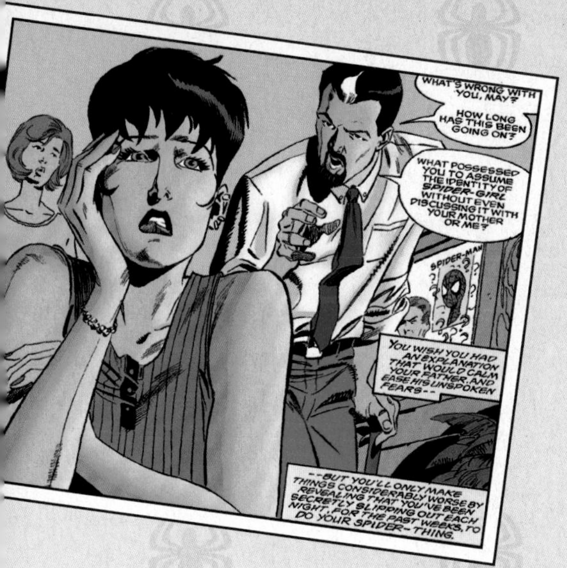
WHAT'S WRONG WITH YOU, MAY?
HOW LONG HAS THIS BEEN GOING ON?
WHAT POSSESSED YOU TO ASSUME THE IDENTITY OF SPIDER-GIRL WITHOUT EVEN DISCUSSING IT WITH YOUR MOTHER OR ME?
SPIDER-MAN
YOU WISH YOU HAD AN EXPLANATION THAT WOULD CALM YOUR FATHER, AND EASE HIS UNSPOKEN FEARS--
--BUT YOU'LL ONLY MAKE THINGS CONSIDERABLY WORSE BY REVEALING THAT YOU'VE BEEN SECRETLY SLIPPING OUT EACH NIGHT, FOR THE PAST WEEKS, TO DO YOUR SPIDER-THING.

I don't want to give you the wrong impression. I didn't spend all my time swinging on webs. My parents went nuclear when they first learned about my extracurricular activities. *(Sure, it was okay for* ***Dad*** *to risk his neck when* ***he*** *was a teenager!)* Let me tell you, they never really *warmed* to the idea of me being **Spider-Girl** and they still barely tolerate it.

t I did get some unexpected support m **Phil Urich.** He works in the police lab h my dad, has been a close family friend so long that I call him **Uncle Phil.** *(His e's name is* ***Meredith,*** *and she's a hotshot vyer who works for* ***Franklin Nelson,*** *rmie Osborn's stepdad.)* Anyway, Phil used be a super hero when he was in his late ns and has spent most of his adult life ing to recapture those glory days.

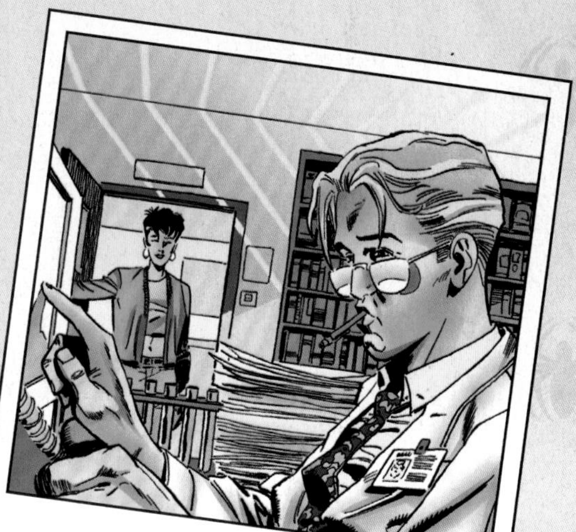

UNCLE PHIL

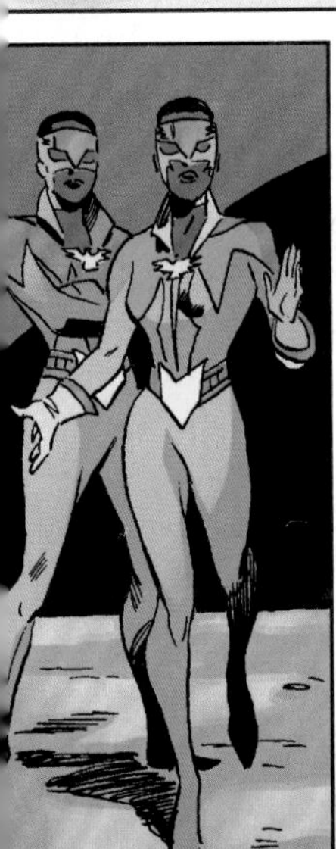

LADYHAWKS

Phil secretly helped train me and even introduced me to the **Ladyhawks**--twin sisters who share the same costumed identity and use a combination of athleticism and martial arts to fight street-level criminals.

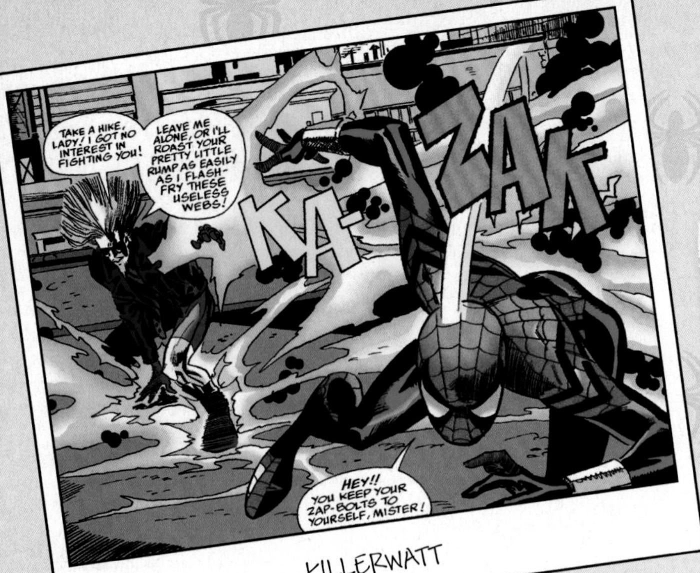
TAKE A HIKE, LADY! I GOT NO INTEREST IN FIGHTING YOU!
LEAVE ME ALONE, OR I'LL ROAST YOUR PRETTY LITTLE RUMP AS EASILY AS I FLASH-FRY THESE USELESS WEBS!
KA-ZAK
HEY!! YOU KEEP YOUR ZAP-BOLTS TO YOURSELF, MISTER!

KILLERWATT

My dad finally began to realiz that I wasn't going to quit bei **Spider-Girl,** so he took me under his wing. That training really paid off when I battled **Killerwatt,** a former band roadie who gained electrical powers in a freak accident.

I eventually grew so confident in my abilities that I even applied for membership with the **Avengers.** *(Okay, so maybe I was a little full of myself!)* While I didn't make the starting team, I did score a reserve spot and eventually became pretty close with **Stinger, American Dream** and **J2.**

My relationship with the other Avengers hasn't always been the best, mainly because I'm constantly butting heads with **Mainframe,** a living robot with a heart of steel.

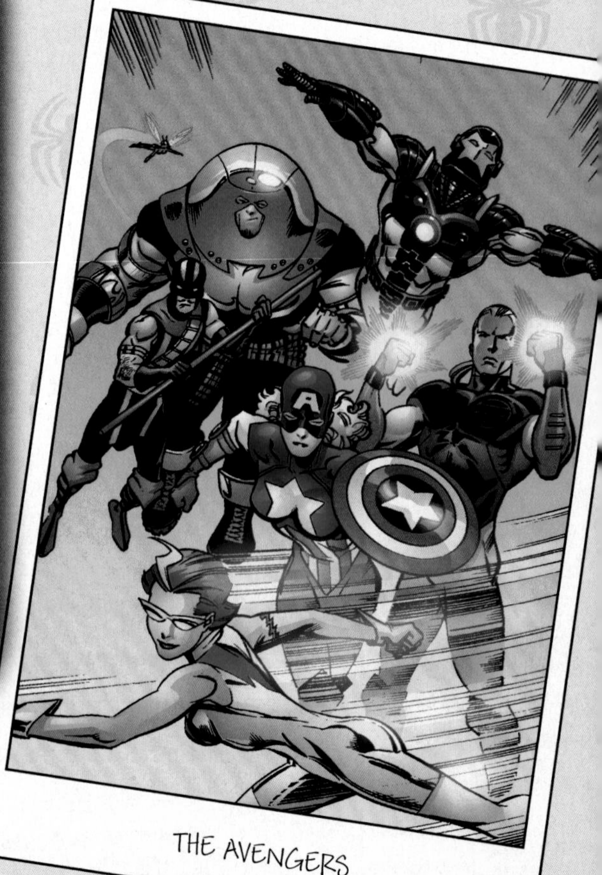

THE AVENGERS

I also had a very bad experience
en I bumped into a relative of my
ather's called **Kaine,** a mercenary
o is super-strong, extremely agile
and often battled my father in the
past. Our first few meetings were
rather vicious, but *(lucky for me)*
aine seems to have mellowed over
me. He is currently trying to atone
his past mistakes and we've gone
m uneasy allies to almost friends.
(Maybe I'll even call him "Uncle" someday.)

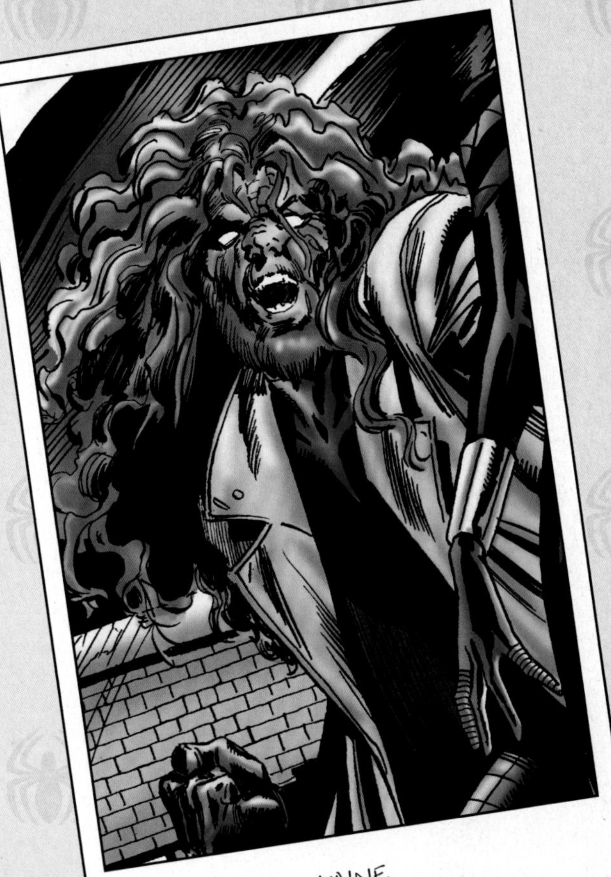

KAINE

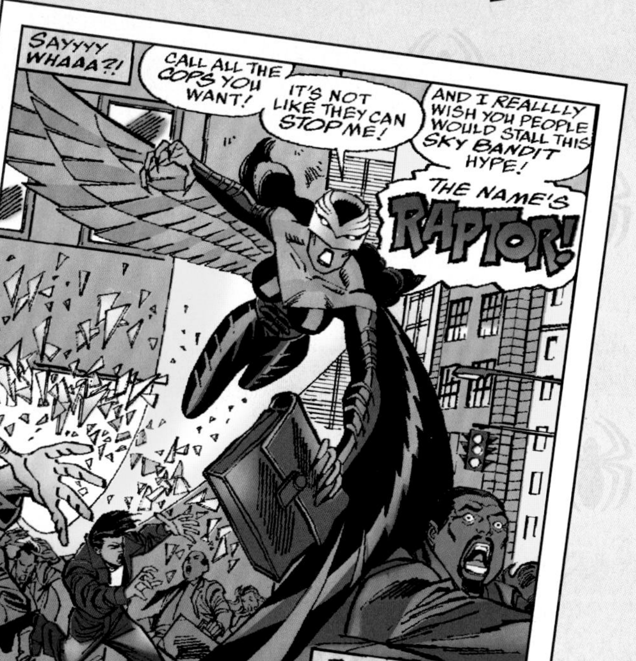
SAYYYY WHAAA?!
CALL ALL THE COPS YOU WANT!
IT'S NOT LIKE THEY CAN STOP ME!
AND I REALLLLY WISH YOU PEOPLE WOULD STALL THIS SKY BANDIT HYPE!
THE NAME'S RAPTOR!
T-THIS ISN'T MR. BIG EYES!

RAPTOR

Another former enemy who eventually turned friendly is **Brenda Drago,** otherwise known as **Raptor.** She used to be a winged thief in an abusive relationship, but soon realized the error of her ways, renounced crime and upgraded boyfriends. *(In fact, she's currently married to* ***Normie Osborn,*** *but I'll get to that later!)*

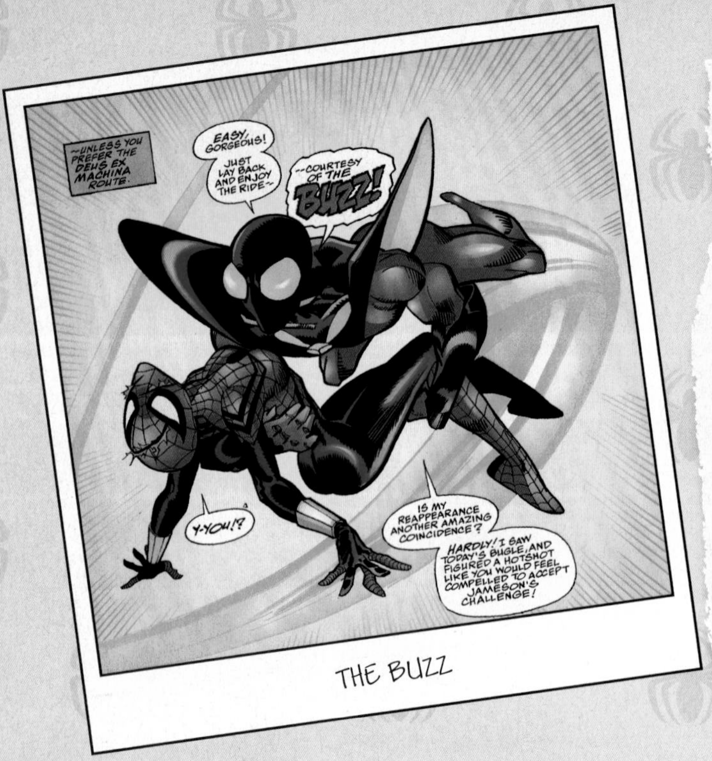
~UNLESS YOU PREFER THE DEUS EX MACHINA ROUTE.
EASY, GORGEOUS! JUST LAY BACK AND ENJOY THE RIDE~
--COURTESY OF THE BUZZ!
Y-YOU!?
IS MY REAPPEARANCE ANOTHER AMAZING COINCIDENCE?
HARDLY! I SAW TODAY'S BUGLE, AND FIGURED A HOTSHOT LIKE YOU WOULD FEEL COMPELLED TO ACCEPT JAMESON'S CHALLENGE!

THE BUZZ

I also met the **Buzz,** who empl a high-tech, armored battle sui to fight crime. Thanks to some brilliant detective work on my p *(actually it was pure dumb luck),* learned that he's secretly **Jack Jameson,** a guy in my class at **Midtown High.** While his parent are off in Europe, **JJ** lives with his grandparents--*Daily Bugle* publisher **J. Jonah Jameson** ar his wife **Marla!**

JJ and I even dated for awhile *(which had an added side benefit of twisting my dad wayyyyy out of shape),* but we broke up because the guy is, *like,* a total dog and can't be trusted! *(Although he's still a major cutie!)*

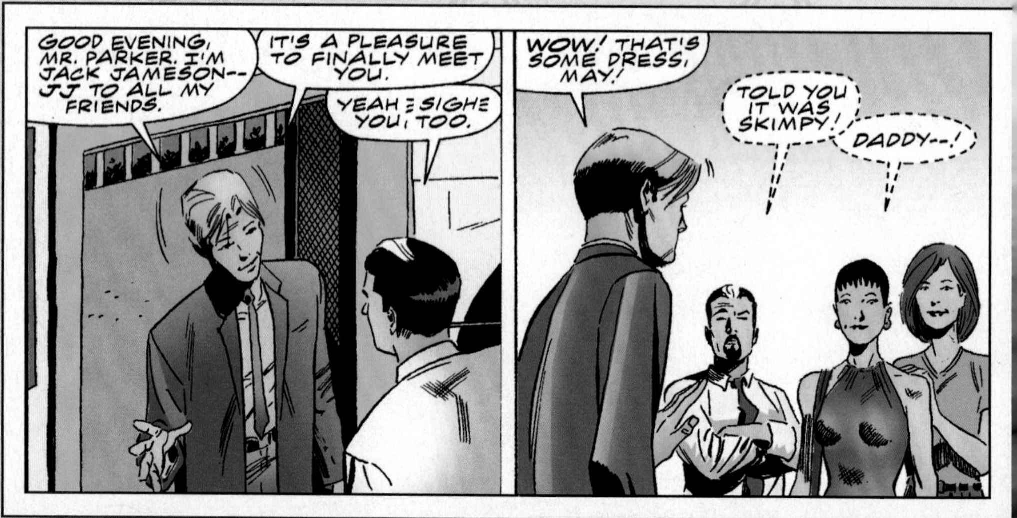
GOOD EVENING, MR. PARKER. I'M JACK JAMESON-- JJ TO ALL MY FRIENDS.
IT'S A PLEASURE TO FINALLY MEET YOU.
YEAH =SIGH= YOU, TOO.
WOW! THAT'S SOME DRESS, MAY!
TOLD YOU IT WAS SKIMPY!
DADDY--!

to choose the most
ic villain I've ever fought,
wer would have to be **Funny**
complete nutjob with no
for human life. He dresses
lown and carries an arsenal
ly weaponry designed to
umiliate and destroy you. I
now if he's completely
-or if it's just an act--but
o named his stupid wand
and he treats it as if it were

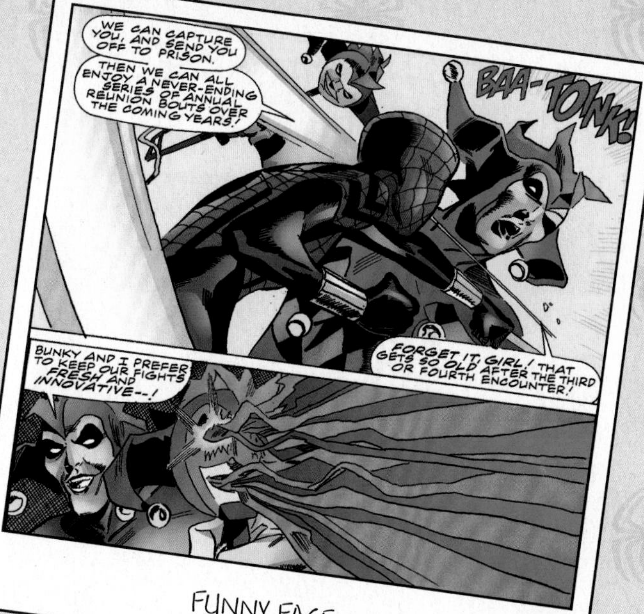
WE CAN CAPTURE YOU, AND SEND YOU OFF TO PRISON.
THEN WE CAN ALL ENJOY A NEVER-ENDING SERIES OF ANNUAL REUNION BOUTS OVER THE COMING YEARS!
BAA-TOINK!
BUNKY AND I PREFER TO KEEP OUR FIGHTS FRESH AND INNOVATIVE--!
FORGET IT, GIRL! THAT GETS SO OLD AFTER THE THIRD OR FOURTH ENCOUNTER!

FUNNY FACE

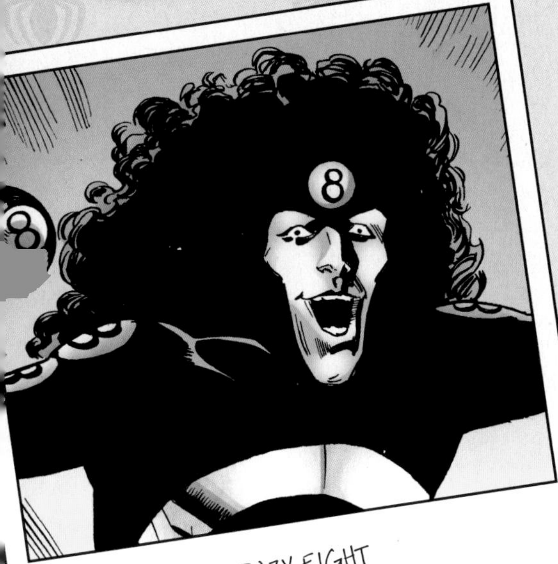

CRAZY EIGHT

He also holds me responsible for the death of his older brother, another super-criminal called **Crazy Eight,** who was killed in the middle of a gang war.

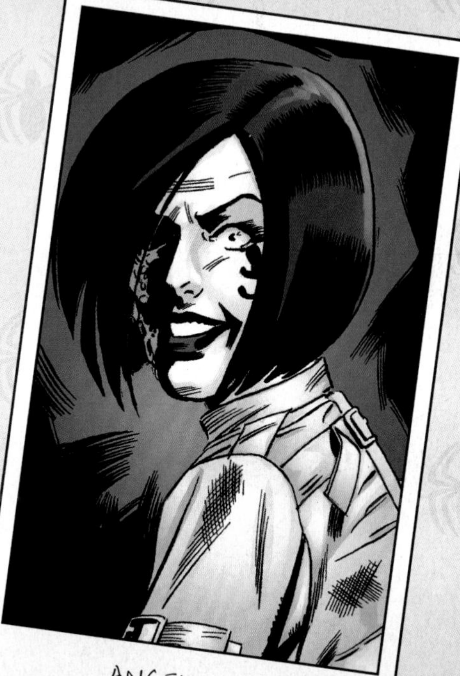

ANGEL FACE

I hate to admit it, but **Funny Face** and I actually have something in common. I'm trying to emulate my dad, and he's sort of the male version of his mom--a ruthless killer who calls herself **Angel Face** and has spent most of her life behind bars.

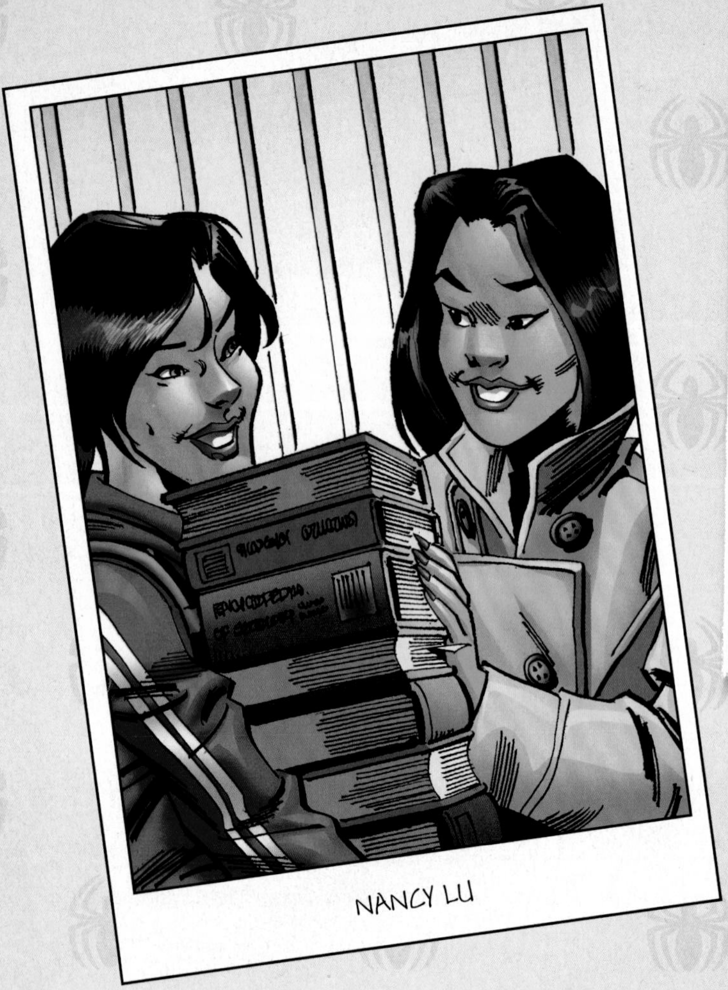
NANCY LU

On the plus side, there's **Nancy Lu**--a teenage telekinetic who just wanted to be left alone and to live a normal life. Things didn't quite work out the way she planned. After accidentally being "outed", Nancy signed on with the uncanny **X-People** to learn how to control her powers, and she adopted the codename of **Push.**

Want to hear something ironic? I think my best spider-day was the one when **Normie Osborn** returned as the **Green Goblin,** captured me and threatened to kill me. This marked a real turning point in our relationship. It gave us a chance to talk, to bond, to explain our feelings and to finally end the war between the **Parkers** and the **Osborns**...the **Spiders** and the **Goblins.**

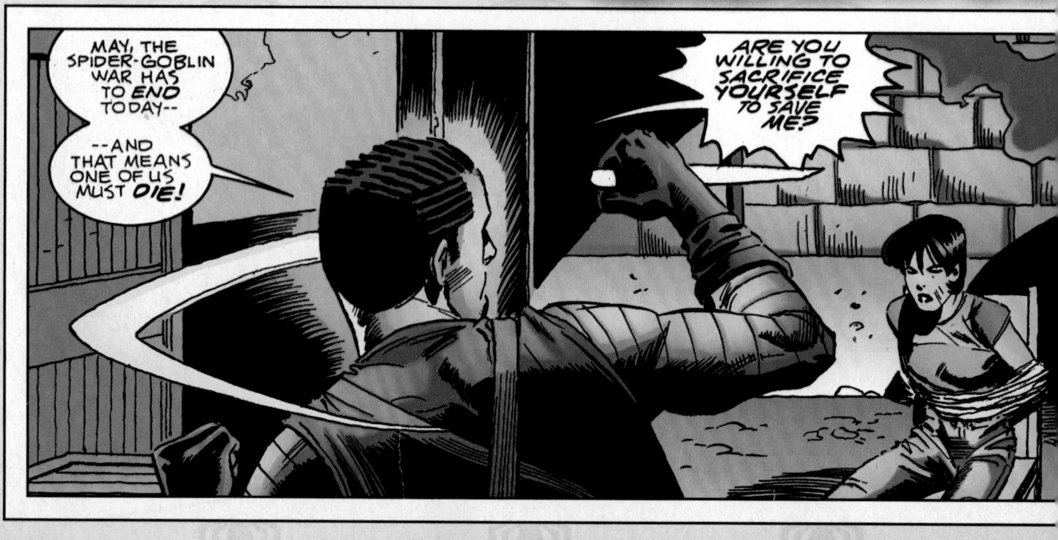
MAY, THE SPIDER-GOBLIN WAR HAS TO END TODAY--
--AND THAT MEANS ONE OF US MUST DIE!
ARE YOU WILLING TO SACRIFICE YOURSELF TO SAVE ME?

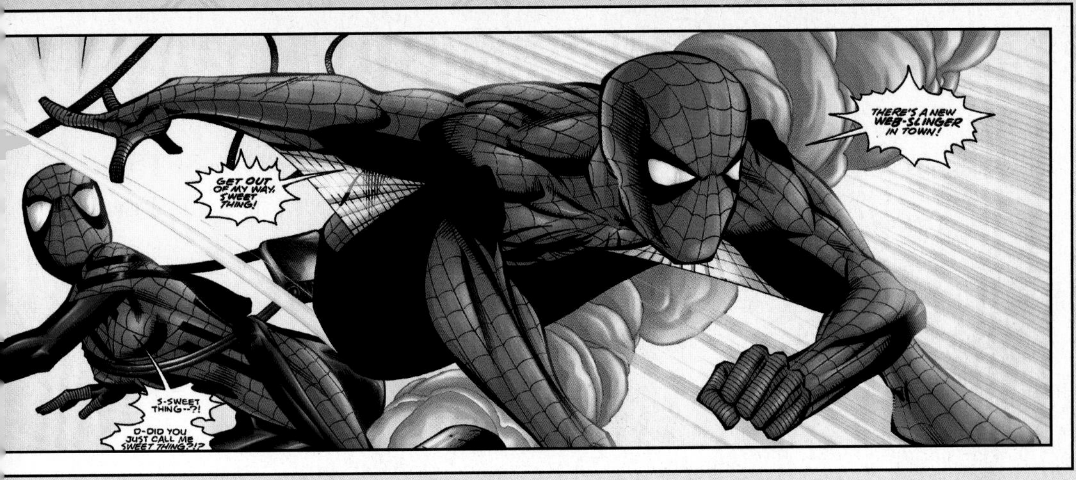
THERE'S A NEW WEB-SLINGER IN TOWN!
GET OUT OF MY WAY, SWEET THING!
S-SWEET THING--?!
D-DID YOU JUST CALL ME SWEET THING?!?

round that time, a **fake Spider-Man** appeared on the scene. I later learned his real name was **erry Drew,** and he was the son of **Jessica Drew,** the original **Spider-Woman. Gerry** was born with rare blood disease that was slowly killing him. He gained spider-powers when his mom tried an xperimental process on him. But he continued to deteriorate and is currently undergoing treatment. *wish him the best!)*

n ambitious crimelord called **Canis** attempted to replace **Wilson Fisk** as the new **Kingpin of Crime** and almost succeeded. **Canis** possesses enhanced reflexes and strength. *(And I always thought he was part wolf!)* After masterminding **Fisk's** assassination, **Canis** was captured and is urrently in prison. *(For e rest of his life, I hope!)*

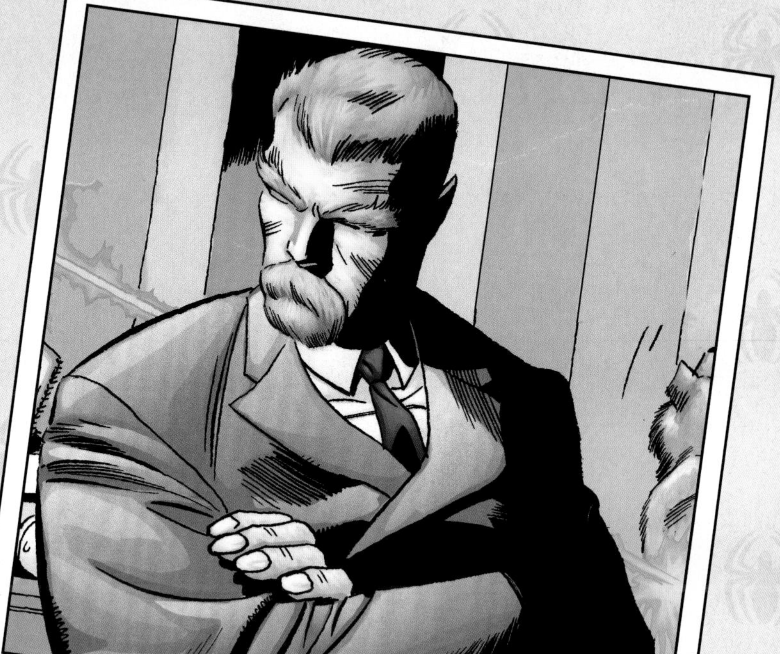

CANIS

Meanwhile, anxious to make up for his past mistakes, **Normie Osborn** became my biggest supporter and even allowed **Phil Urich** to fulfill his lifelong dream and take over as the new **Green Goblin.** (Although, as much as I love **Uncle Phil,** I'm still not convinced he's prime hero material.)

Felicity Hardy is the daughter of **Coach Thompson** (more on him later) and **Felicia Hardy,** who's better known as the **Black Cat.** Felicity must have inherited her mom's detective skills. She discovered my secret identity and tried to blackmail me into letting her become my partner as the **Scarlet Spider.** (A couple of close calls convinced her to retire her costume...at least for now!)

FELICITY AND HER MOM

MOM AND BEN

By the way, while all this was going on, my mom had another baby-- **Benjamin Richard Parker**--who is absolutely the cutest little bundle of joy this world has ever seen! (Although I may be a tad biased!)

Remember **Kaine** and **Raptor?** Well, they somehow got recruited into a top secret government super-team that's run by **Special Agent Arthur Weadon**, a true bureaucrat's bureaucrat. The team also includes **Quickwire** and **Big Man,** two other former super-criminals who chose serving the public over rotting in prison.

Weadon seems obsessed with capturing **Fabian LeMuerto.** Also known as the **Black Tarantula,** LeMuerto is based somewhere in South America and currently rules a criminal empire that has been passed down from father to son for over a hundred years. *(His dad even fought my dad!)*

BLACK TARANTULA

For reasons he's never really explained, the **Tarantula** seems to have taken a special interest in my career. *(Maybe it's my sparkling personality?!?)* His assistant **Chesbro** even temporarily helped equip me with my own **Team Spider.**

CHESBRO

TEAM SPIDER

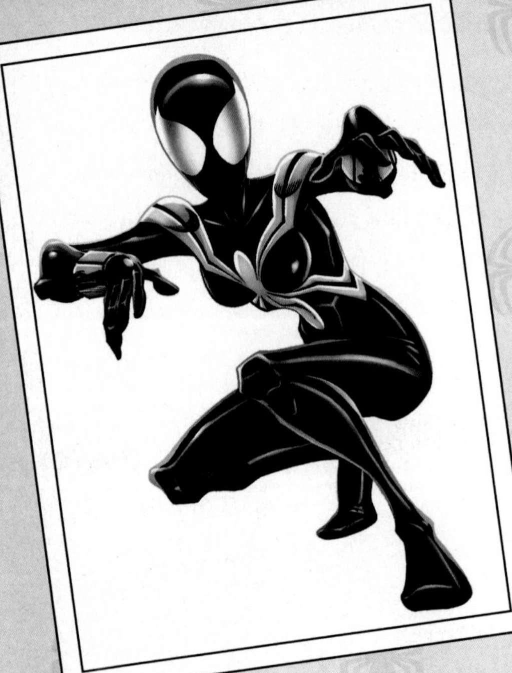

Since every girl likes to enhance her wardrobe, I temporarily adopted a new look--a black costume that was based on something my dad once wore back in his day! *(Switching costumes was kind of cool. I might even try it again.)*

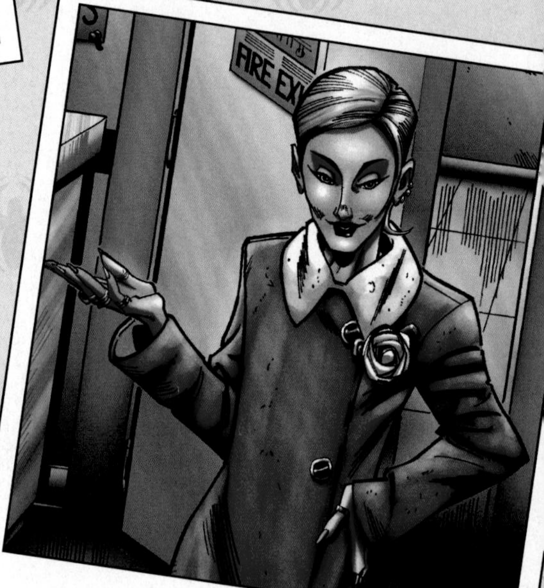
FIRE EX

ELAN DEJUNAE

Elan DeJunae appeared out of nowhere, claiming she was **Normie Osborn's** wife. *(A lie!)* We later found out that she was secretly **Fury, the Goblin Queen,** and a member of a crime cult that worshipped Normie's grandfather.

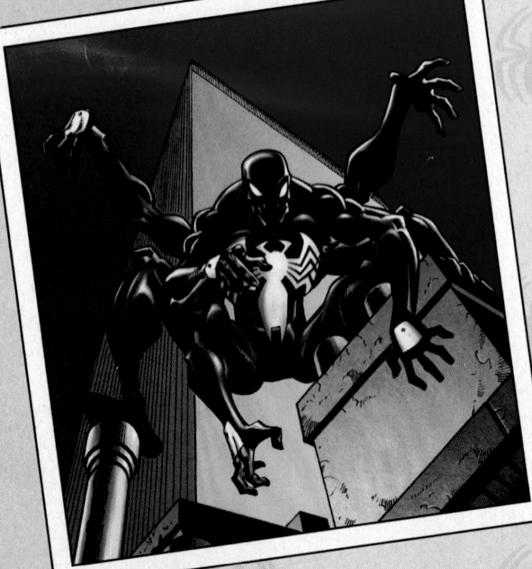

When she failed to convert **Normie** back to the dark side, she bonded him to the **Venom Symbiote,** an alien creature that had often tried to possess my dad. **Normie** eventually learned to control the symbiote and use its powers for good.

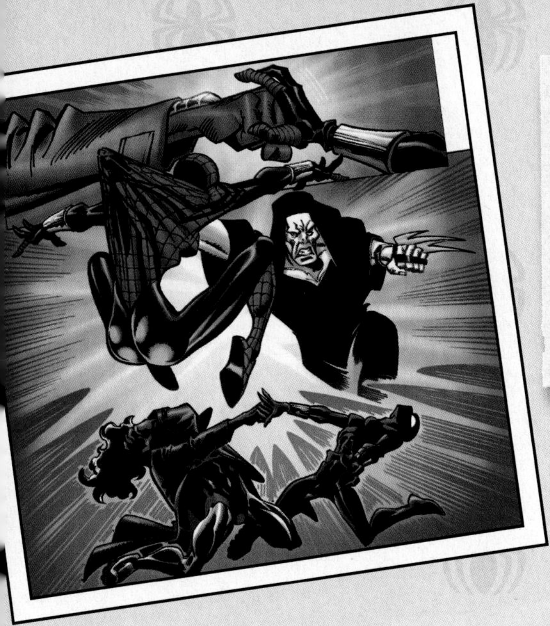

Kaine recently had a vision that showed me being stabbed by a **Scrier.** (*Yeah, still another crime cult!*) Needless to say, I was pretty freaked. I even switched back to my black costume in an effort to outsmart destiny.

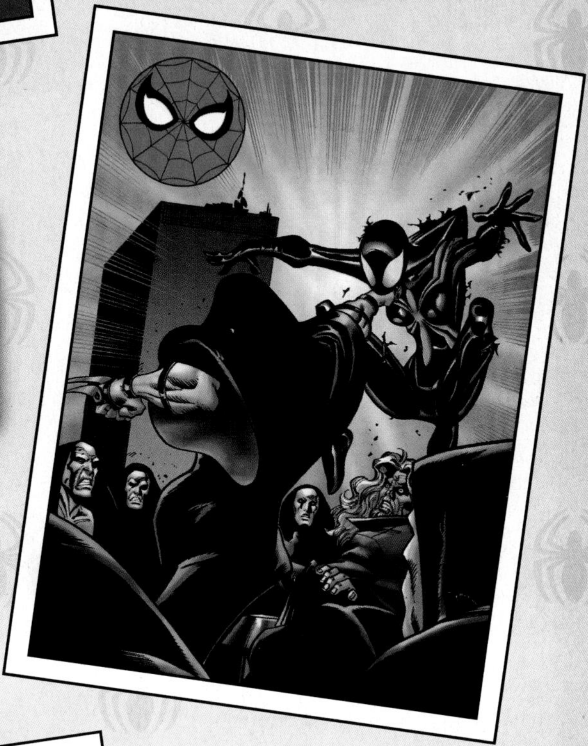

But my plans rarely work! (*Luckily,* ***Normie*** *saved my life by using the* ***Venom Symbiote*** *to heal me!*)

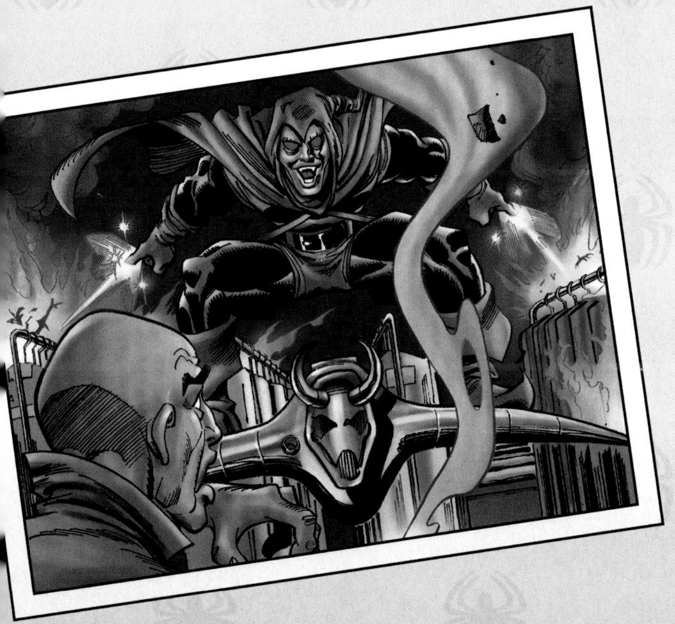

The Scriers were so desperate to kill me that they even broke **Roderick Kingsley,** the legendary **Hobgoblin,** out of prison. (*Definitely the most ruthless and calculating foe I've ever faced!*)

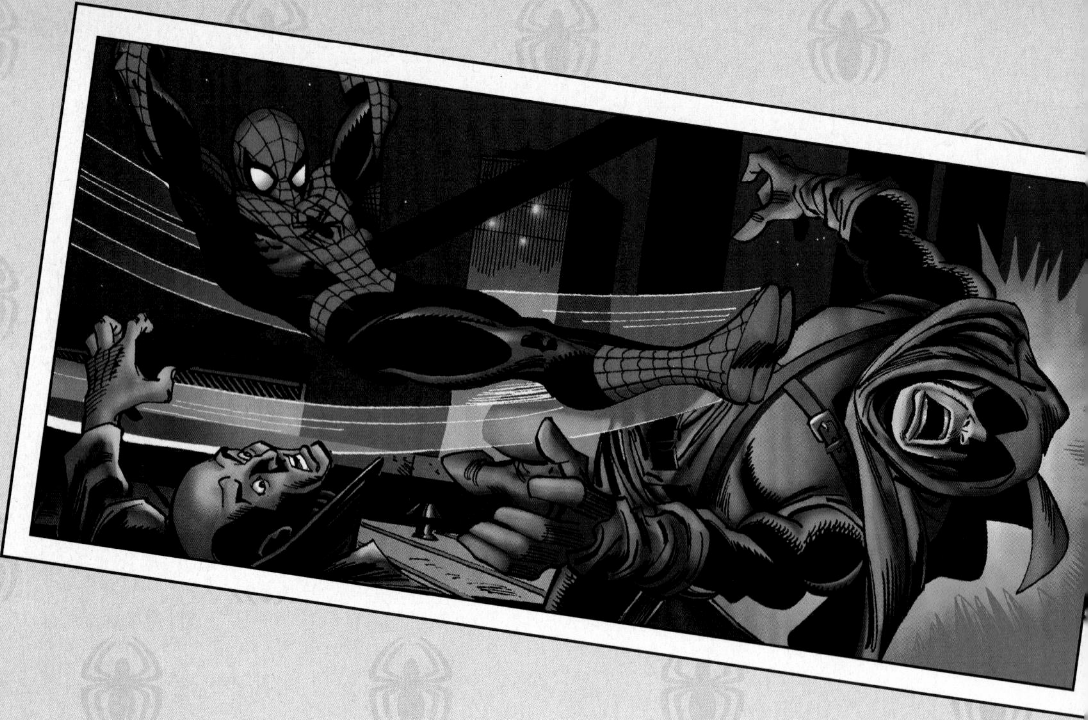

Knowing that I was completely out of my league, my dad came out of retirement to help me. *(It's a stunt he's tried before, and it almost NEVER works! He even once donned a* ***bionic leg,*** *if you can believe it!)* Thanks in no small part to the **Venom Symbiote,** who sacrificed herself to save us, we finally managed to drive the **Hobgoblin** away. *(But he is* ***still*** *at large!)*

Though I don't know exactly how he managed it, the **Black Tarantula** somehow convinced the **Scriers** to back off and leave me alone. The timing worked out because **Normie Osborn** and **Brenda Drago** were married later that night. *(The ceremony was conducted at the Midtown Medical Center, where she was still recuperating from an attack by* ***Hobgoblin.)***

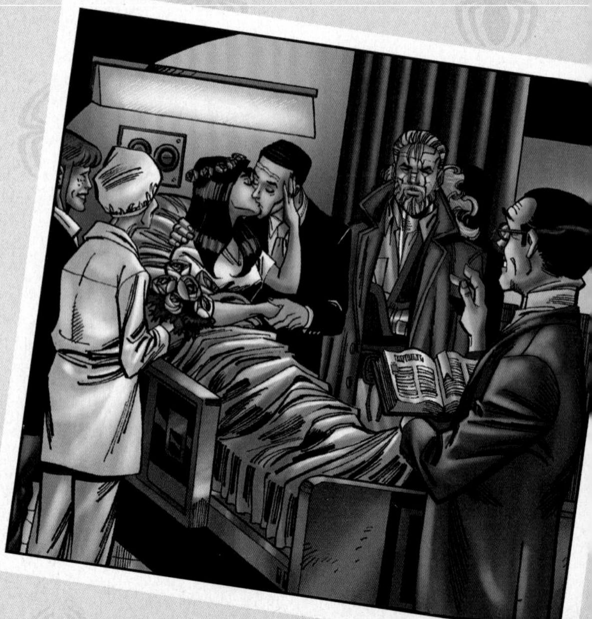

Unfortunately, the stress of **Hobgoblin's** return and the idea of almost losing us really got to my mom and she told me and Dad to hang up our webs for good. I figured she'd eventually calm down and things would go back to normal.

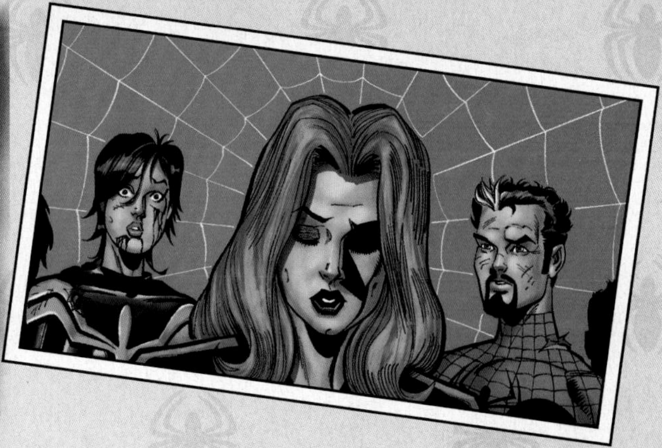

Or maybe they *would* have...but that's when some psychotic space god called **Galactus** came to town. I'm not sure what he was really trying to accomplish, but he did make a big mess of the city and killed a whole bunch of innocent people.

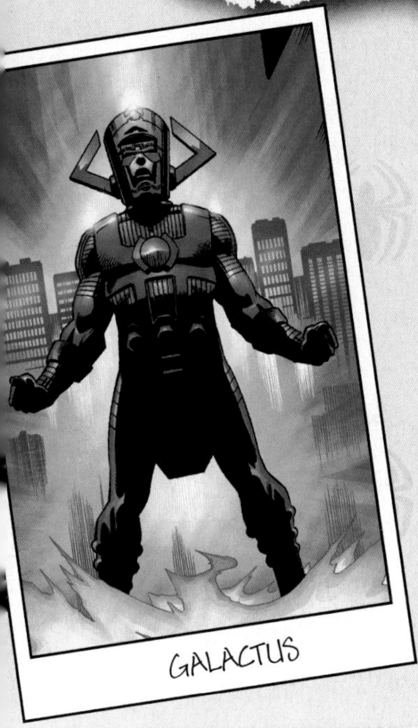

GALACTUS

r, **American Dream, J2** and I eventually managed e the day! *(Okay, so maybe there were also a few other costumed heroes involved, but this is* ***my*** *diary!)* when I decided to take my mother's advice and my webs. What can I say? After risking my neck t Hobgoblin, the Scriers and the biggest space of all, I desperately needed a break. Trouble e discovered that I really like living a villain-free e. I enjoy being a normal teenager. *(Well, as normal n get!)* How long will I feel this way? Will I ever my mind? Is **Spider-Girl** gone forever? We'll just o wait and see...

Goodbye for now!

Mayday Parker

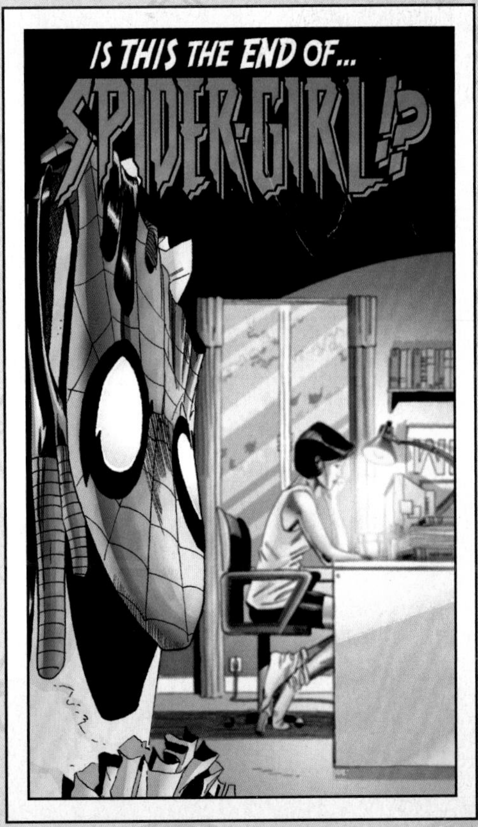

IS THIS THE END OF...
SPIDER-GIRL!?

MY AMAZING FRIENDS

Courtney Duran

I met Courtney on my first day of pre-school when a nasty second-gra_
(who had obviously been born to be a future suspect) decided to bully_
Courtney rushed to my aid and bit him on the leg. It was the beginning_
beautiful friendship. Not only is Court a straight-A student, but she's p_
heart. She's also completely comfortable in her own skin. She's been da_
Moose Mansfield recently, though she seems to spend an awful lot of ti_
with JJ Jameson. (Especially since Moose moved to New Jersey!)

I spent most of grade and high school thinking that Moose was a bully and
a blockhead. And he is...sort of. But he's also a big old teddy bear! Moose is
open, honest and always speaks from the heart. He's sensitive in a very manly
way and always guards his friends' backs. (Okay, he does have temper issues
and can be awfully stubborn, but the guy means well.) Unfortunately, poor
Moosie has been having a hard time. Cancer claimed his mother when he was
just a kid, and his dad was recently diagnosed with prostate cancer. Moose,
his two younger brothers and his sister have gone to live with their Uncle
Billy in New Jersey while their dad undergoes treatment. I originally thought
he and Courtney would be able to survive a long-distance relationship. I'm
not so sure anymore...

Maurice "Moose" Man_

Davida Kirby

I think I was about to enter second grade when my mom signed me up
soccer. I was standing on the side of the field, waiting my turn to kick th_
when the girl behind me loudly proclaimed that she could kick it farthe_
anyone else on the team. She did, too. (But only because my spider-po_
hadn't developed yet.) Davida has only grown more confident over the y_
She knows what she wants and goes for it. I know this makes her sound_
centered, and she can be. (Especially when it comes to boys!) But she i_
a loyal friend and a team player.

Jimmy, Courtney and I used to belong to the science club together. (Now that
I think of it, I was the only member who could hang with both the geeks and
the jocks!) He's one of the sharpest guys I know and will probably be a multi-
zillionaire someday. (If he can learn to control the sarcasm!) Courtney used
to have a bit of a crush on him, but he was focused on me. At least he was
until he started dating Heather Noble.

Jimmy Yama

Okay, I never much liked Heather. She is way too cute for her own good, knows it and often uses it to her advantage. She used to collect boys the way the rest of us accumulated hair scrunchies. I swear that she was determined to date every cute guy in Midtown High (and every other school in the tri-state area!) until she unexpectedly stalled on Jimmy Yama. I just don't understand it. He's so brainy and she's...not. But something's working here! She's helped Jimmy dress better and socialize more, and he's helped improve her grades. But I still feel there's a timer on this relationship and it's ticking down...

Heather Noble

...used to have the biggest crush on Brad. It began in grade school and ...d all the way to my sophomore year of high school. He was *Mr. Cool* as ...s I was concerned. But some relationships should never go beyond the ...stage. We dated for awhile and discovered that we had almost nothing ...ommon. I also learned that he has problems with mutants, and that's a ...turnoff. But I haven't given up on Brad. I still think he can be fixed. He just needs the right girl...

Brad Miller

Meagyn's really an odd duck, and I can't really say that she's a member of my usual crowd. To tell you the truth, most of the time I barely notice her. I was once surprised to discover how many classes we share together. I've heard rumors that she has issues with her mom, but don't we all? Anyway, Meagyn seems to hang a lot with Felicity Hardy. Meagyn also seems to know practically everything that's going on at Midtown High. Everyone speaks freely in front of her--as if she wasn't even there! It's like she's practically invisible. *Whatever!* I just know that Meagyn has often provided me with crucial intel at critical times, and I'm very appreciative. I often intend to spend time with her, but can never seem to find her.

Meagyn Brady

...ndra has had her share of problems. We had shared a few classes and ...changed a few words over the years. One day, after a super-battle that ...t end too well, I was in the girl's room, applying makeup to cover some ...acial bruises. Sandra saw me and asked, "Was it your boyfriend or your ..." I later learned that her boyfriend was physically abusing her and her ...wasn't a prize, either. She finally ditched the boyfriend, but is still stuck with the father. Needless to say, I keep my eye on her.

Sandra Healy

Chris Jarkoer

Chris is a really sweet guy, and we dated for awhile. Unfortunately, duri[ng] of our dates, a super-villain appeared and Chris reacted the way I'd ex[pect] any average person to behave. He got good and scared. No biggie! I did, however, get a little annoyed when I heard him bragging about his "brav[ery]" and portraying himself as quite the hero. What can I say? He's a norma[l] teenage boy! I knew he was no Captain America and shouldn't have exp[ected] him to portray himself in a less than flattering light. Chris assumed I b[roke] up with him because he exaggerated his heroism. The truth is I just did[n't] think he fit into my world. But my world has recently changed and who knows what the future could bring?

Coach Eugene "Flash" Th[ompson]

Coach used to go to high school with my dad and I gather they've had a very complicated relationship over the years. That's their business! Coach was always good to me and I loved playing high school basketball for him! (At least until my spider-powers emerged and I finally realized it wasn't fair to compete with non-powered teens.) Since the girl's basketball team has been on a losing streak, Coach has been under some major pressure recently and may have to teach a few extra courses to guarantee himself a job. Coach also used to be married to Felicia Hardy, the Black Cat. (Talk about an odd coupling!) They have two children—Felicity, who lives with her mom, and Eugene, who...y'know, I think I'm going to hold off on him for now.

Mr. Slattery

Mr. Slattery is Midtown's assistant principal. He teachers English and / Literature, and is also in charge of discipline and detention. I think he [kind of] likes me (as much as he's capable of liking **any** student), but I have a h[unch] my occasional disappearances (to do my web-thing) may force us to sp[end a] lot of time together. (In the detention room!)

Talk about a fixture at Midtown High! Winterhalter has been there forever. She even taught my dad, and he swears that she hasn't aged a day in the last twenty years. I always thought there was something weird about her and wouldn't be surprised if she had a picture hidden up in her attic or we learned that she was sucking the life energy out of her students. Okay, so I'm not her biggest fan! Can you blame me? She gave me a "C" in Political Science last term and I busted tail to complete every one of her assignments. If I get her in junior year, KILL ME NOW!

Ms. Winterhalter